SEA BATTLES

SEA BATTLES

A Reference Guide

MICHAEL SANDERSON

WESLEYAN UNIVERSITY PRESS

Middletown, Connecticut

TO

Adelheid, Peter and Nicholas

Published in Great Britain by David & Charles (Holdings) Limited, Devon

Designed by John Leath

Printed in Great Britain

First American edition

L C 74-21927

ISBN 0-8195-4080-3

Contents

Foreword

The aim of this book has been to give a concise account of the principal sea battles of history. It is designed mainly as a reference guide to readers whose interest in the subject has been awakened and who require a short narrative of each event. The main text is supported by appropriate illustrations, sketch maps and plans. All the illustrations have come from originals held in the National Maritime Museum, Greenwich, and I am very grateful to the Trustees of the Museum for their permission to reproduce them.

A word about the content and arrangement of the book will be helpful. The number of sea battles throughout history is so large that obviously some limits must be set. Therefore the term sea battles has been rather strictly defined to mean those fought between considerable forces in the open sea. Exceptions have of course been made in certain cases but, in principle, naval bombardments, combined operations, inland-waters engagements and single-ship actions have been excluded. Even so, there are accounts of over 250 battles in the book.

Since the battles are presented in alphabetical order, clearly some indication of the wars to which they belong and their relationship with other engagements during the same period is desirable. For this reason the main text is preceded by a comprehensive chronology, which lists each battle according to its proper sequence in time. Note, too, that whenever relevant the dates are given in old style rather than new. The difficult problem of the numbers of ships engaged requires mention. In many battles, authorities differ widely in this respect; some include ships of all sizes within the fleets, others distinguish between the various types. The figures given in the entries attempt to account for these divergencies and retain accuracy but they should be read with this problem in mind. Finally, plentiful use has been made of cross-references in the text, because a number of sea battles have alternative names and many are closely linked with each other.

Michael Sanderson

Chronology

date		battle	remarks
Ancient			
GRAECO-PERSIAN WARS 499–448 BC			
494 BC		LADE	Darius crushes the Ionians
480	30 August–1 September	ARTEMISIUM	
	September	SALAMIS	
479		MYCALE	
466		EURYMEDON RIVER	
435		AMBRACIAN GULF	Corinth v. Corcyra (Corfu)
PELOPONNESIAN WAR 433–404 BC			
433	September	SYBOTA ISLANDS I	
429		PATRAS	*or* Chalcis ⎫ Phormio's
		NAUPACTUS	*or* Panormus ⎭ victories
427	Spring	SYBOTA ISLANDS II	
427	Autumn	PYLOS	
414–13		SYRACUSE	the failure of the Sicilian expedition
411		ABYDOS	
	Autumn	CYNOSSEMA	⎫
410	Spring	CYZICUS	⎬ Alcibiades' two great victories
407	Spring	NOTIUM	⎭
406	August	ARGINUSAE ISLANDS	
		MYTILENE	
405	August	AEGOSPOTAMI	Athenian catastrophe
394		CNIDUS	⎫ War of Independence against
376	September	NAXOS	⎬ the hegemony of Sparta
306	Spring	SALAMIS	in Cyprus

date		battle	remarks
date		*battle*	*remarks*

FIRST PUNIC WAR   265–241 BC

260		LIPARI ISLANDS	
		MYLAE	Caius Duilius' victory
256		ECNOMUS	
249		DREPANUM	Trapani (Sicily)
242	Summer	AEGATES ISLANDS	Carthaginian disaster

SECOND PUNIC WAR   219–202 BC

| 217 | Spring | IBERUS | |
| 212 | | TARENTUM | |

MACEDONIAN WARS   215–167 BC

201		CHIOS	defeat of Philip V of Macedon
		LADE	
191	September	CISSUS	⎫
190	July	SIDE	⎬ Roman victories
		MYONNESSUS	⎭

| 74 or 73 BC | | LEMNOS | Third Mithridatic War (75–65) |
| 56 | | MORBIHAN GULF | Caesar's Gallic Wars |

ROMAN CIVIL WAR   50–44 BC

| 49 | | CURICTA | Pompeians' success in the Adriatic |
| 48 | | ALEXANDRIA | Caesar v. Ptolemy |

SECOND TRIUMVIRATE WAR   43–34 BC

36	13 August	MYLAE	⎫
	15 August	TAUROMENIUM	⎬ Octavian v. Pompeian forces
	29/30 August	NAULOCHUS	⎭ in Sicilian waters

ANTONY-OCTAVIAN WAR   33–30 BC

| 31 | 2 September | ACTIUM | |

| AD 323 | July | HELLESPONT | Constantine the Great's victory over Licinius |

| 551 | Summer | SINIGAGLIA | Justinian's defeat of the Ostrogoths in the Adriatic |

MEDIEVAL

1213	end of May	DAMME	
1217	24 August	DOVER	*or* the fight off Sandwich
1263	Spring	SETTEPOZZI	⎫ Genoa v. Venice
1266	June	TRAPANI	⎭
1284	6 August	MELORIA	Pisa–Genoa War
1298	7 September	CURZOLA	Genoa v. Venice
1304	18 August	ZIERIKZEE	Grimaldi against the Flemish
1340	24 June	SLUYS	

date		battle	remarks
1350	29 August	WINCHELSEA	*or* 'Les Espagnols sur Mer'
1372	22/3 June	LA ROCHELLE	
1379	7 May	POLA	} the War of Chioggia (Genoa v. Venice)
	23 December	CHIOGGIA	
1416	15 August	HARFLEUR	
1499	12 and 14 August	ZONCHIO	*or* Lepanto. Venice against the Ottomans

16th CENTURY

1512	10 August	BREST	
1513	25 April	BREST	
1538	26–8 September	PREVEZA	Andrea Doria v. Barbarossa II
1545	18/19 July	SPITHEAD	
1571	7 October	LEPANTO	
1573	11 October	ZUYDER ZEE	*or* Enkhuizen
1588	July–August	SPANISH ARMADA	
1591	31 August/1 September	AZORES	last fight of the *Revenge*
1592	June	FUSAN	} Japan–Korea War
	9 July	YELLOW SEA	
1598	November	CHINHAE BAY	

17th CENTURY

1639	11 October	THE DOWNS	Tromp v. Oquendo

FIRST DUTCH WAR   1652–4

1652	19 May	DOVER	Tromp v. Blake
	16 August	PLYMOUTH	de Ruyter v. Ayscue
	28 August	ELBA	van Galen v. Badiley
	28 September	KENTISH KNOCK	de Witt v. Blake
	30 November	DUNGENESS	Tromp defeats Blake
1653	18–20 February	PORTLAND	'The Three Days' Battle'
	4 March	LEGHORN	van Galen v. Appleton
	2/3 June	THE GABBARD	*or* North Foreland
	31 July	SCHEVENINGEN	*or* First Texel

1655	4 April	PORTO FARINA	
1657	20 April	SANTA CRUZ	
1658	29 October	THE SOUND	the Dutch against the Swedes

SECOND DUTCH WAR   1665–7

1665	3 June	LOWESTOFT	Obdam's defeat
1666	1–4 June	THE FOUR DAYS' BATTLE	
	25/6 July	ORFORDNESS	*or* St James's Day; *or* North Foreland

THIRD DUTCH WAR   1672–4

1672	28 May	SOLEBAY	*or* Southwold Bay – Duke of York v. de Ruyter

date		battle	remarks
1673	28 May	SCHOONEVELD I	⎫ Prince Rupert and d'Estrées v.
	4 June	SCHOONEVELD II	⎬ de Ruyter
	11 August	TEXEL	⎭
1676	8 January	STROMBOLI	*or* Alicudi
	22 April	AUGUSTA	
	1 June	ÖLAND	
	12 June	PALERMO	
1677	1 July	KJÖGE BIGHT	

WAR OF THE ENGLISH SUCCESSION 1689–97

1689	1 May	BANTRY BAY	
1690	30 June	BEACHY HEAD	Torrington v. de Tourville
1692	19 May	BARFLEUR	⎫ Russell destroys the French
	22–4 May	LA HOGUE	⎭

18th CENTURY

WAR OF THE SPANISH SUCCESSION 1702–13

1702	20–4 August	SANTA MARTA	Benbow v. Ducasse
	12 October	VIGO BAY	Rooke
1704	13 August	MALAGA	*or* Velez Malaga. Rooke
1705	10 March	MARBELLA	Leake v. de Pointis
1708	28 May	CARTAGENA	'Wager's action'

1718	11 August	CAPE PASSARO	

WAR OF 1739–48

1744	11 February	TOULON	
1746	25 June	FORT ST DAVID	*or* Negapatam
1747	3 May	FINISTERRE I	Anson v. de la Jonquière
	14 October	FINISTERRE II	*or* Ushant. Hawke v. de l'Etenduère
1748	1 October	HAVANA	Knowles

SEVEN YEARS' WAR 1756–63

1756	20 May	MINORCA	
1757	21 October	CAP FRANÇOIS	Forrest v. de Kersaint
1758	4 April	ILE D'AIX	
	29 April	CUDDALORE	*or* Sadras. Pocock v. d'Aché I
	3 August	NEGAPATAM	Pocock v. d'Aché II
1759	18/19 August	LAGOS	Boscawen v. de la Clue
	10 September	PONDICHERRY	Pocock v. d'Aché III
	20 November	QUIBERON BAY	

1770	5/6 July	TCHESME	Russo-Turkish War

AMERICAN WAR OF INDEPENDENCE 1775–83

1778	27 July	USHANT I	Keppel v. d'Orvilliers
	15 December	ST LUCIA	Barrington v. d'Estaing

date		battle	remarks
1779	6 July	GRENADA	Byron v. d'Estaing
1780	16 January	CAPE ST VINCENT	'The moonlight battle'
	20 March and 20 June	MONTE CHRISTI	
	17 April	DOMINICA I	Rodney v. de Guichen
1781	16 March	CHESAPEAKE I	or Cape Henry
	16 April	PORTO PRAYA	Cape Verde Islands
	29 April	MARTINIQUE	Hood v. de Grasse
	5 August	DOGGER BANK	Hyde Parker v. Zoutmann
	9 September	CHESAPEAKE II	Graves v. de Grasse
	12 December	USHANT II	Kempenfelt v. de Guichen
1782	25/6 January	ST KITTS	or Frigate Bay
	17 February	SADRAS	Hughes v. Suffren I
	9 April	DOMINICA II	⎫
	12 April	LES SAINTES	⎬ Rodney v. de Grasse
	12 April	PROVIDIEN	⎭
	6 July	NEGAPATAM	⎫ Hughes v. Suffren II–V
	3 September	TRINCOMALEE	⎬
1783	20 June	CUDDALORE	⎭

RUSSO-SWEDISH WAR 1788–90

1789	26 July	ÖLAND	
1790	3/4 June	STYRSUDDEN	
	3/4 July	VIBORG BAY	
	9/10 July	SVENSKUND	

FRENCH REVOLUTIONARY WAR 1793–1802

1794	1 June	GLORIOUS FIRST OF JUNE	
1795	13/14 March	GULF OF GENOA	'Hotham's first action'
	17 June	BELLE ISLE	'Cornwallis's retreat'
	23 June	ÎLE DE GROIX	'Bridport's action'
	13 July	HYÈRES	'Hotham's second action'
1797	14 February	CAPE ST VINCENT	
	11 October	CAMPERDOWN	
1798	1 August	THE NILE	or Aboukir Bay
	12 October	DONEGAL	'Warren's action'

19th CENTURY

1801	2 April	COPENHAGEN	
	6 July and 12 July	ALGECIRAS AND THE STRAITS	'Saumarez's action'

NAPOLEONIC WAR 1803–15

1805	22 July	FINISTERRE	'Calder's action'
	21 October	TRAFALGAR	
	4 November	CAPE ORTEGAL	'Strachan's action'
1806	6 February	SAN DOMINGO	Duckworth v. Leissègues
1809	11–16 April	BASQUE AND AIX ROADS	Cochrane and Gambier
1811	13 March	LISSA	Hoste v. Dubourdieu

1827	20 October	NAVARINO	
1853	30 November	SINOPE	

date		battle	remarks
1857	1 June	FATSHAN CREEK	Second China War

AMERICAN CIVIL WAR 1861–5

1862	8/9 March	HAMPTON ROADS	
1864	5 August	MOBILE BAY	

1866	20 July	LISSA	von Tegetthoff v. Persano
1879	21 May	IQUIQUE	Chile–Peruvian War

SINO-JAPANESE WAR 1894–5

1894	25 July	ASAN	
	17 September	YALU RIVER	

SPANISH-AMERICAN WAR 1898

1898	1 May	MANILA BAY	
	3 July	SANTIAGO DE CUBA	

20th CENTURY

RUSSO-JAPANESE WAR 1904–5

1904	9 February	CHEMULPO	
	10 August	YELLOW SEA	
	14 August	JAPAN SEA	
1905	27/8 May	TSUSHIMA	

WORLD WAR I 1914–18

1914	28 August	HELIGOLAND BIGHT	
	1 November	CORONEL	
	8 December	FALKLAND ISLANDS	
1915	24 January	DOGGER BANK	
1916	31 May/1 June	JUTLAND	
1917	20–1 April	DOVER STRAITS	

WORLD WAR II 1939–45

1939	13 December	RIVER PLATE	*Graf Spee* action
1940	10 and 13 April	NARVIK I AND II	
	3 July	ORAN	*or* Mers El-Kebir
	9 July	CALABRIA	
	27 November	CAPE SPARTIVENTO	
1941	28 March	MATAPAN	
	23–7 May	'BISMARCK' ACTION	including Denmark Strait
	17 December	SIRTE I	
1942	27 February	JAVA SEA	
	28 February/1 March	SUNDA STRAIT	
	22 March	SIRTE II	
	6–8 May	CORAL SEA	
	4–6 June	MIDWAY	

date	battle	remarks
August–November	SOLOMON ISLANDS	including Savo Island; Eastern Solomons; Cape Esperance; Santa Cruz Island; Guadalcanal and Tassafaronga
31 December	BARENTS SEA	
1943 January–November	SOLOMON ISLANDS	including Rennell Island; Kula Gulf; Kolombangara; Vella Gulf; Vella Lavella; Empress Augusta Bay and Cape St George
2–5 March	BISMARCK SEA	
26 March	KOMANDORSKI ISLANDS	
26 December	NORTH CAPE	*Scharnhorst* action
1944 19/20 June	PHILIPPINE SEA	
23–6 October	LEYTE GULF	including Surigao Strait; Samar and Cape Engaño

Sea Battles

ABOUKIR BAY *see* THE NILE

ABYDOS   late 411 BC

Fourteen Rhodian ships under Dorleus approached the entrance of the Hellespont in order to reinforce the Peloponnesian fleet under Mindarus. There they were driven off by Athenian ships and forced to beach near Rhoeteum. Mindarus came to the aid of the Rhodians and pursued the Athenians up the Hellespont to Abydos, where his ninety-seven ships engaged seventy-four Athenians. The arrival of eighteen more Athenian vessels under Alcibiades induced Mindarus to beach his ships under the protection of the cavalry and infantry of his Persian ally, the satrap Pharnabazus. The Athenians then seized thirty empty ships and took them to Sestos.

ACTIUM   2 September 31 BC

Octavian – the future Emperor Augustus – could not reward his supporters adequately without access to the riches of the East, which his brother-in-law Mark Antony controlled through his alliance with Queen Cleopatra of Egypt. Antony's support of Egyptian autonomy against Rome was a further source of discord.

In the summer of 33 BC, Cleopatra came to Ephesus at Antony's summons with money and 200 warships. The next year Antony took his large fleet to the Ambracian Gulf, while Octavian's 260 ships assembled at Tarentum and Brundisium under his admiral, Agrippa. After a series of successful minor actions against Antony's supply routes, Agrippa established an advanced base at Corcyra. In May 31 BC Agrippa's ships took the island of Leukas and then seized Patras and Corinth, threatening Antony with starvation. Antony thereupon decided to abandon Actium and sail for Egypt, if possible defeating Agrippa on the way. Lacking sufficient rowers to man his whole fleet, Antony destroyed many of his ships, reducing the total to about 180 – including sixty of Cleopatra's. His vessels were generally larger than Agrippa's and well equipped with artillery towers and grappling irons. Agrippa, on the other hand, had

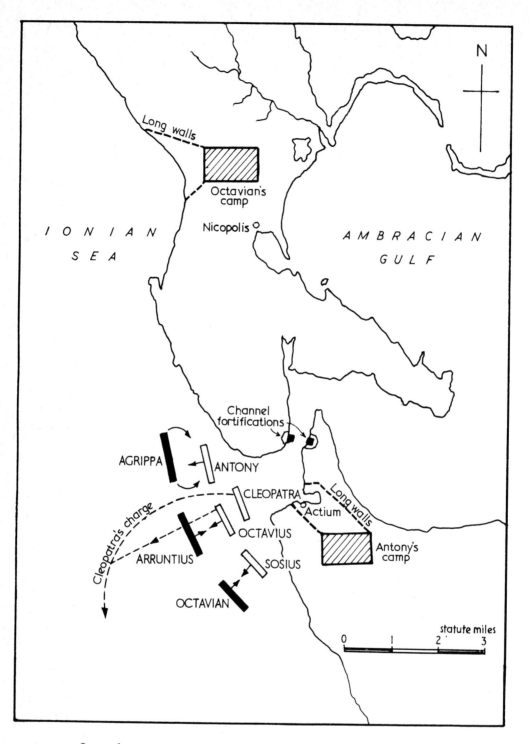

N

Long walls

Octavian's camp

I O N I A N
S E A

Nicopolis

A M B R A C I A N
G U L F

Channel
fortifications

AGRIPPA ANTONY

CLEOPATRA

Long walls

Actium

Cleopatra's charge

OCTAVIUS

ARRUNTIUS

Antony's
camp

SOSIUS

OCTAVIAN

statute miles

0   1   2   3

ACTIUM   2 September 31 BC

more soldiers on board and his ships were fitted with devices for throwing fire.

Both fleets embarked on 2 September 31 BC, Octavian leading the right squadron of his fleet, Arruntius the centre and Agrippa the left, facing Antony. Cleopatra's squadron formed a reserve at the rear of the main fleet. Antony's left wing advanced to battle about noon but the slowness of his ships and short range of their artillery limited their effectiveness. Some time after 1 pm Cleopatra's squadron hoisted sail and ran through the centre of both battle lines. Antony pursued her in a light craft but only a few of his ships followed. Agrippa then used his rams to good effect on the remainder and, having encircled his opponents, began shooting flaming charcoal and pitch at the crowded galleys. By 4 pm the remnants of Antony's fleet had fled.

Many Romans on both sides attributed Cleopatra's manoeuvre to fear but it may be that she hoped by charging the enemy under sail to force the issue and enable Antony's main fleet to follow her. Once to leeward of the action she could not re-engage nor could Agrippa's ships pursue, as they were not carrying sails. Whatever Cleopatra's purpose, Antony knew as he sat in the bows of her ship that he had lost both the battle and his reputation. He then fled to Egypt, where his remaining ships and men deserted him at Alexandria and he later committed suicide.

AEGATES ISLANDS 242 BC

By the summer of 242 Rome had raised a fleet of 200 ships to hasten the capture of the Carthaginian strongholds at Lilybaeum and Drepanum in Sicily. The Roman consul Catullus gained control of the entrances to both ports and awaited the arrival of the Carthaginian fleet under Hanno. Hearing that Hanno had anchored at Hiera in the Aegates Islands, Catullus moved to Aegusa, another island in the same group. Hanno had sailed hastily without a proper complement of fighting men, hoping to make up the deficiency from the Sicilian garrisons. Catullus therefore had the advantage of better trained oarsmen and ships unburdened with cargo. Both fleets rowed themselves into line of battle; in the action which followed the Romans captured seventy ships and sank fifty. A sudden change of wind however enabled Hanno to take the rest of his fleet back to Hiera. When Hanno returned to Carthage he was crucified for his failure. Shortly afterwards Carthage sued for peace and paid a heavy war indemnity.

AEGOSPOTAMI September 405 BC

Although her fleet had been victorious at the ARGINUSAE ISLANDS (qv) in 406, Athens' resources were severely strained. Moreover Lysander, the Spartan commander, had been able with Persian aid to fit out another fleet in Asia Minor. In August 404, Athens assembled with difficulty 180 ships. Under the command of six *strategoi* the fleet sailed up the Hellespont to challenge Lysander, who had besieged and taken Lampsacus.

For four days the opposing fleets watched each other. On the morning of the fifth Lysander sent out scouts, who signalled to him by raising shields to their mastheads. Their message was that the Athenians had beached their ships on the opposite shore, at the mouth of the Aegospotami five miles away, and dispersed to buy provisions. This was the opportunity for which Lysander had waited. He moved his fleet at once across the Hellespont to attack. Caught unawares, only nine Athenian crews reached their ships in time and sailed away. All the rest – 171 ships – were taken. Aegospotami finally broke Athenian naval power and the Peloponnesian War ended the following year.

AIX, ILE D' 4 April 1758

An action of the Seven Years' War, in which Admiral Hawke effectively prevented a French squadron from setting out from Rochefort to escort an important convoy to North America. On the afternoon of 4 April, Hawke with seven of the line and three frigates discovered the enemy lying off Ile d'Aix. The French numbered five 74s and 64s, six or seven frigates and the convoy comprising forty merchantmen. After a confused action and general chase, many of the enemy were driven into shoal water and ran aground. After lightening ship the French were able to refloat many of them next day but the convoy never reassembled.

AIX ROADS *see* BASQUE AND AIX ROADS

ALEXANDRIA 48 BC

Shortly after his arrival in Egypt in July 48 BC, Julius Caesar became involved in the struggle for power between Cleopatra and her brother Ptolemy. Ptolemy and the eunuch Ganymede attempted to seize the city of Alexandria and the Egyptian fleet lying in its harbour. This was prevented but afterwards, during Caesar's temporary absence, Ganymede prepared a naval squadron to intercept his return. In the ensuing action Ganymede was defeated. However the eunuch escaped and formed another squadron – twenty-seven vessels and many lighter ones to oppose Caesar's fifteen large and nineteen small galleys. Action was joined off Pharos Island and Ganymede was again defeated, losing five *tetreres*. However, the fortunes of war then changed. The next day Caesar's ships in the Great Harbour of Alexandria attacked the second bridge and the mole but were repulsed with the loss of 800 men. Later some of Caesar's transports were lured ashore by false lights at the western mouth of the Nile Delta and the ships he sent under Tiberius Nero to aid them were driven off. It was not until January 47 that Alexandria surrendered to Caesar.

ALGECIRAS 6 July and 12/13 July 1801

Two separate actions fought by a squadron under Rear-Admiral Sir James Saumarez against French and Spanish ships of the line near Gibraltar.

The first took place on the morning of 6 July. Saumarez, wearing his flag in the *Caesar*, 80, and with five 74s in support, attacked Admiral Linois's squadron of three ships of the line and one frigate as it lay anchored in Algeciras Bay. Linois was forced to run his ships ashore but during the action the *Hannibal*, 74, went aground near the Spanish batteries and was forced to surrender. After repairing his damaged ships with remarkable speed and energy at Gibraltar, Saumarez got his revenge six days later in a second encounter, sometimes known as the action of the Straits or Gut of Gibraltar.

On this occasion Saumarez met a combined Franco-Spanish squadron of eight ships of the line and three frigates under Linois and Moreno. The action began after dusk on 12 July and continued through the night. At midnight the two Spanish first-rates *Real Carlos* and *San Hermenegildo*, both of 112 guns, caught fire, collided with each other and then sank with very heavy loss of life. Both Linois and Moreno escaped, having earlier transferred to the Spanish frigate *Sabina*. Soon afterwards the French 74, *St Antoine*, was taken. Several of Saumarez's

ALGECIRAS   6 July 1801   *Aquatint by Captain J. Brenton, showing the capture of the* St Antoine

ships – especially the *Venerable* – were disabled but he got them safely into Gibraltar. When the news of Algeciras reached England, Saumarez was hailed as a national hero.

ALICUDI   *see* STROMBOLI

AMBRACIAN GULF   435 BC

An immediate cause of the outbreak of the Peloponnesian War in 436 BC was the quarrel between Corinth and Corcyra (Corfu). Corinth felt the latter was threatening her trade route to Italy. In 435 BC seventy-five Corinthian ships carrying soldiers for the relief of Epidamnus, besieged by the Corcyreans, were heavily defeated by eighty Corcyrean triremes in the Ambracian Gulf. Both sides then appealed to Athens for help. Athens was afraid that a Corinthian victory would ruin her own trade with the Western Mediterranean and therefore made a defensive alliance with Corcyra.

ANGAMOS   8 October 1879

During the Chile–Peruvian war of 1879–81, the Peruvian turret-ram *Huascar* (2,000 tons; two 10in guns) caused havoc by hit-and-run raids on shipping and ports along the Chilean coast. Chilean warships constantly hunted for her and she was eventually trapped on the morn-ning of 8 October 1879 in Angamos Bay, forty miles north of Antofagasta. The *Huascar* was outnumbered, being opposed by the two Chilean armoured central-battery ships *Almirante Cochrane* and *Blanco Encalada* (each of 3,500 tons, four 9in guns). But she fought gallantly in the ninety-minute running battle which ensued and was hit twenty-seven times before surrender-ing. After this engagement, the Chileans held secure command of the sea and they proceeded to blockade the Peruvian ports.

ANTIUM   30 May 1378

With fourteen galleys, the Venetian admiral Vittorio Pisani engaged and defeated a Genoese squadron under Fieschi off Antium (the Anzio of today). Six Genoese galleys were sunk and Fieschi was taken prisoner.

ARGINUSAE ISLANDS   406 BC

At the end of 407 BC Callicratidas replaced Lysander as Spartan commander-in-chief of the Peloponnesian allies. With a fleet of 140 ships he first sailed to attack the Athenian settlement at Methymna on the island of Lesbos. Conon followed him with seventy Athenian ships but was unable to prevent Methymna's fall and lost thirty of his ships in a chance action. Having now collected 170 ships, Callicratidas blockaded Mytilene by land and sea but two Athenian ships managed to slip out. One reached Athens with the news and an urgent call for reinforcement for Asia Minor. Athens responded by raising a fleet of 100 ships and added forty more from Samos and other allies.

Leaving part of his fleet blockading Mytilene, Callicratidas took 120 ships to Malea Point on the coast of Asia Minor, where he sighted the Athenians off the Arginusae Islands seven miles to the south. At daybreak he formed line of battle while his opponents, more numerous but with older ships, manoeuvred into a double line centred on West Arginusae Island. When action was joined the Peloponnesians attacked in two separate groups, so that the Athenian centre suffered little. Callicratidas fell fiercely upon the galleys of the Athenian vice-admiral, Lysias, and sank them but was himself killed in the mêlée. Then the Peloponnesian right wing broke and their left was routed after stiffer resistance. Altogether they lost seventy ships to the Athenians' twenty-five.

Bad weather prevented the Athenians from reaching the blockading squadron at Mytilene and, as the Peloponnesian commander Eteonicus concealed the defeat from his men, they embarked for Chios in good order. After the battle Sparta sued for peace but the Athenian terms were too high and the war continued into the AEGOSPOTAMI campaign (qv).

ARMADA   *see* SPANISH ARMADA

ARTEMISIUM   30 August–1 September 480 BC

Having decided that the pass of Thermopylae was the best place to block the Persian land invasion, the Greek allies looked for a suitable naval base nearby to protect it. They chose Artemisium at the northern end of the island of Euboea and commanding the entrance of the Euripus channel. The Greek fleet of 278 ships (including 147 from Athens) was under the command of the Spartan Eurybiades and it reached Artemisium about 18 August. Immensely superior in numbers – with over 1,300 *trieres* and hundreds of transports – the Persians lay concentrated around Aphetae at the head of the Pagasaean Gulf.

The weather was very stormy and many Persian ships were lost before the action began. On 30 August the Greeks attacked, capturing thirty ships, but withdrew at nightfall. That night a Persian squadron attempting to circumnavigate Euboea was lost in a storm. The Greeks attacked again on 31 August with little result. Next day at noon the Persians came out in crescent formation and tried unsuccessfully to encircle the Greek fleet. Both sides suffered heavily: half the Athenian ships were damaged but the Persian losses were even greater.

ASAN   25 July 1894

A clash between Chinese and Japanese naval units off the west coast of Korea before the official declaration of war on 1 August 1894. The war arose out of both countries' claims upon the sovereignty of Korea. A Japanese flying squadron under Rear-Admiral Tsuboi – protected cruisers *Yoshino*, *Naniwa* and *Akitsushima* – was despatched to the port of Asan with orders to stop the disembarkation of Chinese troops. Early on 25 July Tsuboi met the Chinese cruiser *Tsi-Yuen* and sloop *Kwang-Yi* returning home, having convoyed transports to Asan. After a brief engagement the *Tsi-Yuen* was severely damaged but escaped to Wei-hai-wei and the *Kwang-Yi* was sunk. The same day the Japanese met another Chinese sloop escorting the British steamer *Kowshing*, which was crowded with Chinese troops for Asan. The commander of the *Naniwa* (Captain Togo of future fame) ordered the steamer to follow him but her master was prevented from doing so by threats from the Chinese on board. After hours of fruitless negotiation Togo opened fire and sank the *Kowshing*, an act which provoked an international incident.

AUGUSTA   22 April 1676

The second of three actions fought between the French fleet and combined Dutch and Spanish squadrons in Sicilian waters during 1676 (*see also* STROMBOLI and PALERMO). In 1674 the Sicilians had risen against their Spanish rulers and appealed to Louis XIV, who sent a fleet under Duquesne and troops to garrison Messina. Then Spain, under the terms of the Triple Alliance, sought help from the Dutch, who despatched a squadron to the Mediterranean, commanded by the veteran Admiral de Ruyter.

After an indecisive action off Stromboli in January 1676 the combined fleet made an unsuccessful attack on the French at Messina. It then sailed south, hoping to draw Duquesne into the open. He duly accepted the challenge and on 22 April both fleets met off Augusta on the east coast of Sicily. Duquesne had twenty-nine ships of the line against the Allies' twenty-seven but his advantage was not only numerical. De Ruyter was no longer in chief command. Before the battle he had been joined by ten Spanish ships of the line under Don Francisco de la Cerda, who insisted on forming the centre of the allied line. Leading the van squadron, de Ruyter attacked vigorously but was entirely unsupported by de la Cerda. The Spaniards fought at long range and their position in the centre prevented the rear squadron of Dutch ships under Vice-Admiral Haan from getting into action until evening. Finally Duquesne retired with his fleet to leeward and darkness terminated the action. De Ruyter himself was seriously wounded and died at Syracuse a week later.

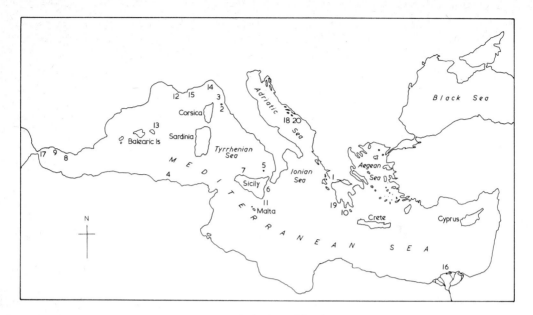

MEDITERRANEAN SEA   1570–1870   *principal naval battles*

1	*Lepanto, 7 October 1571*	11	*Cape Passaro, 11 August 1718*
2	*Elba, 28 August 1652*	12	*Toulon, 11 February 1744*
3	*Leghorn, 4 March 1653*	13	*Minorca, 20 May 1756*
4	*Bugia, 8 May 1671*	14	*Gulf of Genoa, 13/14 March 1795*
5	*Stromboli, 8 January 1676*	15	*Hyères, 13 July 1795*
6	*Augusta, 22 April 1676*	16	*The Nile, 1 August 1798*
7	*Palermo, 12 June 1676*	17	*Algeciras, 6 July and 12/13 July 1801*
8	*Malaga, 13 August 1704*	18	*Lissa, 13 March 1811*
9	*Marbella, 10 March 1705*	19	*Navarino, 20 October 1827*
10	*Matapan, 19 July 1717*	20	*Lissa, 20 July 1866*

AZORES, THE   31 August/1 September 1591

In the summer of 1591 an English squadron under Lord Thomas Howard – *Defiance*, *Revenge* (with Sir Richard Grenville as vice-admiral), *Nonpareil*, *Bonaventure*, *Lion*, *Foresight* and *Crane* – sailed to Flores in the Azores. For many weeks it waited there in vain for the Spanish treasure fleet. Instead, Howard was surprised on 31 August by the sudden appearance of a powerful Spanish fleet of fifty-three ships under the command of Don Alonso de Bazan, who was waiting to escort the treasure fleet home. The English admiral hurriedly weighed from the anchorage, all his ships following except the *Revenge*.

Why Grenville chose to stand and fight has never been fully explained. It may be because he still had men ashore or mistook Don Alonso for the treasure fleet; more probably he was seized by a courageous recklessness. Whatever the reason, the *Revenge* was soon surrounded and under attack.

From 3 o'clock that afternoon until dawn the next day, the *Revenge* fought alone for fifteen hours against overwhelming odds. After engaging the great galleon *San Felipe*, she took on in

AUGUSTA   22 April 1676   *Lithograph by P. Schotel*

turn fifteen Spanish ships and sank two of them. By daybreak she was a shambles but still defiant, with her upperworks shot away, not a mast standing, six feet of water in her hold and the last barrel of powder gone. Forty of her crew were dead and Grenville severely wounded. Eventually the *Revenge* struck and the Spaniards treated her survivors with honour. Grenville himself died of his wounds two days later and the *Revenge* foundered shortly afterwards in a storm.

BADOENG STRAIT   19/20 February 1942

This action arose out of an attempt to destroy Japanese transports which had landed troops on the island of Bali. It was made by a combined Dutch and American naval force against the Japanese anchored off the western shore of the narrow Badoeng Strait separating Bali from Nusa Besar Island. During the night of 19 February the Dutch cruisers *Java, de Ruyter* and three destroyers arrived off the anchorage but found that all but one transport and two destroyers had already sailed. Both sides opened fire: the transport was damaged but the Dutch destroyer *Piet Hein* was sunk by the *Asashio*. A second attack made a few hours later by the Dutch cruiser *Tromp* and four destroyers met with little success. The *Tromp* and US destroyer *Stewart* were severely damaged.

As this force was leaving the Badoeng Strait it was intercepted by two Japanese destroyers. In the ensuing action, one of them – the *Michishio* – was disabled. In a third allied attack, five Dutch torpedo boats failed to make contact with the enemy.

BALIKPAPAN   24 January 1942

Also known as the Macassar Strait action. During the Japanese landings in Borneo the Americans learned of an enemy invasion force anchored off the important oil port of Balikpapan. In the early hours of 24 January, four American destroyers – *John D. Ford, Pope, Parrott, Paul Jones* – made a high-speed torpedo attack on the enemy ships, which were illuminated by the burning oil installations ashore. Thinking they were being attacked by submarines, the Japanese escorts steamed into the Macassar Strait to intercept, leaving the transports unprotected. Despite numerous misses – due possibly to faulty torpedoes – the American destroyers sank four transports and one torpedo boat. *John D. Ford* was slightly damaged by shell-fire. Balikpapan was a tactical victory for the Americans but the Japanese invasion of Borneo was not interrupted.

BANTRY BAY   1 May 1689

Two months after the exiled James II's landing in Ireland in March 1689, Louis XIV gave further support to his cause. He despatched a powerful fleet of twenty-four of the line and ten fireships under le Comte de Châteaurenault, carrying supplies and reinforcements for James. Wearing his flag in the *Ardent*, 66, Châteaurenault sailed from Brest and arrived in Bantry Bay on the SW coast of Ireland at the end of April. There he was found by an English fleet under Admiral Arthur Herbert (later the Earl of Torrington), which had been hurriedly assembled at Portsmouth and sent to Ireland in search of the enemy. Herbert had with him the *Elizabeth*, 70 (flag), sixteen more of the line (mainly 50s and 60s) and three bomb-vessels.

As the English ships entered Bantry Bay on the morning of 1 May, Châteaurenault weighed to meet them. Being to leeward, Herbert had difficulty in working up towards the French, who bore down in good order and began the engagement about 10.30 am. Too late Herbert discovered he was outnumbered and had little room to manoeuvre in the narrow waters of the bay. He could not get the wind to escape and fighting continued until 5 pm, with the English fleet in serious danger of defeat. It was saved from disaster by two fortunate circumstances: the French fireships were still landing stores and did not participate; moreover, a serious dispute arose between Châteaurenault and his two immediate subordinates, who were jealous of him and refused to co-operate. So hampered, the French admiral broke off action in the evening and returned to his anchorage. Having completed his mission, he sailed for Brest on 6 May.

BARENTS SEA   31 December 1942

At the end of 1942, the Admiralty determined to effect the passage of convoys to Russia in smaller groups. Despite the severity of Arctic weather during the winter months, lack of daylight would minimise German aerial reconnaissance and reduce the danger of air and submarine attacks. On 25 December convoy JW 51A reached Kola inlet after a safe passage. The second half – convoy JW 51B comprising fourteen merchantmen – sailed from Loch Ewe on 22 December, escorted by six destroyers and five smaller warships under the command of Captain Sherbrooke in the destroyer *Onslow*. All went well until 27 December when a severe gale scattered some of the convoy. That day Admiral Burnett left Kola with the cruisers *Sheffield, Jamaica* and three destroyers to provide support but bad weather prevented him from establishing contact.

BANTRY BAY   1 May 1689   *Oil painting by Willem Van de Velde*

On 30 December *U.354* reported sighting the convoy south of Bear Island and the German squadron in Alten Fjord – heavy cruiser *Admiral Hipper* (Vice-Admiral Kummetz), pocket battleship *Lützow* and six destroyers – immediately put to sea. In the early hours of 31 December Kummetz divided his forces, planning to approach on both flanks, draw off the escort with the first attack and leave the convoy at the mercy of the second. However for several reasons the action that day developed into a series of confused engagements. Bad weather, stragglers, the German reluctance to press home the attack and the difficulty both sides experienced in distinguishing friend from foe – all contributed to the confusion. In her first attack at 9.30 am the *Hipper* severely damaged the *Onslow* (blinding Captain Sherbrooke in one eye) and overwhelmed the minesweeper *Bramble*. But the destroyers kept her at bay. An hour later the *Lützow* got dangerously close and only sudden snow squalls and the timidity of her captain saved the convoy from destruction. At 11 am the *Hipper* attacked again and crippled the *Achates*, who gallantly continued to defend her charges until capsizing two hours later. Suddenly fortunes changed. The *Hipper* found herself confronted by Burnett's cruisers, who damaged her with three hits and quickly sank the destroyer *Friedrich Eckoldt*. This was enough for Kummetz. At 11.50 am he turned for home and, although *Lützow* later fired at the convoy from long range, the action was virtually over. It had been a remarkable British success. The convoy reached Kola inlet unharmed, and at minimal cost, the escort and Burnett's cruisers had beaten off a greatly superior enemy force. By contrast Kummetz had displayed

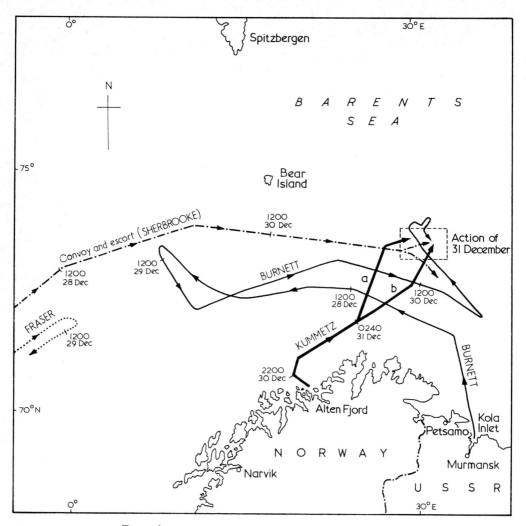

BARFLEUR SEA   31 December 1942

➤ *Vice-Admiral Kummetz, with* Admiral Hipper *(a),* Lützow *(b) and 6 destroyers*

-·-·-➤ *Convoy JW 51B (14 merchantmen) and escort – Captain Sherbrooke with destroyers* Onslow, Obedient, Obdurate, Orwell, Achates; *2 corvettes; 1 minesweeper; 2 trawlers*

➤ *Admiral Burnett with cruisers* Sheffield, Jamaica *and 3 destroyers*

·······➤ *C-in-C Home Fleet with battleship* Anson, *heavy cruiser* Cumberland *and 3 destroyers*

hesitancy and lack of determination, hampered though he undoubtedly was by restrictive orders.

BARFLEUR   19 May 1692

This battle – and its sequel at LA HOGUE (qv) a few days later – decided the Anglo-French naval struggle during the War of the English Succession (1689–97). They put an end to French

BARFLEUR 19 May 1692 *Grisaille by A. van Salm*

superiority in the Channel, temporarily gained after Tourville's victory off Beachy Head two years before. In the spring of 1692 the exiled King James II was at Cherbourg, preparing an expeditionary force to invade England and regain his throne. The main English fleet under Admiral Russell lay at Portsmouth, where it was reinforced in May by a Dutch squadron, bringing the total allied strength up to ninety-six ships of the line. In considerably less force, Comte de Tourville had forty-four of the line at Brest. After waiting in vain for reinforcements from Toulon under Admiral d'Estrées, the French commander-in-chief weighed from Brest and entered the Channel on 17 May. With his flag in the *Britannia*, 100, Russell sailed from Portsmouth on 18 May. Early next day he sighted the enemy fleet off Cap Barfleur, the NE point of the Cotentin peninsula in Normandy.

With the wind in his favour Tourville decided to fight, unaware of the numbers against him. Proceeding SSW he formed line and the action began about 10.30 am. Fierce fighting developed in the centre, during which Tourville's flagship the *Soleil Royal*, 106, was badly damaged. All morning it had been misty and at 3 pm a dense fog enveloped the scene, just when Russell's great superiority in numbers was beginning to tell. Under cover of the fog Tourville conducted a skilful retreat and took his fleet westwards. Action ceased about 8 pm and both fleets anchored at nightfall, with neither having lost a ship. The following morning the fog lifted and Russell ordered a general chase as the French fleet continued to retire west towards the Channel Islands. The events which followed in the next four days form part of the subsequent action of La Hogue (*see* map on page 102 for Barfleur action).

BASQUE AND AIX ROADS 11–16 April 1809

In February 1809 Rear-Admiral Willaumez sailed from Brest with ten of the line and proceeded south to the anchorage of Basque and Aix Roads near Rochefort, where he joined a smaller

BASQUE AND AIX ROADS 11–16 April 1809 *Engraving by Robert Dodd – the French fleet aground after being forced from its anchorage by fireships*. HMS Mediator *in the foreground*

French squadron already there. Admiral Gambier with the Channel fleet followed him and blockaded the approaches to the Roads. However the presence of this strong enemy force in the Bay of Biscay – athwart British communications to Portugal and the Mediterranean – constituted a threat which had to be eliminated. The Admiralty therefore appointed Captain Lord Cochrane to the task of expelling the French from their anchorage by fireships and other means. At the beginning of April Cochrane joined Gambier off Rochefort.

The attack by Cochrane's fireships and explosion vessels (each containing many hundreds of barrels of gunpowder) was launched on the night of 11/12 April. With wind and tide in their favour they penetrated the boom and bore down on the enemy line. In the confusion and panic the French ships cut their cables, fouled each other and many ran aground. At the decisive moment, however, Gambier refused to intervene and completely ignored Cochrane's many signals for assistance. Throughout the next morning – as the tide turned and the enemy strove to refloat their ships – Gambier still did not send in his ships. When he at last did so later in the day, the *Varsovie*, 80, *Aquilon*, 74, and *Tonnerre*, 74, were taken or burnt. Further attacks were made during the next four days but were far less successful as the French had had time to recover.

BATUM 25/6 January 1878

The final naval action of the Russo-Turkish War of 1877–8. During the night, two Russian torpedo-boats, the *Tchesme* and *Sinope*, entered the Turkish anchorage of Batum in the Black Sea. Undetected by the defences they launched their torpedoes and sank the Turkish guardship, a large gunboat. They then retired undamaged. The port of Batum passed into Russian hands under the terms of the Treaty of Berlin (13 July 1878) which concluded the war.

BEACHY HEAD   30 June 1690   *Engraving by Skelton, after Théodore Gudin*

BEACHY HEAD   30 June 1690

An Anglo-Dutch defeat during the War of the English Succession (1689–97) at the hands of the French, by whom it is known as the Battle of Bévéziers (a corruption of Pevensey). In the summer of 1790 the allied fleet guarding the English Channel was commanded by Arthur Herbert, Earl of Torrington, with the Dutch van squadron under Eversten. Naval support for William III's expedition to Ireland and the despatch of a squadron to the Mediterranean had seriously weakened the Channel fleet. Thus when a powerful French force of seventy-seven ships under Comte de Tourville was sighted off the Lizard on 21 June, Torrington could only muster fifty-six ships to oppose him. Both fleets were in contact off Dunnose Head on 25 June, as the French proceeded slowly up Channel with the intention of blockading the Thames. There followed four days of manoeuvring as Torrington with his inferior force gave ground. Then on the evening of 29 June he received orders to engage the enemy and next morning action was joined off Beachy Head.

Torrington with his flag in the *Royal Sovereign*, 100, had the wind in his favour but the attack miscarried. Owing to faulty dispositions by the English admiral, only the Dutch ships in the van really got to grips with the enemy and they suffered severely. Eversten was beset first by the French van under Châteaurenault and then by de Tourville himself with the *Soleil Royal*, 98, and the centre squadron. Fortunately for the Dutch the wind dropped completely about 3 pm and action ceased. That evening the allied fleet retreated eastwards with several disabled ships in tow. Although only one Dutch vessel and some fireships had been lost during the battle, Torrington was compelled next day to destroy his damaged ships to prevent their falling into the hands of the pursuing enemy. They included the *Anne*, 70 – beached near Winchelsea and burnt – and the Dutch *Wapen van Utrecht*, 64, *Maagd van Enkhuizen*, 72, *Tholen*, 60, and *Elswout*, 50. De Tourville lost no ships.

After the battle the French were temporarily masters of the Channel and news of Torrington's defeat caused panic in London. However de Tourville failed to exploit his advantage. On the grounds of growing sickness and shortage of stores aboard his ships, he abandoned the pursuit off Dover and sailed back home down the Channel, burning Teignmouth on the way. The allied fleet, still in great confusion, anchored at the Nore on 10 July and Torrington was relieved of his command. He was acquitted in the court martial which followed but never employed again.

BELLE ISLE   17 June 1795

Known by British authorities as 'Cornwallis's Retreat', although as will be seen in no sense derogatory. On the morning of 16 June a powerful French squadron under Admiral Villaret-Joyeuse (twelve ships of the line, two 50s and nine frigates), sighted a much smaller squadron under Vice-Admiral William Cornwallis north of Belle Isle in the Bay of Biscay. Cornwallis had with him only the *Royal Sovereign*, 100, four 74s and two frigates. As soon as he realised the enemy's strength, he retired south under full sail.

Fortune however was against him; the wind shifted in the enemy's favour and the 74s *Bellerophon* and *Brunswick* sailed so slowly they had to jettison some of their gear during the night. By dawn on the 17th, Villaret-Joyeuse had caught up and action was joined. Having fallen astern with damage aloft, the *Mars*, 74, was in danger of capture until Cornwallis gallantly interposed the *Royal Sovereign* and rescued her. Meanwhile Captain Robert Stopford

BELLE ISLE   17 June 1795   *Aquatint by Richard Livesay, showing Admiral Cornwallis retreating from the French fleet*

– ahead of the squadron with the frigate *Phaeton* – had begun making signals which cleverly tricked Villaret-Joyeuse into thinking he was in touch with the main British fleet. Eventually the French gave up the pursuit. In the face of a superior enemy force, Cornwallis had conducted a masterly retreat without loss.

'BISMARCK' ACTION, THE 23–7 May 1941

On 18 May 1941 the powerful German battleship *Bismarck*, commanded by Vice-Admiral Lütjens, and heavy cruiser *Prinz Eugen* sailed from Gdynia to attack allied shipping in the Atlantic. The British Admiralty soon learned of their departure; cruisers were stationed at the northern approaches into the Atlantic and intensive aerial reconnaissance was mounted. On the evening of 21 May the German ships were sighted lying in Korsfjord south of Bergen. Twenty-four hours later a further reconnaissance, made under difficult flying conditions, established that Lütjens had left the anchorage. Admiral Tovey, commander-in-chief Home Fleet, immediately ordered the battlecruiser *Hood* and newly commissioned battleship *Prince of Wales* from Scapa Flow to reinforce his patrolling cruisers. In misty weather on the evening of 23 May, the heavy cruiser *Suffolk* sighted the German warships entering the Denmark Strait near the Greenland ice-edge. Her sister-ship *Norfolk* made contact soon afterwards and both cruisers began skilfully shadowing the enemy and reporting their movements.

Vice-Admiral Holland with *Hood* and *Prince of Wales* was then some 220 miles away to the SE and he changed course to intercept the German squadron early next day. Shortly before 6 am on 24 May, all four ships came into action south of Denmark Strait and opened fire at a range of 25,000 yards. After a ten-minute engagement – in which *Bismarck*'s fire was heavy and accurate – the *Hood* blew up and sank, as a result of a 15in shell penetrating one of her magazines. Only three men out of her complement of over 1,400 survived. Fire was then concentrated on the *Prince of Wales* and she was forced to break off the action. However she had scored two hits on the *Bismarck*, one of which caused a severe fuel leak. As a result Lütjens decided to abandon his plans for a foray into the Atlantic and make for a French port instead.

Meanwhile Admiral Tovey was concentrating all available forces in the area. He had sailed from Scapa Flow late on 22 May with the *King George V*, *Repulse*, *Victorious*, five cruisers and six destroyers. Admiral Somerville's 'Force H' – *Renown*, *Ark Royal*, *Sheffield* and six destroyers – were coming north from Gibraltar and the battleships *Rodney* and *Ramillies* had been taken from escort duty.

On the evening of 24 May Lütjens detached the *Prinz Eugen* and she reached Brest independently on 1 June. About midnight 24/5 May torpedo-bombers from the *Victorious* unsuccessfully attacked the *Bismarck*. Three hours later Lütjens altered course towards the SW and the shadowing cruisers suddenly lost radar contact. Throughout 25 May intensive air searches were made to find her and anxiety grew as the hours passed without result. At last early next morning a Catalina of Coastal Command sighted the enemy steering due west only 700 miles from Brest. Tovey at once detached the *Sheffield* to shadow and ordered the launching of a strike by *Ark Royal*'s aircraft. Swordfish took off from the aircraft carrier during the afternoon but mistook the *Sheffield* for the *Bismarck* and tried to torpedo her. Fortunately the cruiser took prompt evasive action and a fault in the firing mechanism of the torpedoes was rectified. Between 8.45 and 9.25 pm that evening, fifteen Swordfish from *Ark Royal* carried out a second attack. One torpedo struck the *Bismarck* right aft, damaging her propellers and jamming the

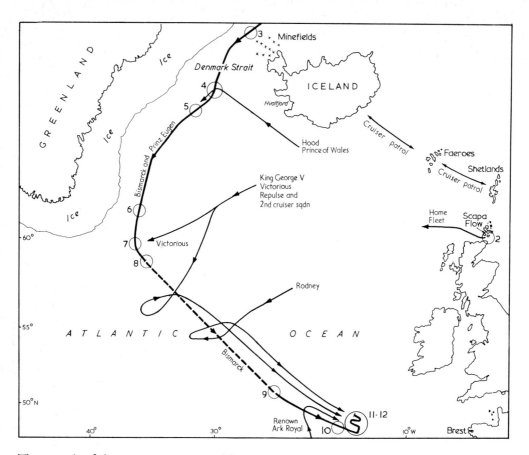

The pursuit of the BISMARCK   24–7 May 1941

1   *Lütjens sails from Korsfjord, south of Bergen, evening 21 May*
2   *Home Fleet sails from Scapa, 10.45 pm 22 May*
3   *Suffolk sights enemy at ice-edge, 7.22 pm 23 May and shadows with* Norfolk
4–5   *Action of Denmark Strait. Admiral Holland with* Hood *and* Prince of Wales. Hood *sunk 6 am 24 May*
6   Prinz Eugen *detached 6 pm; reached Brest evening 1 June*
7   *Unsuccessful torpedo-bomber attack by aircraft from* Victorious, *midnight 24/25 May*
8   *Contact with* Bismarck *lost, 3 am 25 May*
9   *Catalina aircraft regains contact, 10.30 am 26 May*
10   *Successful torpedo-bomber attack by aircraft from* Ark Royal, *which obtained vital hit on* Bismarck's *steering and rudder, 8.45–9.25 pm 26 May*
11   *Night attack on Bismarck by 4th Destroyer Flotilla, 10.30 pm–midnight*
12   *Final gun action between* Rodney, King George V *and* Bismarck, *8–10.36 am 27 May. Finally sunk by torpedoes from cruiser* Dorsetshire *in position 48°10′N, 16°12′W, 400 miles due west from Brest*

rudder. This crucial hit sealed the German battleship's fate, as her speed was drastically reduced and steering became very erratic.

During the night of 26/7 May, the 4th Destroyer Flotilla led by Captain Vian made further torpedo attacks and scored two hits under heavy fire. Meanwhile Tovey, with *King George V*

The BISMARCK sinking   27 May 1941   *Oil painting by C. E. Turner*

and *Rodney*, had closed with the enemy but decided against a night attack. In the final two-hour gun action next morning the *Bismarck* was set on fire and her guns silenced. After receiving three torpedoes from the cruiser *Dorsetshire*, she finally sank at 10.36 am some 400 miles from Brest with her colours still flying. Only 110 men out of her company of 2,400 were rescued. So ended one of the most dramatic and prolonged naval actions of modern times.

BISMARCK SEA   2–5 March 1943

As the Allied forces slowly advanced up the north coast of New Guinea in the first months of 1943, the Japanese made every effort to reinforce their key garrison at Lae in the Huon Gulf. On 1 March a convoy of eight transports, escorted by an equal number of destroyers under the command of Rear-Admiral Kimura, left Rabaul in New Britain for Lae. Next morning shore-based American and Australian aircraft began a three-day attack on the convoy. During the night of 3/4 March American motor torpedo boats from Milne Bay joined the attack. The following night two of them drove off a Japanese submarine which was picking up survivors. By the end of the battle the Japanese had lost all eight transports, the destroyers *Shirayuki*, *Arashio*, *Asashio* and *Tokitsukaze* and 3,000 troops. They never again attempted to reinforce New Guinea by sea.

BREST   10 August 1512

One year after his accession in 1509 the young King Henry VIII made an alliance with Spain and the Empire against Louis XII of France. In 1512 he ordered the Lord Admiral Edward Howard to fit out a fleet of twenty ships at Portsmouth. Its purpose was to convoy an English army under the Earl of Dorset to Guipuzcoa, where it would co-operate with Ferdinand of Spain against the French in the south. Lord Howard successfully disembarked the expedition and then raided the coast of Brittany on his way home. In the first week of August he put out again from Portsmouth with twenty-five ships and came upon the French fleet under Jean de Thénouënol lying outside Brest harbour. An indecisive engagement was fought on 10 August, which has remained memorable owing to a catastrophe. Two of the largest ships engaged, the *Regent* (Sir Thomas Knyvett) and 'the great carrack of Brest' *Marie la Cordelière* collided. While they grappled together and the English archers and French cross-bowmen exchanged fire, the French ship's powder magazine suddenly blew up. Both ships were engulfed in flames and shortly afterwards sank. Knyvett, the *Cordelière*'s captain Primauget and most of their crews perished.

BREST   25 April 1513

Preparatory to his invasion of France in 1513, King Henry VIII planned to attack the French fleet in their main base at Brest in order to secure the safe passage of the English army across Dover Straits. Lord Admiral Howard sailed from Plymouth on 10 April with a fleet of twenty-four ships. On arrival before Brest, Howard found the harbour strongly fortified. Moreover, the able French admiral Prégent de Bidoux had arrived with galleys from the Mediterranean to take command in the Channel.

Unable to enforce a blockade because of insufficient material, the Lord Admiral decided to attack Prégent at his moorings. On the afternoon of 25 April he rashly attempted to cut out the enemy flagship with a small flotilla of galleys and barges. With seventeen followers the admiral boarded from his galley alongside; but the cable was cut and it drifted away, leaving them to be overwhelmed by the enemy and hurled over the side where they drowned. The attack on the French fleet was repulsed and after the loss of their admiral the demoralised English returned to Plymouth.

'BRIDPORT'S ACTION'   *see* GROIX, ÎLE DE

BUGIA   8 May 1671

In a celebrated exploit, Admiral Sir Edward Spragge's Mediterranean squadron attacked and burned eight Algerine corsairs (three armed with thirty-four guns) and three of their prizes. The action took place in Bugia Bay (later Bougie and now Bejaïa) on the north coast of Algeria.

Spragge's first attack with fireships on the night of 2 May failed. Success followed six days later, when the boom which the pirates had thrown across the harbour entrance was pierced in broad daylight.

CABRITA POINT see MARBELLA

CALABRIA 9 July 1940

The first capital-ship action between the Italian navy and the British Mediterranean fleet, after Italy's entry into the war on 10 June 1940. Admiral Cunningham with battleships *Warspite*, *Malaya*, *Royal Sovereign*, aircraft carrier *Eagle*, supported by cruisers and destroyers, was covering the passage of two convoys from Malta to Alexandria. Similarly the Italian fleet under Admiral Campione was providing distant escort for a troop convoy bound for North Africa.

Contact was established off Calabria on 9 July, followed by unsuccessful torpedo attacks by aircraft from *Eagle*. In the afternoon a 105-minute gun action took place at long range, during which *Warspite* hit the Italian battleship *Giulio Cesare* and the heavy cruiser *Bolzano* was slightly damaged. The Italians hurriedly retired under cover of smoke and contact was never regained, although Admiral Cunningham pursued to within twenty-five miles of the Calabrian coast. Finally Italian aircraft heavily bombed the fleet without success. Although brief and inconclusive, the encounter off Calabria first indicated the Italian fleet's reluctance for prolonged action.

CALDERA BAY 23 April 1891

An engagement during the Chilean Revolutionary War of 1891. Early on the morning of 23 April, two Government torpedo boats, *Almirante Condell* and *Almirante Lynch*, steamed into Caldera Bay, 230 miles south of Antofagasta. There the Congressional ironclad *Blanco Encalada* lay at anchor. The *Almirante Condell* led the attack and launched her torpedoes which missed. The ironclad then opened fire but her gunners failed to notice the approach of the second torpedo boat. The *Almirante Lynch* was thus able to come to within fifty yards before releasing her torpedoes. After being struck by the second torpedo the *Blanco Encalada* sank within three minutes.

'CALDER'S ACTION' 22 July 1805

Also known as the action off Finisterre or Ferrol. On 9 June 1805 Admiral Villeneuve with the Combined Fleet sailed from Martinique to return to Europe after an abortive cruise in the West Indies. Nelson after a long chase had missed him by four days. Lord Barham at the Admiralty then made skilful dispositions to prevent the concentration of Franco-Spanish squadrons and awaited Villeneuve's return. Off Ferrol lay Vice-Admiral Sir Robert Calder with ten ships of the line. He was reinforced by a further five and ordered to cruise 100 miles of Cape Finisterre in order to intercept Villeneuve and forestall his junction with the Spanish squadron in Ferrol. Calder reached his appointed station on 19 July and there three days later encountered Villeneuve in a thick fog. Because of the weather the fleets did not engage until 5 pm and a confused and indecisive action then followed. Although Calder took the Spanish line ships *San Raphael*, 80, and *Firme*, 71, and temporarily barred Villeneuve's approach to Ferrol, he signally

CALDER'S ACTION   22 July 1805   *Aquatint by Thomas Whitcombe*

failed to bring the enemy to decisive action both on 22 July and the following two days. At the subsequent court martial he was severely reprimanded for failing to do so and for being more concerned with the safety of his prizes.

CAMPERDOWN   11 October 1797

Throughout the summer of 1797 Admiral Duncan had maintained a continuous blockade of the Dutch fleet in the Texel, despite many desertions as a result of the naval mutinies. In compliance with orders from the Admiralty Duncan on 1 October took his battered squadron to Yarmouth for refit and stores, leaving frigates to keep vigilant watch over the Dutch. Early on 9 October a British lugger arrived in Yarmouth Road with the urgent news that the enemy were coming out of the Texel. Duncan at once weighed with the *Venerable*, 74, and ten of the line and stood over to the Dutch coast, leaving the rest of his squadron to follow. Vice-Admiral de Winter had put to sea early on 8 October with his whole fleet. Since then he had been constantly shadowed by a small inshore squadron under Captain Trollope in the *Russell*, 74. Duncan joined the latter early on 11 October and shortly after noon the opposing fleets came into action about three miles NW of Camperdown (Kamperduijn) on the Dutch coast. Both were evenly matched – sixteen ships of the line each – but the British were heavier-gunned and the Dutch had more frigates. De Winter, too, had the advantage of position and was fighting in his own waters. Because the day was advancing, the wind on shore and the water shoal, Duncan wasted no time on tactical manoeuvring and closed at once with the enemy. He approached with his fleet in two columns in line ahead – each comprising eight of the line – to break the Dutch line

CAMPERDOWN 11 October 1797 *Engraving by T. Hellyer, after Thomas Whitcombe*

at right-angles. About 12.30 pm Vice-Admiral Onslow, his second-in-command with the *Monarch*, 74, led the weather division into action and cut through the rear of the Dutch line of battle. After two hours' severe fighting, the *Jupiter*, 72 (Rear-Admiral Reijntjes, who later died of wounds), *Haarlem*, 68, *Alkmaar*, 56, *Delft*, 54, and the frigate *Monnikendam* surrendered.

Meanwhile Duncan, with the *Venerable* leading the lee division and *Triumph* and *Ardent* in close support, had struck against the Dutch van. He soon engaged de Winter's flagship the *Vrijheid*, 74, which was lying fifth in line. Fighting became extremely fierce and for a while the *Venerable* was surrounded by several Dutch ships and nearly overwhelmed, until others came to her assistance. Action continued for $3\frac{1}{2}$ hours as the Dutch fought with the greatest obduracy. Four more of their battleships then struck – *Hercules*, 64, *Gelijkheid*, 68, *Admiraal Tjerk Hiddes de Vries*, 68, and *Wassenaer*, 64. At length about 3.15 pm de Winter surrendered the *Vrijheid*, by then reduced to a shambles and he himself the only unwounded man on deck. The battle was over and casualties on both sides were very heavy. So badly damaged were the Dutch prizes that none saw sea service again and two sank on the way back to England. Partly because of his own damage but also on account of the gathering darkness on a lee shore, Duncan did not pursue the remaining Dutch ships. Eventually Rear-Admiral Storij with the *Staaten Generaal*, 74, and six of the line reached the Texel. (*See map on next page.*)

CAPE BON AD 468

A Roman fleet of 1,100 galleys and transports commanded by Basiliscus was lying at anchor off Cape Bon, having landed troops on the peninsula in preparation for an assault on Carthage.

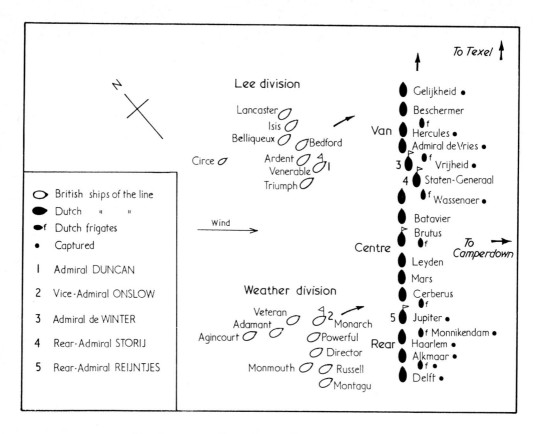

CAMPERDOWN 11 October 1797 *Duncan's attack*

Suddenly a large fleet appeared, led by Gaiseric (also known as Genseric), the celebrated king of the Vandals. The Vandals sent in fireships and over half the Roman fleet was destroyed. The action was further proof of the extent to which control of the Mediterranean had passed to the Vandals, following Gaiseric's sack of Rome in 455.

CAPE BON 13 December 1941

A brilliant night action carried out by a flotilla of allied destroyers under Commander G. H. Stokes, RN. The Tribal class *Sikh* and *Maori*, the *Legion* and the Dutch destroyer *Isaac Sweers* were on passage from Gibraltar to Alexandria. In the early hours of 13 December they sighted and surprised two Italian light cruisers close off Cape Bon. They were the *Alberto di Giussano* and *Alberico da Barbiano*, carrying urgently needed petrol supplies to the Axis forces in North Africa. After a swift torpedo attack, both enemy ships were sunk.

CAPE ENGAÑO *see* LEYTE GULF

CAPE ESPERANCE   11/12 October 1942

The third of six bitterly fought engagements between American and Japanese naval forces in the Solomons during the latter half of 1942 (*see also* SAVO ISLAND; EASTERN SOLOMONS; SANTA CRUZ ISLANDS; GUADALCANAL and TASSAFARONGA). Each reflected the desperate struggle by both sides to gain control of Guadalcanal Island and its surrounding waters.

During the afternoon of 11 October a considerable enemy force under Rear-Admiral Goto (heavy cruisers *Aoba*, *Kinugasa*, *Furutaka*, eight destroyers and two seaplane carriers used as transports) was sighted by reconnaissance aircraft, proceeding down the Slot on direct course for Guadalcanal. The Japanese planned to bombard the American beachhead that night – especially the vital Henderson airfield – and also disembark troops and supplies. Alerted to their presence, Rear-Admiral Norman Scott – with heavy cruisers *Salt Lake City*, *San Francisco*, light cruisers *Boise*, *Helena* and five destroyers – sailed to intercept. Contact was made shortly before midnight off Cape Esperance. A violent gun action then ensued, during which the Japanese destroyer *Fubuki* was blown out of the water and the heavy cruiser *Furutaka* set on fire and later sunk. Admiral Goto was killed on the bridge of his flagship the *Aoba* and the next day two of the retiring Japanese destroyers – *Natsugumo* and *Murakumo* – were caught by American aircraft off Savo Island and sunk. Admiral Scott lost the destroyer *Duncan* and two of his cruisers were damaged but he had successfully repulsed the Japanese attack.

CAPE HENRY   *see* CHESAPEAKE   16 March 1781

CAPE KALIAKRA   11 August 1791

An action during the Russo-Turkish War of 1787–91, when both powers fought for control of the Black Sea. A Russian fleet under Admiral Ushakov sailed from Sevastopol on 8 August and three days later found the Turks under Hussein Pasha at anchor south of Cape Kaliakra, twenty-five miles NE of Varna. The fleets were evenly matched. The Russian attack succeeded in driving Hussein Pasha from his anchorage and by nightfall he was in full retreat. Neither side however lost a ship.

CAPE ORTEGAL   4 November 1805

Also known as 'Strachan's action' and a fitting postscript to the victory of Trafalgar. Near Cape Ortegal, the north-west tip of Spain, on 4 November a British squadron commanded by Captain Sir Richard Strachan – *Caesar*, 80, three 74s and four frigates – met and engaged four of the French ships of the line which had escaped from Trafalgar. These were the *Formidable*, 80, wearing the flag of Rear-Admiral Dumanoir Le Pelley, *Duguay Trouin*, 74, *Mont Blanc*, 74, and *Scipion*, 74. After a long chase in bad weather, Strachan's frigates came up with the slow-sailing *Scipion*. Dumanoir then turned to fight. In the ensuing action all his ships were dismasted and taken after suffering 750 casualties. They were eventually added to the Royal Navy and the *Duguay Trouin*, as the *Implacable*, served as a boys' training ship at Devonport from 1855 to 1949.

CAPE PASSARO   11 August 1718   *Oil painting by Richard Paton*

CAPE PASSARO   11 August 1718

After the Spanish seizure of Sicily in the summer of 1718 the Quadruple Alliance was signed against her by England, France, Holland and the Empire. Admiral Sir George Byng (later Viscount Torrington) was despatched to the Mediterranean with a large fleet – *Barfleur*, 90 (flagship) and nineteen of the line – and reached the Bay of Naples on 1 August. There he learned that although almost all Sicily had fallen to the Spanish troops, the Savoyards were still holding out in the fortress of Messina. Having taken reinforcements on board at Naples, he weighed with his fleet and arrived off Messina on 9 August.

At this juncture Spain and England were not officially at war and the actual declaration did not take place until 17 December. Nevertheless on 10 August Byng came into contact with the Spanish fleet outside Messina. It comprised twelve of the line and several smaller warships including galleys under the command of Vice-Admiral Castañeta flying his flag in the *Real San Felipe*, 74. Both in numbers and discipline the Spaniards were markedly inferior to their opponents. Byng followed the enemy fleet and on the morning of 11 August battle was joined off Cape Passaro on the southern tip of Sicily, when one of the Spaniards – the *San Isidoro*, 46 – opened fire. Action became general, during which Castañeta's ships were thrown into utter confusion and then overwhelmed. By the end of the day twenty-two Spanish warships had been taken, burned or later sank. Castañeta himself was captured and subsequently died of his wounds.

CAPE ST GEORGE   25 November 1943

The last of seven engagements between American and Japanese naval forces in the Solomon Islands during 1943. Both this action and that of EMPRESS AUGUSTA BAY (qv) arose out of

Japanese attempts to counter the American landings on Bougainville Island, which had begun on 1 November. Operating from their main base at Rabaul in New Britain, Japanese naval forces tried unsuccessfully to reinforce their garrisons.

In the early hours of 25 November, a flotilla of five US destroyers commanded by Captain A. A. Burke – *Charles F. Ausburne, Claxton, Dyson, Converse, Spence* – was patrolling the area between Buka in North Bougainville and Cape St George, New Ireland. They intercepted and attacked five Japanese destroyers, which were returning to Rabaul after having taken stores to Buka. Taken by surprise, the *Onami, Makinami* and *Yugiri* were sunk by torpedo and gunfire without loss or damage to the American force (*see also* SOLOMON ISLANDS).

CAPE ST VINCENT 16 January 1780

Frequently known as 'The Moonlight Battle'. On 29 December 1779 Admiral Rodney set sail from Plymouth with a large fleet. With twenty-two ships of the line and nine frigates, his main purpose was to escort a convoy of reinforcements to Gibraltar, then closely besieged by the Spaniards. The fleet also included the trade for the West Indies, whence Rodney was going to take up command of the Leeward Islands station.

CAPE ST VINCENT 16 January 1780 *Engraving by Robert Dodd*

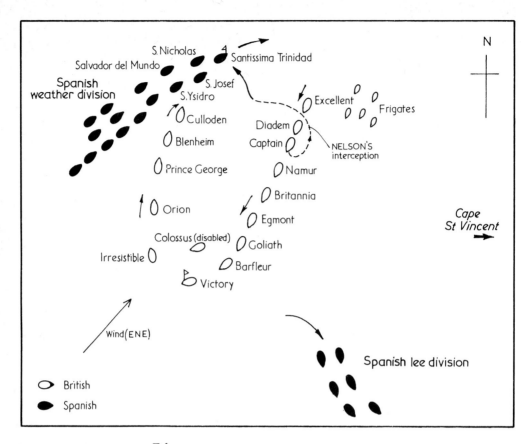

CAPE ST VINCENT   14 February 1797

At daybreak on 8 January he sighted the Spanish Caracca fleet south of Cape Finisterre. The enemy force under Commodore Don Juan de Yardi – *Guipuscoana*, 64, six frigates and a convoy of sixteen merchantmen bound for Cadiz with wheat and naval stores – was chased by Rodney and captured *in toto*. The English fleet then held its course and early on 16 January rounded Cape St Vincent. At noon, when twelve miles south of the cape, enemy ships were sighted bearing SE. Rodney at once crowded on sail and formed his fleet into line abreast. With a strong westerly wind his coppered ships soon overhauled the enemy, which proved to be a Spanish squadron of eleven of the line and two frigates under Admiral Don Juan de Langara. With a two-to-one advantage, Rodney's leading ships were in action with the enemy rear about 4 pm. An hour later the *Santo Domingo*, 70, blew up and only one of her crew of 600 survived. The battle continued throughout the stormy moonlight night, by the end of which the *Fenix*, 80 (Langara's flagship), *San Julian*, 70, *San Eugenio*, 70, *Monarca*, 70, *Princessa*, 70, and *Diligente*, 70, had all been taken. Next morning the weather worsened. Two of the Spanish prizes had to be abandoned and were wrecked near San Lucar; the English fleet was extricated with difficulty from a dangerous lee shore. Curiously Rodney was confined to his bunk with gout throughout the action but this did not seem to impair his ability to defeat the enemy.

CAPE ST VINCENT 14 February 1797 *Oil painting by Robert Cleveley* – Victory *raking the Spanish vice-admiral*

CAPE ST VINCENT 14 February 1797

A resounding British victory during the French Revolutionary War, in which Admiral Jervis's Mediterranean fleet defeated a Spanish force twice its size. At the end of 1796 the French and Spanish ships in the Mediterranean were ordered to Brest to support a projected expedition against Ireland. The former under Villeneuve sailed from Toulon in mid-December and passed successfully through the Straits. Some weeks later the large but undermanned Spanish fleet left Cartagena under Admiral de Cordova to escort valuable mercury ships to Cadiz. He had with him twenty-seven ships of the line – including the very large *Santissima Trinidad*, 136, *Concepcion*, 112, *Mexicano*, 112, *Salvador del Mundo*, 112, *San Josef*, 112, *Condé de Regla*, 112, *Principe de Asturias*, 112 – and twelve frigates. Previously Admiral Jervis had weighed from the Tagus on 18 January with the *Victory*, 100, fourteen of the line and four frigates and was cruising in readiness off Cape St Vincent to intercept. On 13 February he was joined by Commodore Nelson from Gibraltar, who took over command of the *Captain*, 74. That day the enemy's approach was reported to Jervis, who held his course and both fleets drew closer during the night. As the fog lifted off Cape St Vincent next morning the enemy fleet was sighted straggling ESE in two divisions. With admirable precision Jervis thrust his well-disciplined ships in single column through the gap between the two and then, with *Culloden* leading, turned to attack the enemy's weather division. The manoeuvre caused confusion among de Cordova's ships but shortly after 1 o'clock the Spaniards threatened to escape north as they began to pass astern of the British column. At this critical moment Nelson

45

suddenly took the *Captain* – the third ship from the rear – right out of the line and threw her across the path of the advancing Spaniards. Although in danger of being blown out of the water by the huge *Santissima Trinidad*, *San Josef* and *Salvador del Mundo*, Nelson's brilliant tactic forced the enemy to alter course and the ensuing mêlée enabled Jervis to catch up. Soon several ships had come to Nelson's aid, including Collingwood with the *Excellent*. After an hour's action the *Salvador del Mundo*, 112, and *San Ysidro*, 74, struck. Moreover the badly damaged *San Josef*, 112, and *San Nicholas*, 80, ran foul of each other, enabling Nelson to perform a second exploit. In a short space of time he had led a boarding party from the damaged *Captain*, which rushed through both ships and effected their capture – a deed later immortalised as 'Nelson's Patent Bridge for boarding First-Rates'. Even the huge *Santissima Trinidad* was at one time in danger of capture but she lived to fight another day. Action ceased in the late afternoon as Jervis made sure of his four prizes and the defeated de Cordova withdrew to Cadiz.

When news of the victory reached England there was great joy, especially so because at that time the war was going very badly. The battle had been won because of Spanish inferiority, Nelson's daring, and the high pitch of efficiency to which Jervis had brought the Mediterranean fleet – and of these the last was the most important.

CAPE SPADA *see* SPADA

CAPE SPARTIVENTO   27 November 1940

An action south of Sardinia between British forces under Vice-Admiral Somerville (*Renown*, *Ark Royal*, two cruisers and nine destroyers) and units of the Italian fleet. It arose out of operations to ensure the safe passage of a small British convoy of fast transports carrying vital reinforcements to the Middle East. Somerville accompanied the convoy when early on 27 November strong enemy forces were sighted by aerial reconnaissance off Cape Spartivento. This was Admiral Campioni, with battleships *Vittorio Veneto*, *Giulio Cesare*, seven heavy cruisers and sixteen destroyers, who had learned of the convoy's departure. After being reinforced, Somerville turned towards the enemy. Action began at 12.20 pm and lasted one hour, during which the heavy cruiser *Berwick* and the Italian destroyer *Lanciere* were damaged. The Italians then retired and Somerville soon afterwards gave up the chase. At the same time two air strikes by torpedo-bombers from *Ark Royal* failed. The fast convoy got through unharmed but the action was indecisive and unsatisfactory to both sides.

CAP FRANÇOIS   21 October 1757

An Anglo-French engagement in the West Indies during the Seven Years' War. In October 1757 a small squadron under Captain Arthur Forrest – *Augusta*, 60, *Edinburgh*, 64 and *Dreadnought*, 60 – was cruising off the north coast of San Domingo, near the French naval base at Cap François. It awaited the departure thence of a large French homeward-bound convoy. However a superior force under Admiral de Kersaint – *Intrépide*, 74, *Sceptre*, 74, *Opiniâtre*, 64, a 50 and three frigates – came out on the 21st and engaged. After a fierce 2½-hour action, in which the English squadron fought gallantly against odds, de Kersaint retired into Cap François with his damaged ships. Forrest's ships had suffered equally severely, especially in

their rigging, and he took them to Port Royal, Jamaica for a long refit. The ultimate gain lay with the French; long before Forrest got to sea again, the French convoy had sailed from Cap François. (*See map on pages 190–191.*)

CARTAGENA   28 May 1708

Also known as 'Wager's action' and fought in the West Indies during the War of the Spanish Succession. Commodore Charles Wager – with the *Expedition*, 70, *Kingston*, 60, *Portland*, 50, and a fireship – met the Spanish treasure fleet off Cartagena on 28 May. The enemy comprised the *San Josef* and another 64, two fifth rates and eight smaller ships. It was sunset before Wager was able to engage at close quarters and his subordinates failed to support him. After a ninety-minute action between the *Expedition* and the *San Josef*, the Spaniard blew up and sank, taking an immense treasure and nearly 600 men down with her. During the night Wager captured another enemy ship but she carried no treasure. Later another Spanish galleon ran ashore near Cartagena and was burnt by her crew. Subsequently the captains of the *Kingston* and *Portland* were court-martialled for failing to support Wagner and dismissed their ships. (*See illustration on next page, and map on pages 190–191.*)

CATANIA   397 BC

Incensed by Dionysius of Syracuse's destruction of their Sicilian stronghold at Motya in 398 BC, the Carthaginians gave Himilco command of operations the next year. Leptines, Dionysius' brother, intercepted and destroyed fifty transports of the Carthaginian invasion force but the

CARTAGENA   28 May 1708   *Oil painting by Samuel Scott*

rest reached Panormus. The Carthaginians then moved south to attack Syracuse but encountered Dionysius off Catania.

Dionysius ordered Leptines to attack the enemy with his whole fleet of 180 ships. Mago, the Carthaginian admiral, had 500 ships but the majority were transports. Unwisely Leptines opened the attack with only thirty of his best ships – heavy craft armed with catapults. Although initially successful, he was later surrounded and forced to flee. As the rest of his ships came up they were defeated piecemeal, over half being lost. Despite their victory the Carthaginians' later efforts to seize Syracuse failed.

CHALCEDON *see* LEMNOS

CHALCIS *see* PATRAS

CHEMULPO   9 February 1904

The first naval engagement of the Russo-Japanese War, 1904–5, which occurred immediately before the declaration of hostilities. On 8 February, Japanese troop transports arrived off Chemulpo, a port on the west coast of Korea near Seoul, escorted by a squadron of cruisers and torpedo boats under Rear-Admiral Uriu. At anchor in the harbour lay the modern Russian cruiser *Varyag*, sloop *Korietz* and four neutral warships. The Japanese disembarkation was

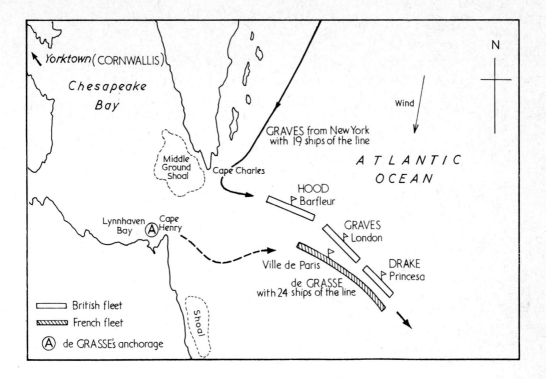

CHESAPEAKE 5 September 1781

completed in the early hours of 9 February and the transports left. Uriu then informed the Russians that war had been declared and he would attack them at their anchorage unless they had sailed by noon. The two Russian ships then tried to break out but were met by Uriu's cruisers. After a brief engagement the *Varyag* was badly damaged. Both ships then returned to Chemulpo and were scuttled by their crews to avoid capture.

CHESAPEAKE   16 March 1781

Alternatively known as the action off Cape Henry. At the beginning of 1781 General Washington repeatedly urged the French squadron at Rhode Island to come south to the Chesapeake and support his scanty forces fighting in Virginia. Eventually des Touches complied and weighed from Newport on 8 March with the *Duc de Bourgogne*, 80, seven more of the line and two frigates. Vice-Admiral Arbuthnot, who was then at Gardiner's Bay, Long Island, with eight of the line and four frigates, followed south two days later.

Off the New Jersey coast on 13 March, Arbuthnot spoke a vessel which had passed the French en route to the Chesapeake and which gave him their course. Three days later both squadrons met in thick haze off Cape Henry. During the day the weather deteriorated with sharp squalls and heavy seas running. In the ensuing action Arbuthnot was completely outmanoeuvred by the French. At the critical moment he failed to give the signal for close action; his van ships – especially the *Robust*, 74 and *Prudent*, 64 – received the brunt of the enemy fire and were badly damaged aloft, as des Touches wore his ships round in succession and then stood away to the east. Arbuthnot could not pursue and went into Chesapeake Bay while the French returned to Newport. No ship was lost on either side. Although des Touches had scored a tactical success, the English squadron was left in temporary command of Chesapeake Bay.

CHESAPEAKE 5 September 1781

The crucial naval battle of the American War of Independence (1775–83), which though inconclusive in itself had the most far-reaching consequences. In the summer of 1781 General Cornwallis was waging his campaign in Virginia; with 7,000 men at Yorktown he awaited the appearance of the British fleet in Chesapeake Bay. Until this time the naval situation in North American waters had remained favourable to Britain. The main opposing fleets under Rodney and de Grasse were in the West Indies; smaller British and French squadrons lay at New York and Newport, Rhode Island. The latter had met in an indecisive action off CAPE HENRY (qv) in March, after which the French returned north.

Quite suddenly the situation changed. In response to entreaties by Washington, de Grasse brought his whole fleet of twenty-four of the line from the Caribbean and reached Chesapeake Bay on 30 August, landing 3,000 troops to aid the rebels. At the same time the French squadron at Newport under de Barras sailed to join him. Washington and Rochambeau crossed the Hudson River and moved towards the head of the Chesapeake. All enemy forces were thus converging upon Cornwallis at Yorktown.

When Rodney learned of de Grasse's departure, he despatched his second-in-command, Rear-Admiral Samuel Hood, with fourteen of the line to reinforce Rear-Admiral Thomas Graves on the North America station. Unfortunately Hood reached the Chesapeake three days before de Grasse and finding the bay empty went on to New York. There Graves assumed command of the whole fleet of nineteen ships of the line. On 31 August he sailed for the Chesapeake with his flag in the *London*, 98, supported by Hood in command of the rear division and Rear-Admiral Drake the van. Finding de Grasse's fleet at anchor just inside the entrance to Chesapeake Bay, Graves saw he must defeat or at least drive away the French, otherwise Cornwallis would be forced to surrender at Yorktown. At the outset on 5 September the British had the advantage of wind and formation, many of the enemy ships being first sighted getting away from their anchorage and rounding Cape Henry. Unfortunately Graves chose to attack in the traditional manner, adopting formal tactics which prohibited initiative and gave de Grasse ample time to react. The battle began at 4 pm and continued for $2\frac{1}{2}$ hours without any decisive result. Indeed Hood's rear division never came into action at all. One British ship of the line, the *Terrible*, 74, was severely damaged and had to be sunk later. For four days after the battle, both fleets remained in spasmodic contact but Graves declined further action. And he rejected Hood's plan to enter the bay and attack the enemy at close quarters. By 10 September Graves had retired north and de Grasse was left in full possession of the Chesapeake, where he was joined by Barras's squadron. The outcome was fatal to British arms. Cornwallis was doomed and he finally surrendered at Yorktown with all his forces on 19 October. This event marked a decisive stage in the war and after it American independence was assured.

CHINHAE BAY November 1598

After the death of the shogun Hideyoshi, the Japanese decided to withdraw their invasion forces from Korea. In November 1598 the troops were embarked at Fusan and the transports sailed with a large naval escort. However a Sino-Korean fleet intercepted the convoy near Chinhae Bay, an inlet on the north shore of the Korean Straits. The fleet was led by the Korean admiral Yi Sun Sin – the victor of FUSAN in 1592 (qv) – who had been restored to command after a Japanese success in 1597. Although heavily outnumbered Yi Sun Sin attacked and a long bitter struggle ensued which ended indecisively. Both fleets suffered severely and Yi Sun Sin was killed. In December Japan and Korea negotiated an armistice.

CHIOGGIA 23 December 1379

The culminating engagement in the long and bitter struggle between Genoa and Venice, known as the War of Chioggia (1350–81). After the Genoese victory at POLA in May 1379 (qv), Pietro Doria's fleet captured the port of Chioggia, twenty miles south of Venice. The doges responded by raising a fleet of forty galleys. Under the command of Vittore Pisani the fleet quietly departed from Venice during the night of 21/2 December 1379. Pisani's plan was to block the harbour entrance of Chioggia by sinking barges laden with stones. Thus the situation there would be reversed, making the Genoese the besieged. The operation succeeded and the blockships were sunk, although the Genoese made strenuous efforts to prevent them. In the ensuing weeks Pisani and Carlo Zeno completely blockaded the Genoese in Chioggia, until they finally surrendered on 24 June 1380. Doria was killed in action and the Venetians took over 4,000 prisoners and seventeen galleys.

CHIOS 201 BC

A battle between the fleets of Philip V of Macedon and Rome's Greek allies in Asia Minor – Pergamum, Rhodes and Byzantium. After an unsuccessful blockade of Elaea, the port of Pergamum, Philip went south to join the rest of his fleet at Samos. Off Chios he was overtaken by the combined Pergamene–Rhodian fleet of seventy-seven warships under King Attalus and Theophiliscus.

Philip ordered his van ships under Democrates to engage the Pergamenes, while he continued towards the small islands in the middle of the Strait of Chios. The Pergamene squadron repulsed Democrates and sank his flagship with all hands. On the other hand the Rhodian ships were harried by Philip's small craft and their commander Autolycus was drowned. Moreover King Attalus became separated from the rest and was forced to abandon his ship and escape on shore. The loss of the royal ship induced the Pergamenes to break off the action, while the Rhodians made for Chios. Philip of Macedon claimed a victory but he had lost nearly half his fleet.

CISSUS September 191 BC

The fleet of King Antiochus of Syria lay at Ephesus in Asia Minor, between Pergamum and Rhodes – his enemies and the allies of Rome. In September 191 his admiral Polyxenidas moved the fleet, seventy triremes and 130 smaller craft, to Cissus on the south coast of the Erythrean peninsula. There he met the combined enemy fleet of 129 heavy ships and about eighty smaller under Eumenes and Caius Livius. In the ensuing battle Polyxenidas was defeated and retired north to Ephesus, having lost twenty-three ships. The Romano-Pergamene fleet then went into

Cissus. On the next day they pursued the Syrians, being reinforced en route by a Rhodian squadron under Pausistratus. However, their challenge to Polyxenidas to emerge from Ephesus and resume battle was unsuccessful. Convinced the Syrians were no longer a threat, the Rhodians and Pergamenes returned home while the Roman fleet wintered at Canae.

CNIDUS 394 BC

In the years following her defeats by Sparta in the Peloponnesian War, Athens sided with Greece's old enemy Persia against Sparta. In 394 a Persian fleet, under the satrap Pharnabazus and the Athenian admiral Conon, crushed a Spartan fleet of 120 triremes under Pisander. The action took place off Cnidus on the SW coast of Asia Minor near Rhodes. Pisander was killed, Sparta's seapower destroyed and the Persian hold on Asia Minor strengthened. But Athens never regained the dominance at sea which she had lost at AEGOSPOTAMI (qv).

COLBERGER HEIDE 1 July 1644

During the Swedish–Danish War of 1643–5, the Swedes captured the island of Fehmarn off the Mecklenburg coast. On 1 July 1644 a Swedish fleet of forty ships was at anchor off Fehmarn when a Danish force of equal size came in sight. A fierce but indecisive action was fought at

COPENHAGEN 2 April 1801

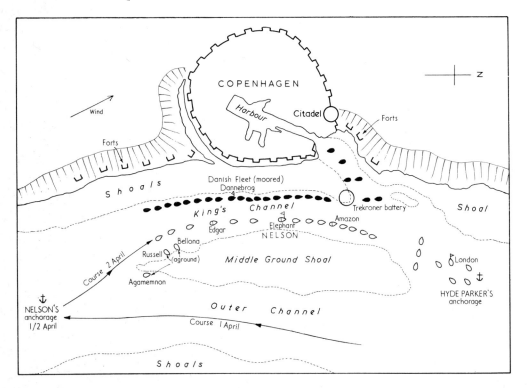

COPENHAGEN 2 April 1801 *Oil painting by Nicholos Pocock*

close quarters until nightfall. Afterwards the Swedes drew off towards Kiel, leaving their op-
ponents in possession of the anchorage. Although no ships were sunk, the Danish King Christian
IV lost an eye in the battle and the admiral of his van diversion, Jorgen Wind, died of wounds.
The name of the battle derives from the bleak stretch of coast between Fehmarn and Kiel Bay.

COPENHAGEN 2 April 1801

After the formation of the Armed Neutrality of the North (Russia, Sweden, Denmark, Prussia)
in December 1800, the Danes placed an embargo on British vessels in their ports and closed the
Elbe. The following February the Admiralty prepared a fleet for the Baltic under Admiral Sir
Hyde Parker and Vice-Admiral Lord Nelson was ordered to join him as second-in-command.
The fleet – eighteen of the line and thirty-five smaller warships – left Yarmouth on 12 March
and anchored off the Danish capital on the 30th. The Danish defences at Copenhagen were
exceptionally strong. Moored near the powerful Trekroner fortress at the harbour entrance,
lay four battleships and supporting ships. A formidable line of eighteen warships, hulks and
floating batteries protected the city's eastern shore. Having reluctantly agreed that Nelson
should lead an immediate attack, Hyde Parker allowed him 12 of the line, 5 frigates, 2 sloops,
5 bomb-vessels and 2 fireships for the purpose. On 1 April Nelson took soundings and then,

having successfully negotiated the Outer Channel, positioned his squadron two miles from the Danish line. He conceived the daring plan of taking ten of his line ships and all the frigates round the Middle Ground shoal and into the narrow and intricate King's Deep channel, immediately opposite the heart of the Danish defences. The *Edgar*, 74, would then anchor opposite the fifth in the Danish line, while each succeeding ship passed close on her disengaged side and took up position.

The manoeuvre began shortly before 10 o'clock on 2 April and an hour later the *Edgar* reached her appointed place. Soon, however, Nelson lost the use of three of his battleships: *Bellona*, 74, and *Russell*, 74, strayed from the narrow channel (from which the Danes had removed every buoy and navigation mark) and were stranded in the Middle Ground shoal. *Agamemnon*, 64, was caught in a strong current and could not get into position. Nevertheless the remaining ships began the bombardment and soon the exchange of fire became very fierce. The Danes resisted stoutly, volunteers replacing their gunners in the batteries as they fell.

At noon the Danish flagship *Dannebrog* was set on fire and Admiral Fischer shifted his flag to the *Holstein*. One hour later Hyde Parker signalled: 'Discontinue the engagement.' Captain Riou of the *Amazon*, 38, obeyed and was withdrawing with the frigates, when he was killed by a shot from the Trekroner battery. In a famous gesture, Nelson chose to ignore the signal by putting a spyglass to his blind eye and exclaiming he could not see it.

Danish resistance gradually began to weaken. The *Nyborg* and *Aggershuus* cut their cables and foundered; the flagship *Dannebrog* drifted away burning and later blew up. By 2.30 pm resistance had almost ceased, although some of the Danish hulks reopened fire when the ships' boats approached to take prizes and rescue survivors. Eventually a ceasefire was agreed and Nelson withdrew his squadron with difficulty, two ships grounding on the way out.

Copenhagen was a desperately fought battle. Casualties on both sides were very heavy and the Danish defence surpassed expectations. The British victory was due to Nelson's meticulous planning and daring and the tenacity shewn by those under his command.

CORAL SEA   6–8 May 1942

In their southward drive in the spring of 1942 to dominate the Coral Sea and threaten Australia, the Japanese planned to seize the key base of Port Moresby, New Guinea. Admiral Inouye, directing operations from Rabaul, planned a three-pronged attack: an invasion flotilla of troop transports and escorting destroyers under Rear-Admiral Kajioka; a covering force of heavy cruisers and the light carrier *Shoho* under Rear-Admiral Shima, linking up with the former north of the Louisiades; finally, a carrier strike group under Vice-Admiral Takagi, which would enter the Coral Sea to prevent any American interference.

On news of the enemy operation, an American task force under Admiral Fletcher – aircraft carriers *Yorktown* and *Lexington*, supported by cruisers and destroyers – was hurriedly assembled and sent into the Coral Sea. Early on 7 May American carrier planes struck at the enemy invasion fleet north of the Louisiades and sank the *Shoho*. Although not realised at the time, this proved a decisive blow: Inouye was afraid to risk his transports further south without proper air cover and ordered them to return to Rabaul.

The first Japanese air strike on 7 May failed to locate the American carriers but sank the destroyer *Sims* and oiler *Neosho*. The principal battle took place next day, when Fletcher's and Takagi's carrier groups finally located each other. It was entirely conducted by the opposing

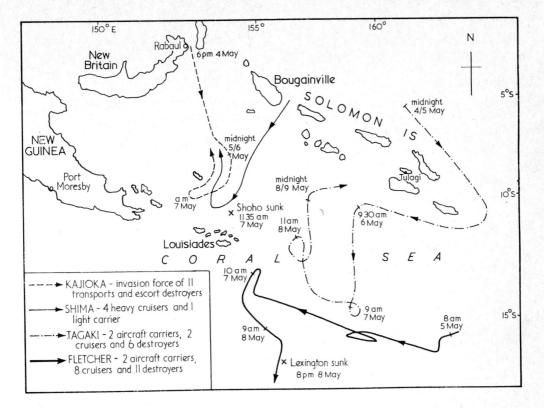

CORAL SEA   6–8 May 1942

carrier aircraft and neither fleet came into contact. Two American attacks that morning, which cost thirty-three aircraft, damaged the large Japanese carrier *Shokaku* and forced her to turn home. In the subsequent counter-strike by seventy Japanese planes, the *Lexington* was hit by torpedoes and bombs and set on fire. Great efforts were made to save her but after two internal explosions she had to be abandoned on the evening of 8 May.

Despite having suffered greater losses, the Americans gained strategically by the battle. For the Japanese thrust had been repulsed and their naval forces never again penetrated the Coral Sea. It was, moreover, an important prelude to the American victory at MIDWAY (qv) a month later.

CORONEL   1 November 1914

On the outbreak of World War I Germany's powerful East Asiatic squadron, based at Tsingtau, was at Ponapé in the Caroline Islands. Its commander Vice-Admiral Graf von Spee realised that Japan's entry into the war on the side of the Allies necessitated his departure from Far Eastern waters. He therefore decided to make the long voyage across the Pacific and operate his squadron off the west coast of South America. Having crossed the ocean with the armoured cruisers *Scharnhorst* (flagship), *Gneisenau* and light cruiser *Nürnberg*, he reached Easter Island

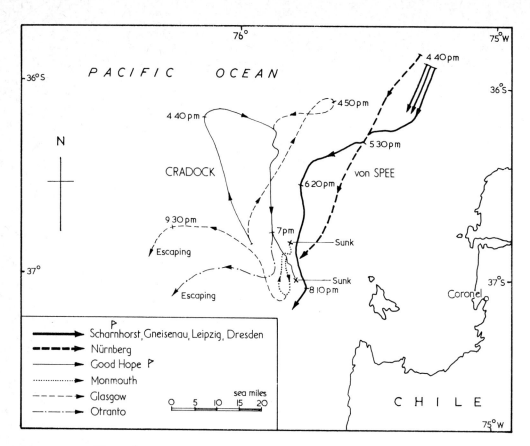

CORONEL 1 November 1914

at the beginning of October and was there reinforced by the light cruisers *Dresden* and *Leipzig*, which had been operating in American waters.

The British Admiralty became aware that von Spee was making for South America and informed Rear-Admiral Sir Christopher Cradock, in command of the South American station. However Cradock's squadron – the old armoured cruisers *Good Hope* and *Monmouth*, the light cruiser *Glasgow* and armed merchant cruiser *Otranto* – was greatly inferior and the Admiralty only sent him the pre-dreadnought *Canopus* as reinforcement. Old and slow as she undoubtedly was, *Canopus* carried a main armament of four 12in guns and Cradock made the fatal error of trying to fight von Spee without her. For reasons which have never been fully explained Cradock sailed from the Falklands on 23 October, passed through the Magellan Straits and steamed north up the Chilean coast with a vastly inferior force in search of the enemy.

Von Spee was at Valparaiso when on 31 October he learned that the *Glasgow* was 200 miles away at Coronel, a Chilean port 17 miles south of Concepción. He at once proceeded south at full speed to attack her, just as Cradock was coming up from the south. Both squadrons met fifty miles off Coronel shortly before 5 pm on 1 November. Cradock was hopelessly outmatched from the start but he did not hesitate to engage. The German admiral used his superior speed to advantage, getting Cradock's ships silhouetted against the setting sun while his own merged into the dark outline of the Chilean coast. The unequal contest did not last long and the German gunnery was deadly in its effect. Repeatedly hit, the *Good Hope* blew up around 8 pm; an hour later the *Monmouth* went down with her flag still flying. There were no survivors from either ship, Cradock and 1,600 of his men being lost. Only the *Glasgow* and *Otranto* managed to escape in the darkness. The German squadron suffered neither casualties nor damage, although a large quantity of irreplaceable ammunition had been expended.

Coronel was a major British naval disaster, redeemed only by the destruction of von Spee's squadron at the FALKLAND ISLANDS (qv) soon afterwards.

CUDDALORE 29 April 1758

The first of two indecisive actions between British and French squadrons in the Indian Ocean in 1758 (*see also* NEGAPATAM). Comte d'Aché with the *Zodiaque*, 74, and eight armed East Indiamen arrived on the Coromandel coast in February 1758. From the French base at Pondicherry he threatened Cuddalore, where there was a British East India Company factory. Vice-Admiral Pocock, the station commander, was then at Madras with the *Yarmouth*, 64, and six small ships of the line. He sailed south from there on 17 April but d'Aché eluded him and anchored off Cuddalore ten days later. There the French admiral surprised the frigates *Bridgwater* and *Triton* and forced them ashore. Early on 29 April he despatched the *Comte de Provence*, 74, and a frigate north to Pondicherry but had no sooner done so than Pocock's squadron appeared over the horizon.

Finding the French at anchor, Pocock tried to attack at once. But d'Aché weighed in time, stood out to sea and signalled the recall of his two detached ships. After a confused chase, the French formed line of battle shortly after noon and Pocock followed suit. The action which followed was fierce but quite indecisive. Eventually d'Aché broke off and retired north to Pondicherry; Pocock tried to follow but many of his ships had suffered damage to their rigging.

CUDDALORE 5/6 July 1782 *see* NEGAPATAM

CUDDALORE 20 June 1783

The last of five remarkable Anglo-French naval actions fought between Admirals Hughes and Suffren in the Indian Ocean during 1782–3 (*see also* SADRAS, PROVIDIEN, NEGAPATAM and TRINCOMALEE). All demonstrated the tactical brilliance of the French admiral.

After defeating Hughes off Madras in February 1782, Suffren landed troops and captured Cuddalore, a key point on the Coromandel coast south of Pondicherry. The following year the English forces launched a counter-attack and by June the port lay under close siege. Admiral Suffren was then at Trincomalee; on learning of the blockade, he hurriedly sailed north with fifteen ships of the line. Upon his approach, Hughes put to sea with the *Superb*, 74, and eighteen of the line and awaited an opportunity to attack. But Suffren eluded him, anchored off Cuddalore on 17 June and embarked 1,200 men from the garrison to supplement his gun crews. Both fleets then spent nearly three days manoeuvring for position before action was finally joined off Cuddalore late on 20 June. The three-hour engagement was sharp but there were no losses on either side. Next day, however, Hughes retired to Madras and Suffren raised the blockade of Cuddalore soon afterwards.

CUMAE AD 38

In this action the fleet of Pompey the Great's younger son – Sextus Pompey – commanded by the Greek Menecrates, encountered Octavian's fleet under Caius Sabinus Calvisius in the bight of Cumae near Naples. Menecrates' 100 ships joined battle soon after dawn, forcing Calvisius' southern wing back to the beach. However, Calvisius' lieutenant Menodorus grappled with the Pompeian flagship and captured her. The wounded Menecrates then jumped overboard to his death. On the northern wing there was a fierce struggle. Demochares – Menecrates' vice-admiral – drove several ships on the rocks and forced others to flee before Calvisius was able to intervene. Eventually the Pompeian fleet retired to Sicily, while Calvisius remained at Cumae to repair his ships.

CURICTA summer 49 BC

Although in the campaign of 49 Julius Caesar had triumphed in Spain and Southern France, his general in Illyria had failed to hold the northern shore of the Adriatic against Pompey's threatened invasion of Italy. Two legions under Caius Antonius, supported by a squadron of forty ships under Gnaeus Cornelius Dolabella, were encamped on the large island of Curicta (the present day Krk) off the Dalmatian coast. The legions' mobility depended on the ability of Dolabella to maintain their line of supply with the coast. Pompey then sent two of his squadrons, under Octavius and Libo, into the attack. After a sharp engagement Dolabella was defeated, leaving Antonius' legions marooned on Curicta. Some of his troops escaped on rafts but fifteen cohorts mutinied and went over to Pompey. In consequence Caesar lost control of the provinces of Dalmatia and Illyria.

CURZOLA 7 September 1298

One of the many battles between Genoa and Venice in their bitter struggle for maritime supremacy in the Mediterranean. It was fought near Curzola (Korcula) Island off the Dalmatian coast between Lamba Doria's seventy-eight Genoese galleys and a Venetian fleet of ninety-eight galleys under Andrea Dandolo.

Doria displayed great strategic skill throughout the battle. At the outset he stationed his galleys with the sun behind them and kept a squadron of twenty ships hidden in reserve. Although Dandolo fought well, Doria threw his reserve galleys against the Venetian flank at the critical moment, causing widespread confusion and terror. This proved decisive and the total Venetian losses were heavy – eighty-four galleys and 7,000 men. Among the many prisoners was Marco Polo. Dandolo himself dashed his brains out against the mast to which he had been chained, rather than be led captive to Genoa.

CYNOSSEMA autumn 411 BC

En route for Sestos an Athenian fleet of seventy-six ships, led by Thrasylus and Thrasybulus, was passing Cynossema Point on the coast of Asia Minor, when it encountered eighty-six Peloponnesian ships under Mindarus. As both fleets rowed past each other, Mindarus began to envelop Thrasybulus and cut him off from the open sea, provoking the Athenian to elongate his formation dangerously. The following squadron under Thrasylus was hidden from view round the point. Mindarus succeeded in driving part of the Athenian centre ashore but then lost close formation. Hampered by the strong current he was attacked and routed by the rest of Thrasybulus' ships. Eventually the Peloponnesians fled to give Athens her first naval victory since the disaster at SYRACUSE (qv).

CYZICUS   spring 410 BC

The Spartan commander Mindarus landed troops in the Propontis and then besieged the island city of Cyzicus, which Athens had seized after her victory off CYNOSSEMA (qv). An Athenian relieving force of eighty-six ships under Alcibiades then reached Cyzicus. Aided by bad visibility, they were able to interpose themselves between the city and Mindarus' fleet of sixty ships, which was on a training cruise. Mindarus retired shorewards but Alcibiades landed the crews of twenty ships to seize the beached Peloponnesian vessels, whilst the rest of his fleet attacked from the sea. In the ensuing battle Mindarus was killed and the victorious Athenians entered Cyzicus next day. It took the Peloponnesians three years to recover from this disaster.

DABUL   March 1508

As the Portuguese expanded their trading interest in the Indian Ocean, Mahmoud Begara of Gujarat and the Sultan of Egypt formed an alliance to expel the European intruders. Early in 1507 the latter despatched to India a fleet manned by Turks and Levantines. The following March the combined Gujarat–Egyptian fleet surprised a Portuguese squadron in the harbour of Dabul (or Chaul), just south of Bombay. The squadron of eight ships, including five carracks, was commanded by Don Lorenzo de Almeida, son of the Portuguese viceroy. After three days' bitter fighting at close quarters the Portuguese were defeated; only two of their ships escaped and Almeida was killed. But the defeat was avenged next year at DIU (qv).

DAMME   late May/early June 1213

An important English naval victory in the war between England, France and the Empire, which culminated in Bouvines. The exact date of the battle remains uncertain. At the beginning of 1213 Philip Augustus of France invaded Flanders and ordered his fleet to Damme, the port of Bruges. The Count of Flanders appealed to England for help and King John sent a large fleet commanded by William Longespée, Earl of Salisbury. Owing to the great size of Philip's fleet and the mud in Damme harbour, many of his ships had to ride at anchor in the estuary whilst others were beached on shore. When Salisbury appeared he found many of the French had left to take part in the siege of Ghent. Salisbury's men took to their boats and attacked the enemy ships lying outside the harbour. The result was a remarkable victory. Contemporary sources on both sides agree that the French lost 400 ships captured or destroyed. Accepting defeat, Philip Augustus ordered the rest of his fleet blockaded in Damme to be burned.

DAN-NO-URA   1185

The battle which marked the culmination of the struggle between the Taira and Minamoto clans for control of Japan in the late twelfth century. The Minamoto victory was largely due to the leadership of Yoshitsuné and to the treachery of a small boy on board the junk in which the six-year-old emperor was being carried by the Taira. The boy hung a yellow cloth over the side to indicate its position. Seven hundred Minamoto war junks attacked the Taira armed convoy off Dan-no-Ura in the narrow Strait of Shimonoseki. Although the Taira held them off for a time by skilful archery and ramming, the capture of the royal junk caused them to lose heart. The emperor's mother jumped overboard with her son, preferring death to capture; the male Taira who survived the battle were executed by their triumphant enemies.

DENMARK STRAIT *see* 'BISMARCK' ACTION

DHAT AL-SAWARI *see* LYCIA

DIU 3 February 1509

After his son's defeat at DABUL (qv), Francisco de Almeida, the Portuguese viceroy of India, had to await naval reinforcements from home before exacting his revenge. On 12 November 1508 he sailed from Cannanore near Calicut with a squadron of nineteen ships. After weeks of searching he found the large Gujarat–Egyptian fleet in the harbour of Diu, which lies on the NW coast of India between the Gulfs of Cambay and Kutch. In a brief but sharp action he utterly destroyed the Muslim fleet in harbour. This victory established Portuguese naval supremacy in the Indian Ocean.

DOGGER BANK 5 August 1781

A stubbornly fought Anglo-Dutch action in the North Sea, which took place nine months after Holland had entered the war on the side of France. The veteran Vice-Admiral Hyde Parker was escorting home a large Baltic convoy when he met the Dutch, also escorting merchantmen, near the Dogger Bank. The opposing squadrons were of equal strength – Hyde Parker had the *Fortitude*, 74, and six of the line; Rear-Admiral Zoutmann the *Admiraal de Ruijter*, 68, and six of the line. Most of the individual ships on both sides were in poor condition and badly manned.

At 8 am Hyde Parker signalled for close action and fighting continued for the next $3\frac{1}{2}$ hours. The British merchantmen had beforehand set course for England and in the middle of the battle the Dutch convoy bore away for the Texel out of harm's way. The struggle developed into a hard slogging match, with neither side able to gain the upper hand; eventually they drew apart, exhausted. Casualties were heavy and included the commander of the *Princess Amelia*, 80. Although no ship was lost in the battle, the Dutch *Hollandia*, 64, sank next day.

DOGGER BANK 24 January 1915

During the night of 23 January 1915, Rear-Admiral Hipper sailed from Wilhelmshaven with battlecruisers *Seydlitz* (flagship), *Moltke*, *Derfflinger* and *Blücher*, supported by light cruisers and torpedo boats. His purpose was to attack British patrols and fishing craft near the Dogger Bank at dawn next day. British Admiralty intelligence knew of the plan and Rear-Admiral Beatty's battlecruiser squadron – *Lion* (flagship), *Tiger*, *Princess Royal*, *New Zealand* and *Indomitable* – was despatched from Rosyth. After joining with the Harwich force, Beatty aimed to position himself between Hipper and his base. Early next morning Hipper was duly sighted

DOGGER BANK   5 August 1781   *Oil painting by Richard Paton*

DOGGER BANK   24 January 1915   *Watercolour by W. L. Wyllie – the sinking of the German battlecruiser* Blücher

NE of Dogger Bank and Beatty took up the pursuit. Soon after 9 am *Lion* opened fire and action became general with both squadrons proceeding at high speed. Fifty minutes later a 13.5 in shell from the *Lion* struck the *Seydlitz*, which put both her rear turrets out of action and killed 160 men. The resultant explosion would have proved fatal, had not the after magazines been promptly flooded. The *Blücher*, unable to keep up with the fleeing squadron, was also hit and badly damaged.

At this critical juncture – when the German battlecruisers seemed doomed – three 12in shells from the *Derfflinger* struck Beatty's flagship in quick succession. As the *Lion* rapidly fell astern, Beatty lost immediate control of his squadron. Command of the pursuit passed to Rear-Admiral Moore in the *New Zealand*, who unfortunately misinterpreted his admiral's intentions. Instead of continuing to pursue the main enemy force, he swung round and concentrated the fire of the whole squadron upon the crippled *Blücher*. After absorbing tremendous punishment for three hours she capsized and sank. But by the time Beatty had rejoined the main force via a destroyer, it was too late to catch Hipper and the great opportunity of destroying his squadron was lost.

DOMINICA   17 April 1780

The most important of three inconclusive actions fought between fleets under Rodney and de Guichen in the Caribbean during April and May 1780. De Guichen reached Martinique at the end of March with strong naval reinforcements and a large convoy from France. The same month Rodney assumed command of the Leeward Islands station. On 13 April de Guichen left Fort Royal with twenty-three of the line, five frigates and a convoy carrying 3,000 troops to attack Barbados. Three days later Rodney, with the *Sandwich*, 90, and twenty of the line sighted the enemy beating to windward in the channel between Martinique and Dominica. By the early hours of 17 April both fleets were on parallel course heading north, well to leeward of Dominica. Rodney planned to turn and attack the enemy's rear and centre with his whole force when the opportunity arose. But, sensing the danger, de Guichen wore his fleet around altogether and steered south. Rodney did likewise and at 11.50 am made the vital signal: 'Every ship to bear down and steer for her opposite in the enemy's line', followed five minutes later by 'Engage'. Unfortunately his captains completely misunderstood him. The whole van division, led by Captain Robert Carkett in the *Stirling Castle*, instead of engaging the enemy ship immediately opposite, carried sail so as to reach station opposite their numerical opponents in the order. Thus the fleet was committed to a dispersed, disjointed attack instead of the massive concentration which Rodney intended. After an indecisive engagement during which the *Sandwich* was severely damaged, the French bore up, ran down the wind and the action ended. Subsequently Rodney bitterly condemned his subordinates for their failure to understand his signals. (*See map on pages 190–191.*)

DOMINICA   9 April 1782

At the end of March 1782, Admiral de Grasse lay at Fort Royal, Martinique, with thirty-five ships of the line, having received substantial reinforcements from Europe. He was assembling a large expeditionary force, preparatory to combining with the Spaniards for an attack on Jamaica. Thirty miles to the south Rodney was at Castries, St Lucia, with thirty-six of the line awaiting developments. On 5 April his look-out frigates reported that troops were embarking

DOMINICA 17 April 1780 *Engraving by unknown artist*

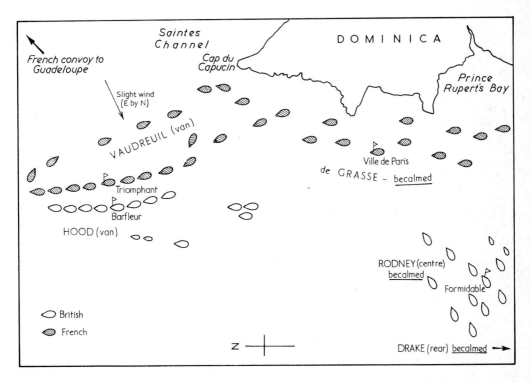

Saintes Channel

DOMINICA

French convoy to Guadeloupe

Cap du Capucin

Prince Rupert's Bay

Slight wind (E by N)

VAUDREUIL (van)

Ville de Paris

de GRASSE - becalmed

Triomphant

Barfleur

HOOD (van)

RODNEY (centre) becalmed

Formidable

○ British

▨ French

Z

DRAKE (rear) becalmed

DOMINICA 9 April 1782 – *the position at 9.45 am*

at Fort Royal and on the 8th de Grasse sailed. Rodney at once got under way and both fleets were in contact by dusk.

Next morning the bulk of de Grasse's fleet and the convoy were becalmed under the lee of Dominica. However his van under Rear-Admiral Vaudreuil had managed to catch the trade wind in the channel north of the island. Rodney then tried to close the enemy but was similarly becalmed. Indeed sixteen of his ships (the entire rear division and four of the centre) never got into action at all. However Rear-Admiral Sir Samuel Hood crept nearer with the *Barfleur*, 90, and eight of the line and was in action by 9.30 am. By then de Grasse had signalled the convoy to make for Guadeloupe, while he began to work to windward, intending to draw Rodney away. But the sight of Hood's division – separated and quite unsupported by the main English body – made him change his mind. For four hours Hood was under attack – but only from Vaudreuil's van division firing at long range. De Grasse thus failed to seize a great opportunity when he was in much superior force. By 1.15 pm it was too late, for Rodney had at last found the wind and came up to support Hood. Soon afterwards firing ceased and the French withdrew to the north, neither side having lost a ship (*see also* LES SAINTES). (*See map on pages 190–191.*)

DONEGAL   12 October 1798

Also known as 'Warren's action'. Following their abortive expedition to Bantry Bay in December 1796, the French made two further attempts to land troops in Ireland in 1798. Commodore Bompart sailed from Brest in September with the *Hoche*, 74, and nine large frigates with 3,000 soldiers on board. Due to prompt action by the frigate *Boadicea*, steps were quickly taken to intercept Bompart before he reached his destination at Lough Swilly.

About noon on 11 October, Rear-Admiral Warren's squadron – three of the line and five frigates – sighted the enemy off Tory Island, Donegal. After a long chase in heavy seas, the French were brought to action at 7 am on 12 October. The *Hoche* put up a gallant fight before striking; pursuit of the rest then followed. *Bellone*, *Coquille* and *Embuscade*, all 36s, were taken that afternoon and *Résolue*, 36, *Loire*, 40, and *Immortalité*, 40, a few days later. The three remaining frigates got back safely to France. The destruction of Bompart's squadron eclipsed the hopes of the Irish revolutionaries. Their leader, Wolf Tone, was captured on board the *Hoche* and later took his life in Dublin gaol.

DOVER   24 August 1217

The first of the great series of medieval naval battles between England and France and sometimes known as 'the fight off Sandwich'. During the minority of Henry III the safety of the kingdom was threatened by the presence in England of Prince Louis of France, in league with the great barons. On 23 August 1217, eighty French ships – mostly transports but including ten armed vessels – sailed from Calais for the Thames. On board were several hundred French knights to reinforce Louis and the fleet was commanded by Eustace the Monk, a renegade priest turned pirate. Off Dover it was met by an English fleet of about forty ships under Hubert de Burgh. The English cleverly let the enemy pass and then attacked from behind. The fight raged round the great ship of Eustace, which lay low in the water crowded with soldiers, horses and stores. An English ship came alongside and grappled; the crew threw powdered lime into the enemy's faces and swept her decks with cross-bow bolts. She was boarded and taken after a fierce struggle. Most of the French transports were seized and then towed back to

DONEGAL 12 October 1798 *Painting by Captain M. Oates showing (left to right):* Melampus, Ethalion, Amelia, Foudroyant, Magnanime, Robust, Canada, L'Hoche, L'Ambuscade, La Coquille, La Loire, La Résolution, Le Romain, La Bellone, L'Immortalité, La Sémillante

Dover. Eustace the Monk was discovered hiding in the bilges of his ship and decapitated. His head was later paraded on a pole through the streets of Canterbury.

DOVER 19 May 1652

The opening engagement of the First Dutch War and actually fought over a month before the declaration of hostilities. A Dutch fleet of forty-two ships under Maarten Tromp was forced by bad weather to seek refuge under the South Foreland. Later on 17 May it anchored in Dover Road, where there was an exchange of musketry with the castle. Nearby Nicholas Bourne, with a small squadron in the Downs, became alarmed and sent an urgent message to Blake, who was anchored off Rye with the main English squadron.

The Dutch sailed from Dover about noon on 19 May to return to Calais. On the way Tromp met a small Dutch warship commanded by Captain Zaanen, with the news that his convoy of seven valuable merchantmen was off Fairlight. The admiral at once turned about and proceeded NW to protect them. About 4 o'clock he ran into Blake's squadron coming up from the south and a fierce fight ensued. During the afternoon Bourne's ships arrived and attacked the Dutch rear. Eventually Tromp withdrew, having lost two ships.

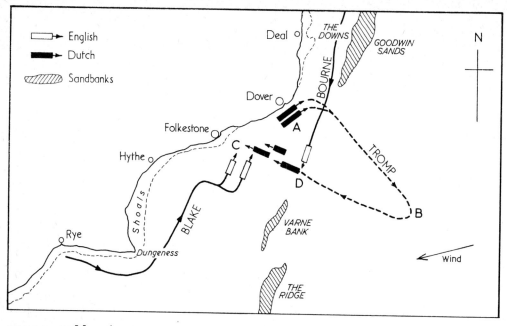

DOVER   19 May 1652

A   *Tromp at anchor in Dover Road*
B   *Van de Zaanen's ship joins Tromp*
C   *Action between Tromp and Blake*
D   *Bourne's attack on the rear of the Dutch fleet*

DOVER STRAITS   20/1 April 1917

Since October 1916 German destroyers based at Zeebrugge had made three night raids on the Dover Straits with varying success. Their targets had been merchant shipping anchored in the Downs and the long line of vulnerable drifters which patrolled the important net barrage stretching from the South Goodwins to the Outer Ruytingen.

A major clash occurred in the Straits on 20/1 April 1917. The Germans planned to attack both ends of the barrage with twelve destroyers in two flotillas. Admiral Bacon at Dover had no inkling of the impending raid and made his usual dispositions. That night six British destroyers, including the flotilla leaders *Broke* and *Swift*, patrolled the barrage. In the early hours of the 21st the German flotilla under Commander Gautier suddenly met the British patrol off Dover. A violent action at close range ensued, which included torpedo attacks, gunfire and even ramming. Both Commander Evans of the *Broke* and Peck of the *Swift* distinguished themselves and by the end of the engagement the German destroyers *G.42* and *G.85* had been sunk. The *Broke* was badly damaged and suffered forty casualties. No further German destroyer raids into the Straits of Dover took place until 1918.

DOWNS, THE   11 October 1639

In the late summer of 1639 an armada of Spanish and Portuguese ships was assembled under the command of Admiral Oquendo. Its purpose was to transport substantial reinforcements to

THE DOWNS   11 October 1639   *Oil painting by Cornelis Verbeeck*

the Spanish army fighting in the Netherlands. Aware of the plan, the Dutch had despatched a scouting force under Maarten Tromp to patrol the English Channel. On 6 September Oquendo was sighted off Selsey Bill. Although he had only seventeen ships with him, Tromp did not hesitate to attack and a brisk engagement took place in the Straits of Dover, in which the *Santiago*, Oquendo's flagship, was damaged.

Despite his immense superiority, Oquendo was shaken by Tromp's determination; he therefore retreated and sought refuge off Dover. Nearby lay an English squadron under Sir John Pennington. A tense diplomatic situation now arose, with three naval forces – two at war with each other and the third neutral – in close proximity. Pennington was strictly forbidden to interfere and while Oquendo sent ashore for water and supplies, Tromp kept vigilant watch to seaward. The impasse continued for many weeks, as Oquendo refused to move and the Dutch were steadily reinforced until their fleet numbered over 100 sail. At last on 11 October Tromp attacked. Having detached a squadron under de Witt to watch Pennington, he bore down with the wind upon the Spanish fleet at anchor in the Downs. Even then, Oquendo refused to fight and the result was annihilation. The greater part of the armada was burned and 7,000 men perished; Oquendo escaped only with the *Santiago* and thirteen other ships. At one stroke Tromp had shattered Spanish naval power in northern waters.

DREPANUM   *see*   TRAPANI

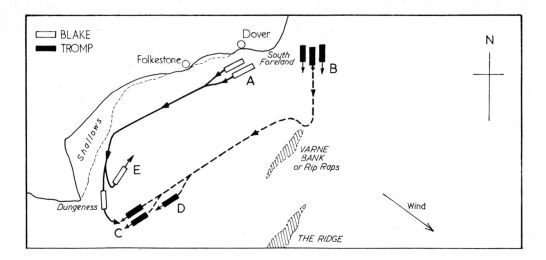

DUNGENESS   30 November 1652

A   *Blake at anchor in Dover Road, evening 29/30 November*
B   *Tromp off South Foreland*
C   *Action between the vans of both fleets, pm 30 November*
D   *Tromp's rear unable to come up*
E   *Blake's rear avoiding action*

DUNGENESS   30 November 1652

An English defeat in the First Dutch War. After de Witt's reverse at the KENTISH KNOCK (qv) in September, the able Maarten Tromp was recalled to command the Dutch fleet. One of his first tasks was to safeguard the outward passage of a very large convoy; to this end he put to sea from the Helvoetsluys on 21 November with seventy-eight men-of-war.

Leaving the convoy off the Flemish coast, Tromp appeared off the Goodwins eight days later with his whole fleet. General-at-Sea Robert Blake was then in the Downs with only forty-two warships but he did not hesitate to sail to meet him. During the afternoon the wind from the NW reached gale force, prohibiting action by the fleets. That evening Blake anchored in Dover Road, while Tromp lay under the cliffs of the South Foreland. The wind having moderated next morning, 30 November, both fleets weighed and steered parallel courses along the Kent coast. There was no engagement until they approached Dungeness, when the trend of the coast brought the English van down upon the Dutch. In the action which followed the leading English ships were hard pressed, many farther back refraining from joining in. Blake's flagship the *Triumph* got away after losing her fore topmast but the Dutch took the *Garland* and *Anthony Bonaventure* and three other English ships were sunk. Having gained command of the Straits, Tromp was able to escort the outward-bound convoy down Channel, the purpose for which he had fought.

EASTERN SOLOMONS   24/5 August 1942

One of the six major engagements fought by American and Japanese fleets in 1942 for control of the Solomon Islands. The Japanese despatched a powerful combined fleet from their main base at Truk to the area NE of the Solomons. Their presence provoked a retaliation from

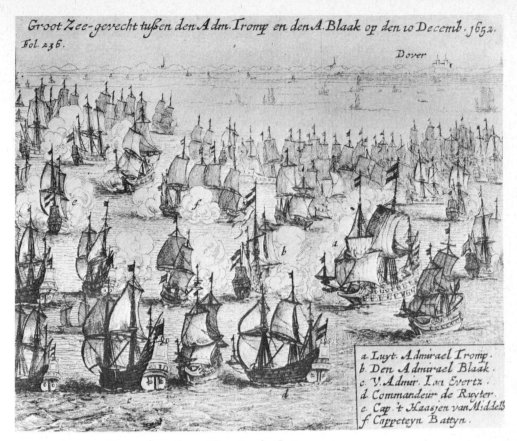

a. Luyt. Admirael Tromp.
b. Den Admirael Blaak.
c. V. Admir. Ian Evertz.
d. Commandeur de Ruyter.
e. Cap. 't Haasjen van Middelb
f. Cappeteyn Battyn.

DUNGENESS   30 November 1652   *Engraving by C. Jansen*

Vice-Admiral Fletcher's carrier group – *Enterprise*, *Saratoga* and *Wasp*. The result was a long-range duel between the opposing carrier planes which lasted for two days. On the morning of 24 August, Fletcher's aircraft torpedoed and sank the light carrier *Ryujo* east of Malaita but that afternoon his own ships came under heavy attack. The *Enterprise* was struck by three bombs and her rudder temporarily jammed. Next day both fleets retired, the battle undecided and the vital carrier groups intact on both sides.

ECNOMUS   256 BC

A major naval battle of the First Punic War. Under the consuls Attilius Regulus and Manlius Vulso, a large Roman fleet – estimated at 250 warships and eighty transports – was assembling on the south coast of Sicily. It had concentrated off Mount Ecnomus, near the mouth of the River Himera, to embark an invasion force for Africa. Nearby lay the Carthaginian fleet under Hanno and Hamilcar, 350 strong according to the historian Polybius.

From the outset the Carthaginians attempted envelopment but the four Roman squadrons deployed to prevent this. By early afternoon a furious action had developed in three places. Although the Carthaginians manoeuvred skilfully, the consuls' determination gave them final victory and the destruction or capture of nearly 100 enemy ships for the loss of twenty-four of their own.

ELBA   28 August 1652

On the outbreak of the First Dutch War there were only eight English warships in the Mediterranean under the divided command of Appleton and Badiley. In July a superior Dutch squadron commanded by Van Galen blockaded Appleton in Leghorn. Leaving four ships to watch
the port, he then sailed with the rest of his squadron in search of Badiley and on 27 August
found him off Elba escorting four Levant merchantmen. Against Van Galen's ten ships,
Badiley had only the *Paragon*, 42, *Constant Warwick*, 30, *Elizabeth*, 38, and *Phoenix*, 38. Nevertheless he conducted a most gallant defence when battle was joined next day. During it the
Phoenix became separated and was boarded and taken. Fighting ended at dusk, both sides
having suffered severely. Badiley's badly damaged ships were then towed into Porto Longone,
Elba. When Van Galen tried to attack him in the port next day, he was refused entry by the
governor and eventually withdrew (*see also* LEGHORN).

EMPRESS AUGUSTA BAY   2 November 1943

The first of two United States–Japanese naval actions fought at the end of 1943 in the Solomon
Islands theatre (*see also* CAPE ST GEORGE). They arose out of vain attempts by the Japanese,
operating from their main naval base at Rabaul, to interrupt the American landings on Bougainville Island.

   A strong Japanese squadron under Vice-Admiral Omori – heavy cruisers *Myoko* and *Haguro*,
light cruisers *Sendai* and *Agano* and six destroyers – sailed to attack the American transports
disembarking troops at Empress Augusta Bay, Bougainville. In a fierce night action on
2 November, Rear-Admiral Merrill's squadron of four light cruisers and eight destroyers prevented the Japanese from reaching their target. After losing the light cruiser *Sendai* and the
destroyer *Hatsukaze*, Omori broke off the action and returned to Rabaul. The only American
casualty was the destoyer *Foote*, which was torpedoed but regained harbour.

ENKHUIZEN   *see* ZUYDER ZEE

ERETRIA   September 411 BC

A Peloponnesian fleet of forty-two ships under the Spartan Agesandridas entered the Saronic
Gulf, raided Aegina and then sailed past Athens en route to support a revolt in Euboea. The
Athenians sent out ships to pursue Agesandridas and join with another of their squadrons on
patrol off Eretria on the west coast of Euboea. The Eretrians however were in league with
Sparta and gave the Athenian crews a hostile reception when they landed on the outskirts of
the city. The Athenian admiral Thyocares hastily called his men out to face the Spartan attack
but they put to sea in disorder and were crushed. Twenty-two ships were captured and the
sailors who fled to the city killed.

ERINEUS   413 BC

During the Peloponnesian War a fleet of thirty Corinthian ships under Polyanthes was operating off Erineus in the Gulf of Corinth, supporting the troops on shore. There the Corinthians
were attacked by thirty-three Athenian ships commanded by Diphilus. Polyanthes had before-

hand ordered the bows of his ships to be strengthened with ἐπωτίδες, or cheek-pieces, to crush those of the enemy and fend off their rams. His foresight was proved when seven enemy ships were disabled by them, although the Corinthians themselves lost three ships. Later the Athenians recovered the wrecks of their ships, which had drifted out to sea and both sides claimed a victory.

'ESPAGNOLS SUR MER, LES' 29 August 1350

A crushing victory inflicted by the fleet of King Edward III of England upon a strong force of Spanish privateers, commanded by the freebooter Don Carlos de la Cerda. The action took place off Winchelsea – the name by which it is alternatively known.

In defiance of an existing truce, Cerda took a number of English ships laden with wine off Bordeaux in November 1349 and murdered their crews. He then sailed north to Sluys, pillaging as he went. By May 1350 King Edward had prepared a fleet to meet the Spaniards in the Channel on their passage home. The English fleet of fifty ships sailed from Winchelsea on 28 August and the following afternoon Cerda was sighted coming down Channel. A fierce engagement began about 5 pm and continued until nightfall. The king's ship was sunk but he transferred to a prize. Great damage was inflicted by the Spanish cross-bowmen and stones and ironbars rained down upon the English decks. Casualties were high on both sides, yet Edward's fleet finally triumphed. Authorities differ on the Spanish losses; some state fourteen ships were taken, others as many as twenty-six – quite apart from those sunk.

EURYMEDON RIVER 466 BC

During the preparations for a third invasion of Greece in 466 BC, a large Persian fleet gathered at the mouth of the Eurymedon River on the south coast of Asia Minor. There it was met and heavily defeated by a combined fleet raised by Athens and her allies in the Delian League. The details of the battle are not known but the Persians certainly lost more than 200 ships and afterwards the Greeks of southern Asia Minor joined the Athenian confederacy.

FALKLAND ISLANDS 8 December 1914

After destroying Rear-Admiral Cradock at CORONEL (qv), Vice-Admiral Graf von Spee took his squadron – armoured cruisers *Scharnhorst* and *Gneisenau*, light cruisers *Nürnberg*, *Leipzig* and *Dresden* – to Valparaiso and remained there until 15 November. Six days later he coaled in St Quentin Bay and then proceeded south towards Cape Horn. Meanwhile the British Admiralty concentrated all available warships under Rear-Admiral Stoddart at Montevideo and ordered the pre-dreadnought *Canopus* and the light cruisers *Kent* and *Glasgow* to join him there. Most important of all, Churchill and Fisher detached the powerful battlecruisers *Invincible* and *Inflexible* from the Grand Fleet. Put under the command of Vice-Admiral Sir Doveton Sturdee, they sailed in great haste from Plymouth on 11 November for South America. In compliance with his secret orders, Sturdee met Stoddart at the Abrolhos Rocks a fortnight later, took his squadron under his command and then proceeded south in company. After several days' delay en route, he entered Port Stanley in the Falkland Islands on 7 December. Von Spee, too, had been delayed: by bad weather off Cape Horn and by the *Dresden* running short of coal. While the latter was being replenished from a captured British collier in

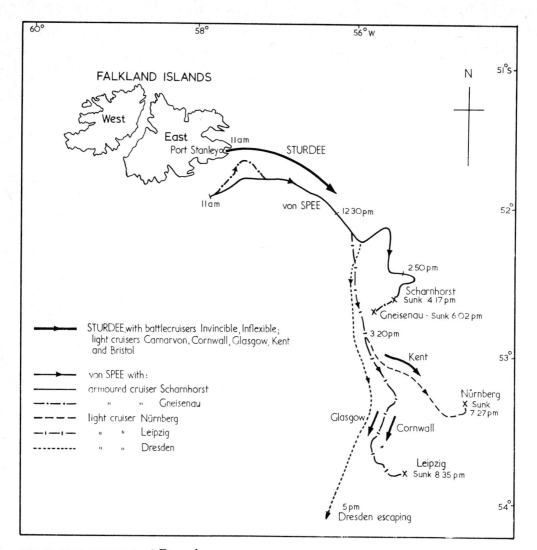

FALKLAND ISLANDS   8 December 1914

a remote Patagonian anchorage, the German admiral made a crucial decision. Believing the Falklands to be undefended, he determined to attack Port Stanley, destroy the wireless station and render it useless as a naval base.

At dawn on 8 December von Spee reached Port Stanley and detached *Gneisenau* and *Nürnberg* to reconnoitre. Shortly after 9 o'clock the former's gunnery officer reported with horror that he had sighted four tall tripod masts in the outer anchorage. They could only belong to battle-cruisers; von Spee turned sharply away and headed east at full speed. In fact his sudden appear-ance had caught the British ships unprepared and several were in the act of coaling. Neverthe-less Sturdee remained cool; he brought his ships out and by 11 o'clock had settled into a long chase, steering SE at 22 knots in pursuit of von Spee. Both admirals knew the British battle-

FALKLAND ISLANDS 8 December 1914 *Watercolour by W. L. Wyllie, showing the last fight of* Scharnhorst *and* Gneisenau

cruisers' superior firepower and speed would be decisive. Just before 1 o'clock they opened fire on the lagging *Leipzig* and twenty minutes later von Spee signalled his light cruisers to break away and try to escape, while he turned at bay with *Scharnhorst* and *Gneisenau*. Sturdee divided his forces likewise and the battle developed into a number of separate actions. After a brave fight von Spee's two main ships were overwhelmed by the battlecruisers. The *Scharnhorst* sank with all hands shortly after 4.15 and the *Gneisenau* at 6 with her flag still flying.

There followed the pursuit of the light cruisers. The *Glasgow* and *Cornwall* accounted for the *Leipzig*, while after a tremendous chase the *Kent* gradually overhauled the *Nürnberg* and sank her. Only the *Dresden* escaped. Three months later she was found hiding at lonely Mas-a-Fuera, Juan Fernandez, and after a brief engagement scuttled herself.

FATSHAN CREEK 1 June 1857

An engagement during the Second China War (1856–8). At the end of May 1857 a fleet of seventy heavily armed Chinese war junks lay at anchor in Fatshan Creek south of Canton. Rear-Admiral Sir Michael Seymour assembled a flotilla – paddle-tenders *Coromandel*, *Hong Kong*, seven gunboats and ships' boats from the squadron – to attack the enemy. Early on 1 June the fort commanding the entrance was captured and the flotilla entered the creek. Most of the gunboats grounded on a barrier of sunken junks filled with stones but the ships' boats continued to pull towards the enemy under very heavy fire. Eventually the Chinese surrendered their fifty junks and later twenty more were captured further upstream.

FATSHAN CREEK   1 June 1857   *Drawing by an unknown artist – Gunboat* Haughty *and leading boats in Fatshan Creek just above Hyacinth Island*

The first battle of FINISTERRE   3 May 1747   *Oil painting by Samuel Scott*

FINISTERRE   3 May 1747

The first of two Anglo-French actions in 1747, both fought off Cape Finisterre on the NW coast of Spain. On 29 April two important French convoys bound for India and North America sailed together from Rochefort, escorted by a combined squadron under de la Jonquière and St-Georges. Aware of the enemy movements, Admiral Anson left Spithead on 9 April with the *Prince George*, 90, and twelve of the line and cruised in the Bay of Biscay. His search was rewarded early on 3 May, when the enemy was sighted twenty-five miles NW of Finisterre. De la Jonquière formed line of battle ahead with his main force, ordering the convoy to escape westward. After a three-hour running fight, the entire French squadron – *Sérieux*, 64, *Invincible*, 74, and ten smaller warships – was taken. Anson then set off in pursuit of the convoy and captured six merchantmen but the remaining twenty escaped in the darkness.

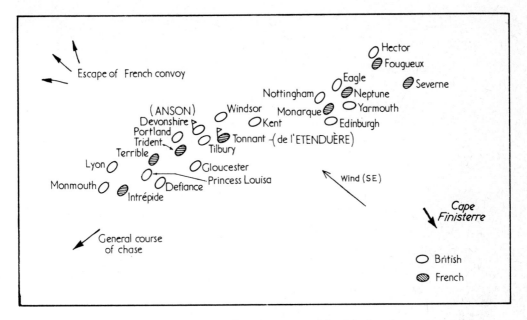

The second battle of FINISTERRE   14 October 1747 – *The situation about 3.30 pm*

FINISTERRE   14 October 1747

In August 1747 the Admiralty learned that a very large French convoy was assembling in Basque Roads, preparatory to sailing to the West Indies under escort of the Brest squadron. Rear-Admiral Sir Edward Hawke was immediately despatched with the Western Squadron to cruise between Ushant and Finisterre. For many weeks Hawke searched fruitlessly and the enemy did not in fact sail from Ile d'Aix until 6 October. Eight days later Hawke sighted them off Finisterre. Admiral de l'Etenduère, in command of the escort squadron, was heavily outnumbered – eight of the line against fourteen. Nevertheless in a nine-hour running fight he fought gallantly to save the convoy. By nightfall Hawke had taken six of the enemy line and only the flagship *Tonnant*, 80, and her second, *Intrépide*, 74, succeeded in regaining Brest badly damaged. As, however, the whole French convoy escaped capture, de l'Etenduère's sacrifice had not been in vain.

FINISTERRE   22 July 1805   *see* CALDER'S ACTION

FLAMBOROUGH HEAD   23 September 1779   *Engraving by Lerpinière and Fittler, after Richard Paton of the famous duel between* Serapis *and* Bonhomme Richard

FLAMBOROUGH HEAD   23 September 1779

The climax of a raid against British coastal trade in 1779 by a squadron under John Paul Jones. Sailing from Lorient on 14 August with the frigates *Bonhomme Richard, Alliance, Pallas* and two smaller ships, Jones cruised along the Irish and Scottish coasts taking several prizes. A foray into the Firth of Forth was unsuccessful. Late on the afternoon of 23 September he met a large convoy off Flamborough Head, which proved to be the Baltic trade. It was escorted by the newly built frigate *Serapis*, 44, (Captain Richard Pearson) and the small sloop *Countess of Scarborough*.

Action began at 7.20 pm, watched by crowds of spectators on shore. The *Pallas* made the *Countess of Scarborough* prize but the *Alliance*, owing to the extraordinary conduct of her captain, took little part. These events, however, were completely dwarfed by the historic duel between the *Bonhomme Richard* and the *Serapis*, which continued until 10.30 pm when the latter struck. Jones's coolness and resource in the numerous crises of the fight enabled him finally to overcome a more powerful adversary. In the course of the action he spoke the famous words: 'I have not yet begun to fight.' With both ships shattered, the *Bonhomme Richard* sank next morning. Jones however succeeded in getting his prizes into the Texel and ultimately to France.

FLORES *see* AZORES

FOOCHOW   23 August 1884

An action during the war of 1883–5 between France and China for control of Annam and Tonkin in Indo-China. In June 1884 a French squadron under Admiral Courbet – the armoured central-battery ships *Volta* and *Triomphante*, six gunboats and two torpedo boats – was sent to blockade the Chinese port of Foochow. Lying in the harbour were eleven warships and nine junks under Admiral Tin. Courbet remained off Foochow for six weeks before receiving permission to attack. In the opening engagement on the afternoon of 23 August, Tin's flagship the *Yanau* was damaged by the torpedo boats and then sunk by shell-fire. Her loss demoralised the Chinese who made little further resistance. After sinking or firing most of their ships, Courbet's squadron silenced the Foochow shore batteries and bombarded the naval arsenal.

FORT ST DAVID   25 June 1746

In the spring of 1746 a small French squadron under La Bourdonnais – *Achille*, 70, and seven armed merchantmen – sailed to the Coromandel coast. Commodore Edward Peyton with the *Medway*, 60, three 50s and two smaller ships was cruising between Fort St David and Negapatam when he sighted the enemy on 25 June. Despite his decided superiority, Peyton failed to take advantage of the situation. Admittedly there was little wind and action did not commence until 4 pm but nonetheless Peyton acted very feebly. La Bourdonnais skilfully extricated himself and Peyton's conduct was later censured by the East India Company.

FOUR DAYS' BATTLE, THE   1–4 June 1666

One of the most prolonged and hard-fought naval battles in history. At a critical juncture in the Second Dutch War, the disastrous mistake was made of dividing the English fleet in the belief that the French were sending a squadron to aid the Dutch. Thus Prince Rupert with twenty-four ships was detached down Channel to intercept, leaving the Duke of Albemarle (Monk) off the Thames estuary with only sixty ships to face de Ruyter and the entire Dutch fleet. Early on 1 June Albemarle sighted the enemy in thick weather off the North Foreland. Although greatly outnumbered he attacked with the wind in his favour.

At first all went well: Cornelis Tromp's squadron was chased in a running fight towards the French coast and de Ruyter was unable to get into action with the main body until noon. But then the situation changed. Forced to turn about as the shoals off Dunkirk drew near, Albemarle became closely engaged with the Dutch centre and rear and was badly mauled. The *Swiftsure*, 64, surrendered after her admiral, Sir William Berkeley, had been killed. Another flagship – Rear-Admiral Sir John Harman's *Henry*, 64 – just escaped being overwhelmed by Evertsen's division and three fireships.

Action was resumed next morning and Albemarle chose to attack once more despite his perilous situation. He again pressed Tromp's division hard but after hours of severe fighting against heavy odds began to withdraw slowly towards the English coast. The retreat continued on 3 June, during which three disabled ships had to be burnt to avoid capture. Then followed another serious loss. Admiral Sir George Ayscue's flagship, the *Royal Prince*, 90 – one of the finest ships in the English fleet – drove ashore on the Galloper Sand, was captured and burnt.

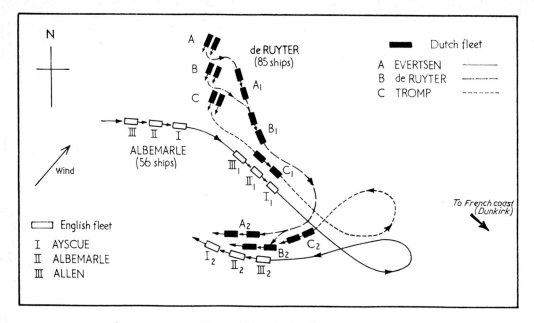

THE FOUR DAYS' BATTLE 1–4 June 1666 – *the first day*

In the early afternoon Prince Rupert's squadron arrived on the scene just in time to save Albemarle from destruction. That evening the joint English commanders conferred and agreed to fight on, although many of their ships were damaged, ammunition was low and the crews approaching exhaustion. The battle on the final day developed into a confused mêlée in which both fleets fought to a standstill. Rupert's flagship, the *Royal James*, 82, and Albemarle's the *Royal Charles*, 80, were badly damaged. Another English admiral, Sir Christopher Myngs, commanding the *Victory* in the van division, was mortally wounded. Eventually de Ruyter had had enough and the Dutch fleet retired that evening.

In this unique battle the English fleet suffered a severe defeat, losing 8,000 men and seventeen ships (including two flagships). Nevertheless the Dutch casualties were also heavy and de Ruyter was astonished at the fighting spirit of the English, who were ready to do battle again at Orfordness seven weeks later.

FRIGATE BAY *see* ST KITTS

FUSAN June 1592

Three engagements during the war between Japan and Korea (1592–3). In 1592 Hideyoshi, shogun of Japan, planned to invade China but Korea refused to allow the passage of his troops through her territory. After Japanese troops had landed at Fusan (or Pusan) on the south coast of Korea, a Korean fleet of eighty ships commanded by Yi Sun-Sin attacked the invasion flotilla. His flagship was a remarkable primitive type of ironclad known as *kwi-sun* or 'tortoise-ship'. It had an iron-plated turtleback deck for protection against missiles and iron

THE FOUR DAYS' BATTLE 1–4 June 1666 *Oil painting by Abraham Storck*

spikes to deter boarders. The stem was strengthened for use as a ram and the sides were pierced for archery ports. In the first action off Okpo, twenty-six Japanese ships were set on fire and the rest put to flight; the same day a smaller Japanese squadron was destroyed off No-Ryang. Next morning Yi Sun-Sin met the main enemy force off Tang-Hang and after a desperate battle won a complete victory.

GABBARD, THE 2/3 June 1653

A major action of the First Dutch War (1652–4). Sometimes known as the first battle of North Foreland but more correctly after The Gabbard sands off Orfordness, where the opposing forces first met. The fleets engaged were far larger than earlier in the war, the English being jointly commanded by Generals-at-Sea Monk and Deane, the Dutch by Maarten Tromp with de Ruyter and de Witt as his vice-admirals.

After various manoeuvrings in the North Sea throughout May, both fleets sighted each other off The Gabbard at daybreak on 2 June. The wind was so light that action was not joined until 11 o'clock. A stubborn fight then took place, in which the English ships were skilfully handled. By 6 pm the Dutch were in full retreat having lost three ships. Next day Tromp renewed battle and fought determinedly for four hours. However, when Blake arrived with a reinforcement of eighteen ships, the Dutch retreated to their own coast. Accounts of

THE GABBARD 2/3 June 1653 *Grisaille by Heerman Witmont*

their loss vary but it probably mounted to twenty ships: eleven taken – including a vice-admiral – six sunk and three blown up. No ships were lost on the English side but the casualties included General Deane, who was killed by the first broadside.

The Gabbard was a decisive encounter of the war. It compelled the Dutch to retire into their harbours and undergo a rigorous economic blockade.

GIBRALTAR 207 BC

In 207 the inhabitants of Gades (Cadiz) plotted to surrender their city to the Romans. A small Carthaginian fleet under Adherbal and Hannibal's brother Mago lay in the harbour. A naval force under Laelius was despatched to Gades but it clashed with the Carthaginians in the Straits of Gibraltar. The manoeuvrability of the triremes on both sides was affected by the strong current but the Roman quinquiremes, which were heavier and carried more rowers, kept better station. As a result three Punic ships were sunk and the remainder retreated to Carthage.

'GLORIOUS FIRST OF JUNE, THE' 1 June 1794

The first great sea battle of the French Revolutionary War. In fact it was a series of engagements spanning five days and culminating in the major action of 1 June over 400 miles into the Atlantic. The battle arose out of the safe passage to France of an immense grain convoy, which had sailed from the Chesapeake for the relief of the starving country.

During April and May 1794 Admiral Earl Howe with the British fleet of thirty-four of the line had scoured the Western Approaches without success in search of the convoy. Off Ushant on 19 May he learned that Rear-Admiral Villaret-Joyeuse had sailed from Brest three days before with twenty-six of the line. In rough seas early on 28 May, Howe's flagship the *Queen Charlotte*, 100, sighted the enemy. The French had the wind advantage and throughout the next

THE GLORIOUS FIRST OF JUNE 1794 *Oil painting by P. J. de Loutherbourg*

three days Villaret-Joyeuse clung tenaciously to preventing Howe reaching the grain convoy, which was far out of sight to the south. That day there was a brief action, during which the *Révolutionnaire* was damaged but escaped. During the next Howe was still to leeward of the French but eventually broke through towards the enemy's rear and cut off two three-deckers. The weather was misty for much of 30/1 May and the opposing forces kept in distant contact. Villaret-Joyeuse was unexpectedly reinforced by four of the line under Rear-Admiral Neilly.

With both fleets some four miles apart, 1 June dawned fine and clear. Howe at once put into action his plan of running his ships straight down upon the enemy and achieving a decisive breakthrough. In the ensuing attack *Queen Charlotte*, *Defence*, *Marlborough*, *Royal George*, *Queen* and *Brunswick* did exactly as Howe intended and brought on a general mêlée. The others in the British line either misunderstood his signals or failed to break through. By the end of the morning six enemy ships of the line, including two 80s, had struck and *Le Vengeur du Peuple*, 74, foundered after a tremendous duel with the *Brunswick*. The French admiral's flagship, the *Montagne*, 120, was badly damaged and had 300 killed. Although the French fleet was in great confusion after the battle, Howe and his men were exhausted and did not pursue.

An attempt by a squadron from Plymouth under Rear-Admiral Montagu to intercept the convoy was beaten off by Villaret-Joyeuse on 9 June, despite the disabled state of his ships. Finally both he and the vital grain convoy reached Brest safely. Although the French lost seven ships of the line, the sacrifice had not been in vain.

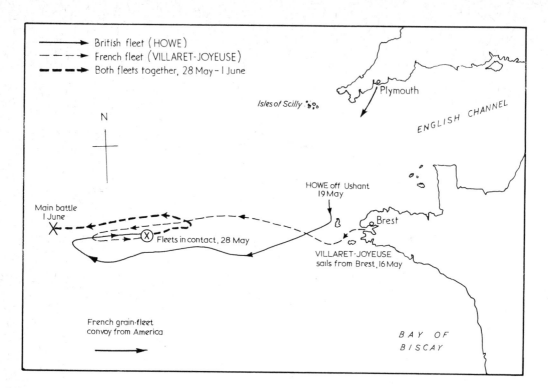

Legend:
→ British fleet (HOWE)
- - → French fleet (VILLARET-JOYEUSE)
━ ━ → Both fleets together, 28 May – I June

N

Isles of Scilly

Plymouth

ENGLISH CHANNEL

HOWE off Ushant
19 May

Brest

Main battle
I June

Fleets in contact, 28 May

VILLARET-JOYEUSE
sails from Brest, 16 May

French grain-fleet
convoy from America

BAY OF
BISCAY

GLORIOUS FIRST OF JUNE 1794 – *approximate movements preceding the main battle*

'GRAF SPEE' ACTION *see* RIVER PLATE

GRAVELINES *see* SPANISH ARMADA

GRENADA 6 July 1779

Vice-Admiral Byron assumed command of the Leeward Islands station in May 1779, at a time when French naval threats in the Caribbean had become very menacing. Admiral d'Estaing had seized St Vincent in June and three weeks later he sailed with twenty-five of the line and a large expeditionary force to attack Grenada. After four days the whole island and thirty merchantmen in the harbour of Georgetown were in his hands.

Byron was at St Lucia when he learned of the enemy's movements and he immediately weighed with his whole fleet, including twenty-one ships of the line. At dawn on 6 July he sighted Grenada and then began to close with the enemy fleet, as it struggled confusedly out of harbour and tried to form line of battle in St George's Bay. However Byron's leading ships suffered damage and he found himself engaged with a superior force. Three more of his fleet – *Cornwall*, 74, *Grafton*, 74, and *Lion*, 64 – were severely damaged and dropped astern. By 11 am both fleets were in line ahead sailing NNW. Shortly afterwards Byron's van came under

GRAVELINES 29 July 1588 *Engraving by Theodor de Bry, published in* 1615

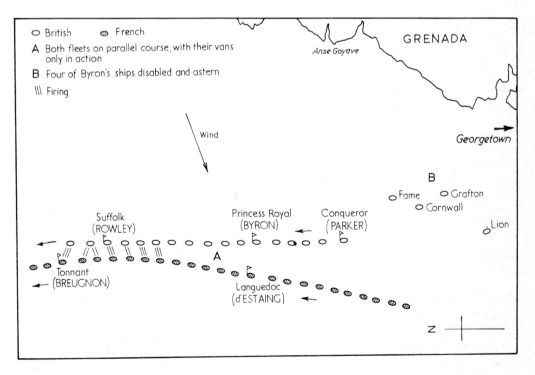

The action off GRENADA 6 July 1779 – *the position at* 10.30 *am*

heavy fire but at the critical moment was supported by Rowley's ships coming up from astern. Thereafter firing became desultory and in the late afternoon the French turned south and broke off the action.

In a difficult situation Byron was saved from disaster by d'Estaing's failure to exploit his advantage; the four disabled English ships should certainly have been taken. Although the battle had been indecisive, strategically the naval initiative in the Caribbean had passed to the French and remained with them until 1782. (*See map on pages 190–191.*)

GROIX, ÎLE DE 23 June 1795

Also known as 'Bridport's action'. In June 1795 a force of French royalist exiles were landed at Quiberon Bay in Brittany. They had been escorted there by Commodore Warren's squadron and Lord Bridport provided distant cover with the Channel Fleet. On 22 June Bridport sighted a French squadron of nine of the line under Admiral Villaret-Joyeuse, who quickly retreated towards Lorient. Early next day the British van overtook the enemy off Île de Groix. The French were thrown into confusion and three of their rear ships struck – *Alexandre*, 74, *Tigre*, 74, and *Formidable*, 74. Bridport, however, failed to take full advantage of the situation and was content to conclude the action and make off with his prizes. Lucky to escape without further loss, Villaret-Joyeuse took refuge in Lorient.

ÎLE DE GROIX 23 June 1795 *Also known as 'Bridport's Action'. Engraving by Robert Dodd, after Captain A. Becher*

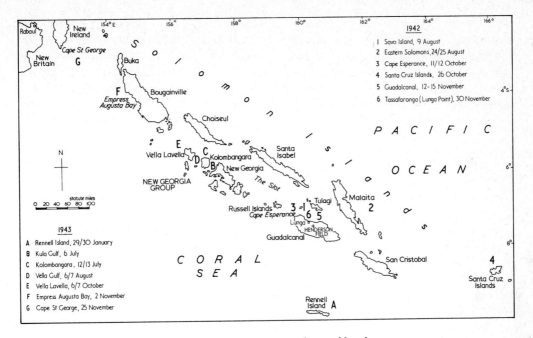

GUADALCANAL AND THE SOLOMONS 1942–3 – *the naval battles*

GUADALCANAL ISLAND August–December 1942

On 7 August 1942 11,000 United States marines landed on Guadalcanal Island in the southern Solomons and established a beachhead. It was the opening move in a desperate struggle for possession, which continued for the rest of the year and involved six naval battles: SAVO ISLAND, EASTERN SOLOMONS, CAPE ESPERANCE, SANTA CRUZ ISLANDS, GUADALCANAL and TASSAFARONGA (qqv).

From the outset the Japanese naval forces in control of the central and northern Solomons reacted violently to the American landings. Operating from their main base at Rabaul, they made constant use of the vital channel between the eastern and western Solomons chain, known as the Slot. Down it they rushed heavily escorted reinforcements to their garrisons on Guadalcanal. So heavy and regular did this nightly traffic through the Slot become, that it came to be called the 'Tokyo Express'. Another focus of naval activity in 1942 was Sea Lark Channel between Guadalcanal and Florida Island, which was renamed Iron Bottom Sound as so many warships were sunk there. Following early defeats, the US naval forces gradually gained supremacy but only after a severe struggle.

GUADALCANAL 12–15 November 1942

One of the most prolonged and bitterly fought naval battles of World War II. It also marked the turning point in the struggle for Guadalcanal, after which the Japanese never again sent large naval forces into the area.

The battle developed in four phases. On the night of 12/13 November, Vice-Admiral Abe led a powerful raiding group – battleships *Hiei* and *Kirishima*, three light cruisers and fourteen destroyers – down the Slot, bent on destroying the United States beachhead. Only Rear-Admiral Callaghan's force of five cruisers and eight destroyers stood in his path. A devastating action followed in the darkness off Guadalcanal, during which the American light cruiser *Atlanta* and four destroyers were sunk and Admirals Callaghan and Scott killed. Next morning the light cruiser *Juneau* was torpedoed by the submarine *I-26* and sunk with the loss of 700 lives. But the enemy never reached Guadalcanal and the damaged *Hiei* was found by aircraft north of Savo Island and sunk.

Both sides then prepared for further action. Japanese heavy cruisers came south from Java to combine with the undamaged *Kirishima* and cover a second assault group, comprising eleven transports and eleven destroyers under Rear-Admiral Tanaka. Meanwhile the Americans rushed in reinforcements and Admiral Kinkaid's task force – battleships *Washington* and *South Dakota* with the aircraft carrier *Enterprise* – reached the scene. During the night of 13/14 November, the Japanese cruisers bombarded Henderson Field while Tanaka approached with the transports. But next day both groups suffered severely from air attacks; the cruiser *Kinugasa* was sunk and no fewer than seven of the transports went down that afternoon. Tanaka however pressed on tenaciously and managed to beach the remaining transports on the island.

The final Japanese attempt was made on the night of 14/15 November. En route to bombard Guadalcanal, Admiral Kondo with the *Kirishima*, four cruisers and destroyers clashed with the American battleships in Iron Bottom Sound shortly before midnight. Although *South Dakota's* firepower was nullified by an electrical power failure at the critical moment, *Washington* made amends. In seven minutes salvoes from her 16in guns had wrecked *Kirishima* and soon afterwards the Japanese retired for the last time.

GULF OF GENOA   13/14 March 1795

Or 'Hotham's first action', named after Vice-Admiral William Hotham who was then in command of the British fleet in the Mediterranean. Fifteen French ships of the line under Rear-Admiral Martin sailed from Toulon on 3 March, carrying 5,000 troops to retake Corsica. Hotham was cruising in the Gulf of Genoa with fourteen of the line (including the *Agamemnon*, 64, commanded by Captain Horatio Nelson) when he sighted the enemy on 11 March. Two days of fruitless manoeuvring followed and Hotham failed to close. On the morning of the 13th, the French *Ça Ira*, 84, fouled her next ahead, the *Victoire*, and fell astern with both fore and main topmasts gone. She was quickly engaged by the frigate *Inconstant* and then by the *Agamemnon*, during which Nelson succeeded in severely damaging his bigger adversary. Next morning both fleets engaged indecisively at long range. By 2 o'clock the French had stood away under full sail to the west and Hotham did not pursue. The helpless *Ça Ira* and the *Censeur*, 74, which had taken her in tow, were captured; nevertheless it was an unsatisfactory outcome for Hotham (*see also* HYERES).

HAMPTON ROADS   8/9 March 1862

The opening major naval engagement of the American Civil War and the first in history between ironclads. After occupying Norfolk, Virginia in April 1861, the Confederate forces found several Federal warships, which had been scuttled to avoid capture, in the navy yard. They raised one of them, the frigate *Merrimac*, and by the following February had converted

HAMPTON ROADS   8/9 March 1862   Monitor *v.* Merrimac *and the sinking of the* Cumberland

her into a formidable ironclad ram. Renamed *Virginia*, she was well protected and mounted ten heavy guns, including three 9in Dahlgrens. On the other hand she was very unwieldy and drew over twenty feet of water. Meanwhile the Federal navy had ordered similar ironclads to be built but only the *Monitor* had been completed by March 1862. She was a raft-like vessel with a revolving turret, mounting two 11in Dahlgrens and protected by thick armour plating. Much smaller than the *Virginia*, she was also faster and more manoeuvrable.

On 8 March Captain Franklin Buchanan took the *Virginia* into Hampton Roads and quickly destroyed two wooden warships of a Federal squadron stationed there. While Buchanan was on the casement of his ship directing the fire, he was hit by a sharpshooter and had to be super-seded in command. During the night the *Monitor*, commanded by Lieutenant John Worden, arrived from New York; next morning she surprised the *Virginia* as she steamed into the Roads to renew the attack. There followed an historic four-hour duel between the ironclads, as both bombarded each other at close range with little effect. At one stage about noon the *Virginia* ran aground but as the *Monitor* approached a Confederate shell burst on her pilot-house, temporarily blinding Worden. Eventually all action ceased. Later that year both iron-clads were lost – the *Virginia* after the evacuation of Norfolk and the *Monitor* in a storm off Cape Hatteras.

HARFLEUR 15 August 1416

In the summer of 1416 a French fleet blockaded the port of Harfleur at the mouth of the Seine. Under the joint command of the Bastard of Bourbon and Robinet de Braquemont, the fleet had been strengthened by eight carracks hired from the Genoese. Determined to raise the blockade, King Henry V of England despatched a fleet from Southampton under Sir Walter Hungerford. On 15 August the opposing forces met in the narrow channel immediately opposite Harfleur and north of the Amfar Bank. After a five-hour fight the French were worsted. Some of their ships took refuge in Honfleur on the other side of the Seine estuary but at least two of the Genoese carracks ran ashore and were wrecked. Some eight French ships were taken, de Braquemont's son was killed and the Bastard of Bourbon captured. Following the battle the siege of Harfleur was speedily lifted.

HAVANA 1 October 1748

The commander-in-chief of the Jamaica station, Rear-Admiral Charles Knowles, learned in September 1748 that the Spanish plate fleet was expected at Havana. He weighed from Port Royal with the *Cornwall*, 80, and five of the line and cruised off the Tortuga banks. Near there

HAVANA 1 October 1748 *Oil painting by Samuel Scott, showing the beginning of the action*

on 1 October he met not the treasure fleet but a Spanish squadron of two 74s and four 64s under Vice-Admiral Reggio. Though Knowles had the wind advantage, he approached very slowly and action was not joined until 2.30 pm. Indeed the *Warwick* and *Canterbury* were so far astern that it took them two hours to come up. After a gallant defence the Spanish *Conquistador*, 64, struck; fierce fighting continued until 8 pm when Reggio withdrew towards Havana. The badly damaged Spanish flagship *Africa*, 74, was unable to reach port and anchored in a cove. Discovered by the English squadron two days after the battle, she was burnt by her crew to avoid capture. In December 1749 Knowles was court-martialled and reprimanded for not bringing his squadron into action earlier and in better order. (*See map on pages 190–191.*)

HELIGOLAND BIGHT 28 August 1914

Late in August 1914 the British Admiralty approved a plan to send a raiding force deep into the Heligoland Bight to attack German destroyer patrols. The operation was to be undertaken by Commodore Tyrwhitt's Harwich force – light cruisers *Arethusa* and *Fearless*, with 1st and 3rd Destroyer Flotillas (thirty-one boats) – and was planned for the early hours of 28 August. In addition to the usual support, 1st Battlecruiser Squadron under Vice-Admiral Beatty was at the last moment detached from the Home Fleet, providentially as it turned out.

In the early morning haze Tyrwhitt began his sweep towards Heligoland but soon ran into trouble. The Germans had some inkling of the impending attack and, instead of sending out their usual patrols, concentrated all available forces. In a series of confused engagements between 8 and 11.30 am, Tyrwhitt was in hot action with six enemy light cruisers, which were later joined by two more. Although the *Frauenlob* was hit and retired, the Harwich force was in danger of being overwhelmed when the *Arethusa* and three destroyers were repeatedly hit and damaged. At 11.25 Tyrwhitt sent out an urgent call to Beatty, who was forty miles north of Heligoland, unaware of the critical situation developing. Fortunately he decided to intervene and came south at full speed straight into the Bight. The arrival of the British battlecruisers on the scene at 12.40 pm proved decisive. The *Köln* (flagship of Rear-Admiral Maas), *Ariadne* and *Mainz* were crippled and later sank; the remaining German light cruisers quickly scattered. Shortly afterwards the British forces set course for home.

HELLESPONT AD 323

During his reign the Roman emperor Constantine the Great repulsed a succession of rivals to the throne, including the dangerous Licinius. In 323 Constantine assembled a large fleet at the Piraeus, while Licinius levied 350 triremes from Egypt, Phoenicia and Asia Minor. After the army of Licinius had been defeated at Adrianople, his fleet under Abantus met the emperor's under the command of his son, Crispus. In two days' fighting at the mouth of the Hellespont, Abantus lost 130 ships and 5,000 men. His defeat enabled Crispus to force the passage of the Dardanelles and blockade Byzantium. Licinius fled across the Propontis but was eventually captured and put to death.

HOGLAND 17 July 1788

Fought during the Russo-Swedish War of 1788–90. In June 1788 King Gustav III of Sweden despatched an expeditionary force of 8,000 men to invade Russian Finland. Supported by the Swedish fleet under Carl, Duke of Södermanland, the troops landed at Helsinki on 2 July. Two weeks later a major engagement took place between the Swedes and a Russian fleet of seventeen battleships under Admiral Greig. It occurred off Hogland in the Gulf of Finland, roughly midway between Helsinki and the Russian naval base at Kronstadt. The action was severe but indecisive and neither side attempted to renew action next day. The Swedes lost their van flagship, the *Prins Gustav*, 70, and the Russians the *Vladislav*, 74.

'HOTHAM'S ACTIONS' *see* GULF OF GENOA and HYERES

HYERES 13 July 1795

Vice-Admiral Hotham's second encounter with the French Mediterranean fleet in 1795. Although reinforcements from home had raised his ship-of-the-line strength to twenty-three against Vice-Admiral Martin's seventeen, he still failed to act decisively. Both fleets met on 13 July near the Hyères Islands off the coast of Provence. The French did their best to get away and Hotham signalled a general chase. However the opposing fleets were scattered over a wide area; indeed at one stage Hotham's flagship – the *Britannia*, 100 – was more than seven miles astern of his leading ships. Only the British van got into close action, during which one enemy 74, the *Alcide*, was taken. Then the wind changed and Hotham, fearful of being blown on shore, at once made the signal to disengage. The order was only reluctantly obeyed by the van squadron, which included Nelson with the *Agamemnon*.

IBERUS   spring 217 BC

Early in the year Hasdrubal the Bald led the Carthaginian army, supported by forty quinquiremes, north from Cartagena to the mouth of the River Iberus (Ebro). The Roman commander Gnaeus Scipio decided to attack Hasdrubal's naval supply lines and sailed with thirty-six quinquiremes to an anchorage eight miles north of the estuary. He hoped his final approach would be concealed behind a promontory but Hasdrubal received advance warning from watch towers, which had been erected along the coast to guard against pirates. However, he could not prevent the Roman attack and many of the Carthaginian crews were forced to beach their ships and abandon them. By the end of the day Hasdrubal had lost twenty-five ships and was compelled to retreat far inland.

IQUIQUE   21 May 1879

At the beginning of the war between Chile and Peru of 1879–81, Admiral Rebolledo's fleet blockaded the Peruvian port of Iquique. In May he left to attack a Peruvian convoy, leaving only the old sloop *Esmeralda* and gunboat *Covadonga* behind to continue the blockade. Learning of the weak force at Iquique, the Peruvians despatched the heavy ironclad rams *Huascar* and *Independencia* to attack. The action which followed on 21 May was memorable for the heroism shown by the Chilean commanders – especially Arturo Prat of the *Esmeralda*. Realising escape from Iquique was impossible, he decided to fight to the last. The *Esmeralda* engaged the *Huascar* until she capsized, after being rammed at the third attempt. Prat himself was killed while attempting to board the enemy, sword in hand. Meanwhile the *Covadonga*, keeping close inshore, broke away to the south hotly pursued by the *Independencia*. However, in attempting to ram for the third time, the *Independencia* ran aground and was wrecked. Although later pursued by the *Huascar*, the gunboat succeeded in making good her escape.

JAPAN SEA   14 August 1904

During the first months of the Russo-Japanese War, the Vladivostok squadron – armoured cruisers *Rossiya*, *Gromoboi* and *Rurik* under Rear-Admiral Yessen – made a number of successful sorties. On 11 August Yessen learned that the main Russian battle squadron had sailed from Port Arthur. He therefore went to meet Admiral Vitgeft in the Straits of Korea, unaware that he had been defeated two days before in the YELLOW SEA (qv) and forced to turn back. At daybreak on 14 August Yessen was thirty-six miles NE of Tsushima when he sighted a Japanese squadron under Admiral Kamimura. His four armoured cruisers *Idzumo*, *Adzuma*, *Tokiwa* and *Iwate* were all better armed and more modern than the Russian warships. Early in the action the *Rurik* was repeatedly hit and her steering gear broke down. Overwhelmed by Japanese fire she eventually sank, taking over 400 men down with her. Kamimura had, however, made the

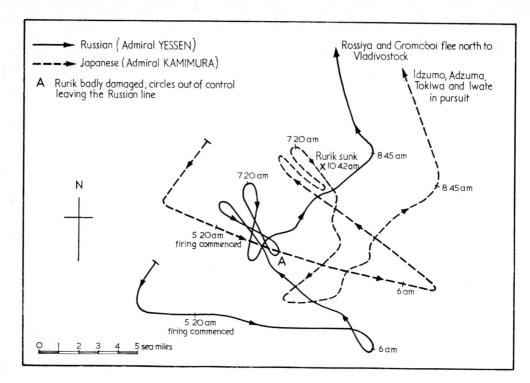

Russian (Admiral YESSEN)

Japanese (Admiral KAMIMURA)

A   Rurik badly damaged, circles out of control
leaving the Russian line

Rossiya and Gromoboi flee north to
Vladivostock

Idzumo, Adzuma,
Tokiwa and Iwate
in pursuit

7 20 am

Rurik sunk
X 10 42am

7 20 am

8 45 am

8 45 am

N

5 20 am
firing commenced

A

5 20 am
firing commenced

6 am

6 am

0   1   2   3   4   5 sea miles

JAPAN SEA   14 August 1904

mistake of concentrating on the doomed *Rurik*, instead of closing determinedly with Yessen's other ships. Thus after a running engagement, the damaged *Rossiya* and *Gromoboi* escaped north at high speed and regained Vladivostok.

JASK   November 1620

In November 1620 two East Indiamen – the *Hart* and *Eagle* – arrived off Jask near the entrance to the Persian Gulf. A Portuguese squadron of twenty-one ships commanded by Admiral Ruy Frere opposed their passage and they returned to Surat for reinforcements. Joined by the *London* and *Roebuck*, they sailed again for Jask. After an indecisive engagement Frere withdrew NW to Ormuz, further into the Persian Gulf. He quickly refitted his squadron and returned but the Portuguese were finally defeated after a long battle.

JASMUND   25/6 May 1676

An action during the war between Denmark and Sweden, 1675–9 (*see also* KJÖGE BIGHT and ÖLAND). In May 1676 a combined Danish and Dutch fleet of thirty-five ships under Niels Juel was cruising between Bornholm and Rügen, awaiting further Dutch reinforcements under Cornelis Tromp. Early on 25 May some ten miles north of the Jasmund peninsula on the NE coast of Rügen they met the Swedish fleet of fifty-nine ships commanded by Lorens Creutz.

Although outnumbered, Juel formed line of battle and engaged. The Swedes were in some disorder, partly owing to Creutz's inexperience, and Juel was able to cut off five small vessels before darkness fell. A partial action took place next day but was indecisive. This gave rise to friction between Juel and Almonde, the commander of the Dutch squadron.

JAVA SEA   27 February 1942

The last obstacle to the Japanese seaborne invasion of Java in February 1942 was a weak allied squadron based at Soerabaya. There Rear-Admiral Karel Doorman had a very mixed force under his command – cruisers *de Ruyter*, *Java* (Dutch); *Exeter*, *Perth* (British); *Houston* (American) and nine destroyers (two Dutch, three British and four American). Already battle-weary and entirely without air support, the squadron was no match for the massive attack about to be launched. On the afternoon of 27 February Doorman received reports of a large enemy convoy eighty miles NE of Soerabaya and immediately sailed to intercept. Shortly after 4 pm he

JAVA SEA   27 February 1942

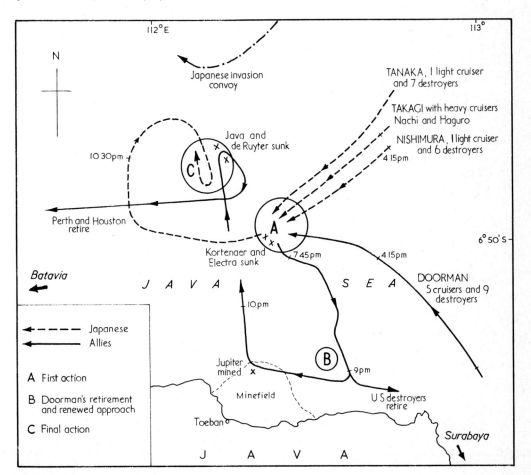

sighted a powerful force of Japanese heavy cruisers and destroyers under Rear-Admiral Takagi. Intermittently over the next seven hours there followed a series of savage engagements. In the first the allied destroyers *Electra* and *Kortenaer* were sunk by torpedo and the cruiser *Exeter* heavily damaged. Then Doorman broke off action and turned south, hoping after nightfall to work round Takagi and reach the enemy transports beyond him. Unfortunately off the Java coast he passed through a newly laid Dutch minefield and the destroyer *Jupiter* exploded. In a final desperate effort Doorman turned north again but shortly after 10 pm encountered the Japanese cruisers. After a gun duel both Dutch cruisers were struck by torpedoes and soon sank, taking Doorman and many men down with them. Only the *Perth* and *Houston* escaped to bring the melancholy news to Batavia (*see also* SUNDA STRAIT).

JUTLAND 31 May/1 June 1916

In January 1916 the appointment of Admiral Scheer to the command of the High Seas Fleet marked the opening of more aggressive German naval activity in the North Sea. After a number of raids the German commander-in-chief finally committed himself at the end of May. He planned to lure the Grand Fleet under Admiral Jellicoe from its bases, with the aim of bringing to action and defeating a detachment of it – in particular Admiral Beatty's battlecruisers. Vice-Admiral Hipper in command of the German battlecruisers would form the spearhead and proceed towards the Skagerrak, while the main fleet gave distant cover off the Jutland coast. Early on 31 May Hipper and Scheer sailed from the Jade estuary to take up their appointed stations. The British Admiralty were aware that major enemy movements were impending and Jellicoe left Scapa Flow and Beatty the Firth of Forth on the evening of the 30th. Neither side, however, realised the full extent of the opposing commitment, with the result that by noon next day immense forces were approaching each other in the North Sea.

Action began shortly before 3 pm after the light cruiser *Galatea* had sighted Hipper's force (five battlecruisers with accompanying light cruisers and destroyers) and Beatty turned SSE to intercept. With his flag in the *Lion*, Beatty had six battlecruisers, supported by four new battleships under Rear-Admiral Evan-Thomas, light cruisers and destroyers. As Beatty ran south in hot pursuit a signalling failure caused Evan-Thomas to lag far behind. A fierce duel followed between the opposing battlecruisers, during which the German fire was extremely accurate. Owing to inadequate magazine protection the battlecruisers *Indefatigable* and *Queen Mary* blew up after being hit and there were very few survivors. Beatty's flagship would have suffered the same fate had not a Royal Marines major given his life in preventing the explosion of her 'Q'-turret magazine. Despite these British disasters, Hipper's outnumbered ships began to be hit hard. Shortly after 4.30 however the light cruiser *Southampton*, scouting ahead of Beatty, signalled she had sighted a large enemy force bearing SE. It was Scheer with the main battlefleet coming up from the south to aid Hipper and close the trap on the British battlecruisers. Ten minutes later Beatty turned away to fall back on Jellicoe, hoping the enemy would follow. During this run to the north the battlecruisers clashed again and Hipper's flagship the *Lützow* was badly damaged. Just before 6 pm the situation became critical, Beatty having joined with Jellicoe and action between both battlefleets appearing imminent.

While the battlecruisers were engaged, Jellicoe had been proceeding south with the main fleet disposed in six parallel columns. With insufficient data on the enemy's position, course and speed, he was faced with the difficult problem as to how best dispose his ships for battle. A rapid decision was imperative and at 6.15 he ordered deployment on the port wing, aiming to

JUTLAND   31 May 1916   *Painting by the German artist Claus Bergen, showing Admiral Hipper's battlecruisers in action*

'cross the enemy's T' and cut off his line of retreat. The manoeuvre was completed successfully, while Scheer held his course towards the Grand Fleet unaware of its approach. About this time the British 1st Cruiser Squadron ran into the path of the German battlefleet and two armoured cruisers were quickly overwhelmed. Soon afterwards Rear-Admiral Hood's 3rd Battlecruiser Squadron engaged Hipper's battlecruisers. After some brilliant shooting Hood's flagship the *Invincible* was blown up in the same way as the two battlecruisers lost earlier.

Meanwhile action had been joined between the main battlefleets and Scheer realised he was facing imminent destruction. In desperation he performed a remarkable *volte face* shortly after 6.30 pm – bringing his whole fleet round in a simultaneous turn under cover of smoke and diversionary attacks by the destroyer screen. This skilful manoeuvre saved Scheer and for the time being firing ceased as the High Seas Fleet withdrew to the SW. In worsening visibility Jellicoe remained unaware for some time that the enemy had turned away. Then just before 7 pm Scheer advanced once more to the attack and the second main action ensued. During this phase the German ships began to suffer heavy punishment but again Scheer succeeded in extricating himself. The critical moment occurred at 7.20 when Jellicoe turned away and steered SE, fearing torpedo attacks, enabling the hard-pressed enemy to continue withdrawing to the SW. This development proved decisive. Although sporadic engagements by individual units continued until nightfall, contact between the opposing battlefleets had been lost and was never regained. The final daylight gun action – between Beatty's and Hipper's battle-cruisers – began at 8.20 pm and lasted twenty minutes.

Although contact had been lost, Jellicoe was athwart the enemy's line of retreat and he still felt confident of being able to bring Scheer to battle next morning. He rejected the idea of a night action, mainly because of the risk of confusion and the presence of large numbers of enemy torpedo boats. Having so decided, Jellicoe was then faced with the problem of where

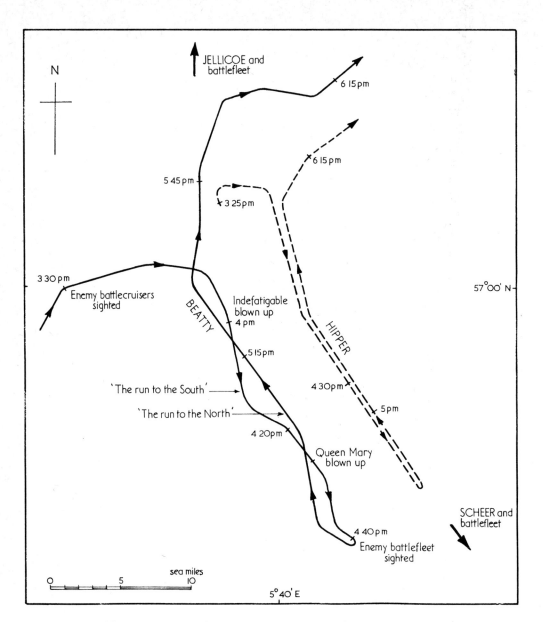

N

JELLICOE and
battlefleet

6 15 pm

6 15 pm

5 45 pm

3 25 pm

57°00' N

3 30 pm
Enemy battlecruisers
sighted

BEATTY

Indefatigable
blown up
4 pm

5 15 pm

HIPPER

'The run to the South'

'The run to the North'

4 30 pm

5 pm

4 20 pm

Queen Mary
blown up

SCHEER and
battlefleet

4 40 pm
Enemy battlefleet
sighted

sea miles

O   5   10

5° 40' E

JUTLAND   31 May 1916 – *the battlecruiser phase, 3.25 to 6.15 pm*

and how best to station his forces to ensure that Scheer did not reach home. Discounting the Skagerrak, the German fleet had three possible routes: SW to the Ems estuary; south via Heligoland to the Jade; and SE via Horn Reef to the Elbe estuary. Jellicoe favoured either of the first two and made his dispositions accordingly. In fact Scheer chose the Horn Reef channel and in following a SE course succeeded in passing through the rear of the British fleet during the night to escape practically unscathed. In the darkness there were a series of violent clashes between the light cruisers and destroyer flotillas, with some losses on both sides, but they did not affect the main issue. By 3.30 am Scheer had reached the safety of the Horn Reef channel and half an hour later Jellicoe realised the enemy had eluded him. There was nothing more to be done except sweep north for stragglers and go home and the Grand Fleet re-entered Scapa Flow that afternoon.

Intense disappointment was felt on the British side at the failure to bring the enemy to decisive action. The battle aroused bitter controversy and recrimination which continued for many years afterwards. The sinking of the three British battlecruisers and the cause of their loss was particularly keenly felt. Materially, British losses and casualties were heavier – three battlecruisers, three armoured cruisers, eight destroyers against one pre-dreadnought, one battlecruiser, four light cruisers and five destroyers; 6,000 men killed against 2,500. On this basis the Germans claimed that the Skagerrak, as they called the battle of Jutland, was a victory. Yet strategically the battle served to underline the maritime supremacy exercised by Great Britain. The High Seas Fleet did not come out again to renew the challenge and henceforth German naval effort turned to unrestricted submarine warfare.

KENTISH KNOCK   28 September 1652

An important action of the First Dutch War. After his engagement with Ayscue off PLYMOUTH on 16 August 1652 (qv), the Dutch Admiral de Ruyter continued to cruise in the Channel looking for homeward-bound Dutch merchantmen. But by mid-September his squadron was running short of provisions and the merchantmen already under convoy were anxious to reach port. De Ruyter therefore turned home and joined up with the main Dutch fleet under Admiral de Witt off Calais. Having crossed the Straits with his combined force, de Witt suddenly appeared off the Goodwins on 25 September. The English fleet anchored in the Downs under General-at-Sea Robert Blake was hastily reinforced until it numbered sixty-eight sail. Early on 28 September Blake weighed from the Downs and sailed in search of the enemy. Having passed the North Foreland, he sighted the Dutch fleet at noon hove-to close under the lee of the Kentish Knock sand. The wind had shifted to the SW and moderated. The main action began late in the afternoon and lasted three hours. It was particularly fierce in the van and two Dutch warships were dismasted; several of Blakes' grounded on the sand but were got off. Trouble and discontent beset the Dutch fleet. The crew of Tromp's old flagship the *Brederode* refused to allow de Witt on board her and many of his ships refrained from going into action. Partly for this reason and partly owing to the suddenness of Blake's attack, the Dutch by nightfall were beaten. (*See map on next page.*)

KJÖGE BIGHT   1 July 1677

A great Danish victory during her war with Sweden, 1675–9. Following their defeat by a combined Danish and Dutch fleet at ÖLAND (qv) in June 1676, the Swedes suffered even more severely a year later. With his flag in the *Christianus V*, 84, and twenty-four of the line, the Danish admiral Niels Juel led his fleet against a larger Swedish force under Admiral Horn. The battle took place in the waters of the Kjöge Bight, a broad bay on the coast of Sjaelland near Copenhagen. It was hard fought but at the end of the day the Swedes were in full flight. Seven of their ships of the line were taken and the *Kalmar*, 62, burnt.

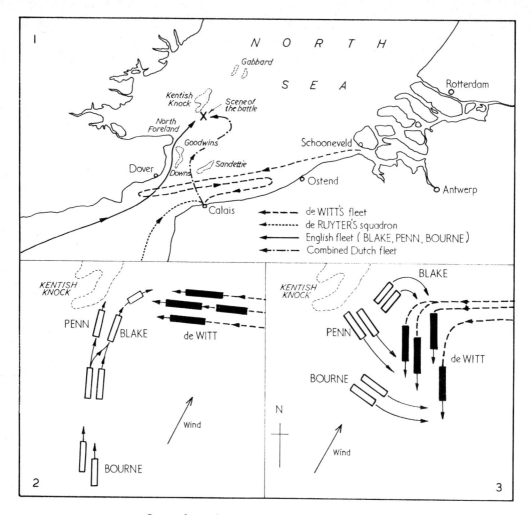

KENTISH KNOCK   28 September 1652 – (1) *Approximate movements of the fleets, 4–28 Sept-ember* (2) *opening of the action,* (3) *close of the action*

KOLOMBANGARA   12/13 July 1943

The second of two sharp night actions fought in the Solomon Islands theatre in July 1943 (*see also* KULA GULF). In order to reinforce their hard-pressed garrison at Vila on Kolombangara Island, the Japanese despatched a strong support group under Rear-Admiral Izaki from Rabaul. To support the four destroyer-transports carrying 1,200 troops, Izaki had the light cruiser *Jintsu* and five destroyers. Receiving intelligence of the enemy movement, an American task force (Rear-Admiral Ainsworth with cruisers *Honolulu* and *St Louis*, New Zealand light cruiser *Leander* and ten destroyers) was quickly assembled at Tulagi and proceeded up the Slot under cover of darkness. In the early hours of 13 July both forces met off the NW tip of Kolombangara Island.

After a fierce engagement the *Jintsu* blew up, Ainsworth's three cruisers were hit by torpedoes and the destroyer *Gwin* sunk. Izaki and many of his men went down with the *Jintsu* but the Japanese transports got through to Vila. American claims of damage inflicted on the enemy were later shown to have been exaggerated. In fact the main feature of the action was the deadly effectiveness of the Japanese 24in 'long-lance' torpedo.

KOMANDORSKI ISLANDS   26 March 1943

An unusual battle of the Pacific war, being a prolonged gun action between surface forces in which neither aircraft nor submarines were involved. Admiral Hosogaya with the heavy cruisers *Nachi* and *Maya*, light cruisers *Tama* and *Abukuma* and four destroyers was escorting two large transports to reinforce the Japanese garrison at Attu in the Aleutian Islands. At dawn on 26 March he was attacked by a US squadron south of the Komandorski Islands, which lie between Attu and the Kamchatka peninsula. Rear-Admiral McMorris, commanding the cruisers *Salt Lake City* and *Richmond* and four destroyers, was inferior in strength but did not hesitate to engage. The weather was clear but extremely cold. Before the engagement began Hosogaya ordered the transports away. In the $3\frac{1}{2}$ hour gun action which followed, the *Salt Lake City* was severely damaged and at one time lay dead in the water. The Americans however fought back with great skill and determination and Hosogaya eventually withdrew. Henceforth no reinforcements by sea reached the Japanese fighting in the Aleutians.

KORČULA   *see* CURZOLA

KUA KAM   20–2 October 1849

The depredations of a Chinese pirate fleet under the notorious Shap-ng-tsai became so serious in 1849 that a naval flotilla was formed under Commander Dalrymple Hay to destroy it. On 8 October he left Hong Kong with the East India Company's armed steamer *Phlegethon*, sloop *Columbine* and paddle-sloop *Fury*. Eventually the pirate junks were located moored in the Kua Kam, one of the numerous creeks in the Song Ka (Red River) estuary near Haiphong. On the morning of 20 October Hay's flotilla entered the labyrinth of channels but did not find the right passage leading to the junks until late afternoon. Then they discovered Shap-ng-tsai's largest junks moored across the entrance, their guns trained. The pirates opened fire at a range of 800 yards and the British vessels replied with shells and rockets. During the brisk engagement a shell from the *Phlegethon* hit the pirate flagship, which blew up, and by nightfall twenty-seven junks were ablaze. By the end of the operation fifty-eight Chinese junks had been destroyed and some 3,000 pirates killed or captured. Shap-ng-tsai himself escaped in one of the six surviving junks but later surrendered.

KULA GULF   6 July 1943

A night action in the Kula Gulf (which divides Kolombangara Island from the New Georgia mainland) during the Solomon Islands campaign. Rear-Admiral Akiyama's force of ten destroyers was carrying troops and supplies to the Japanese garrison at Vila. At 1.40 am 6 July, Rear-Admiral Ainsworth, leading a squadron of three cruisers and four destroyers, made radar contact with Akiyama's destroyers. The contact was made just after the Japanese commander had detached his destroyer-transports, with orders to proceed south down the gulf to Vila, and he himself had reversed course for home. Although the Americans quickly sank the *Niizuki* by gunfire, her consorts *Suzukaze* and *Tanikaze* were able to launch sixteen 'long-lance' torpedoes with deadly effect. Three struck the cruiser *Helena* and she went down, although her severed bow floated for many hours afterwards with survivors clinging to it. Many were rescued. A second Japanese destroyer, the *Nagatsuki*, ran aground on Kolombangara Island during the night. She could not be refloated and was destroyed by American aircraft next day (*see also* KOLOMBANGARA).

LADE 494 BC

In the Ionian revolt of 499 BC, the Greek colonies in Asia Minor rose against Persian rule. Not until 494 was the revolt finally crushed. That year Darius' great fleet of 600 ships under Artaphernes blockaded Miletus, the chief Ionian city. Then over 350 ships from Lesbos, Chios and Samos sailed in an attempt to relieve Miletus. Both fleets met off Lade, thirty miles south of Ephesus on the west coast of Asia Minor. All but eleven of the Samian ships deserted, bribed by the Persians, and although the Chians fought bravely the Greek fleet was destroyed. The victorious Persians then landed and sacked Miletus. Later they used their fleet to reduce the Aegean Islands as a preliminary step to the invasion of Greece.

LADE 201 BC

A battle between a Rhodian fleet under Theophiliscus – who was mortally wounded at CHIOS (qv) later the same year – and a Macedonian fleet under Heraclides. Both sides claimed to have won, though the Macedonians suffered fewer losses.

LAGOS 17/18 June 1693

Better known as 'the disaster of the Smyrna Convoy'. In June 1693 an extremely large and valuable convoy of 400 English, Dutch, German, Danish and Swedish merchantmen sailed down the English Channel bound for the Mediterranean. Protection as far as Ushant was given by the main Anglo-Dutch fleet, which then returned home. The task of escorting the convoy for the rest of the voyage lay with the accompanying squadron under Vice-Admiral Rooke and Rear-Admiral van der Goes. The French knew about the convoy and Admirals Tourville, based at Brest, and d'Estrées at Toulon, were ordered to rendezvous in Lagos Bay on the south coast of Portugal and there lie in wait.

   All went well with the convoy until noon on 17 June when, south of Cape St Vincent, Rooke found himself in the presence of eighty enemy ships. The admiral made every effort to avoid engagement but by the evening the French warships were amongst the convoy. Two of the Dutch escort – the *Zeeland*, 64, and *Wapen van Medemblik*, 64 – gallantly sacrificed themselves in an attempt to save their charges and were at length taken. By next morning the convoy was completely scattered; some took refuge in Cadiz, Malaga and Gibraltar. Rooke could find only fifty-four merchantmen in sight and he proceeded with them to make for the rendezvous at Madeira. The French took, burnt or sunk at least ninety-two ships of the convoy and the total financial loss to the Allies exceeded £1,000,000.

LAGOS   18/19 August 1759   *Oil painting by Thomas Luny*

LAGOS   18/19 August 1759

In May 1759 Admiral Edward Boscawen assumed command in the Mediterranean. While he was at Gibraltar, a French squadron of ten of the line, two 50s and three frigates under de la Clue sailed from Toulon on 16 August with the intention of joining the main French fleet at Brest. As soon as he learned of the enemy move, Boscawen left Gibraltar and set off in pursuit westwards, with the *Namur*, 90, fourteen of the line and several frigates. Seven ships of the French squadron were sighted off the Portuguese coast early on the 18th, the rest having parted company during the night without orders and made for Cadiz. Action began at 1.30 pm in variable winds, during which the French *Centaure*, 74, was taken and the *Namur* disabled. Boscawen then transferred to the *Newark*, 80, and continued the chase through the night. In the darkness two of the enemy ships altered course and escaped but the last four were driven into Lagos Bay. Next day the *Téméraire*, 74, and *Modeste*, 64, were captured and de la Clue's flagship *Océan*, 80, and *Redoutable*, 74, wrecked and burnt. De la Clue himself was carried ashore and later died of his wounds at Lagos. French casualties were severe and in accounting for five enemy ships of the line Boscawen had scored a notable success.

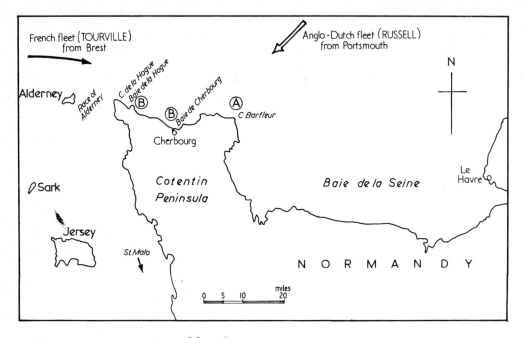

LA HOGUE AND BARFLEUR   May 1692

LA HOGUE 22–4 May 1692

On 20 May 1692 – the day after the Anglo-French fleet action off BARFLEUR (qv) – Comte de Tourville with his forty-four of the line retreated westwards towards the Channel Islands. Admiral Russell and the Anglo-Dutch fleet of ninety-six of the line followed in pursuit. The chase continued for three days, during which some of the French men-of-war managed to escape to the north and eventually got back to Brest. Twenty-two others navigated the danger-ous Race of Alderney under the skilful pilotage of Hervé Riel and reached St Malo. The remain-ing fifteen of the line, however, were caught by the flood-tide. Unable to find suitable anchor, they were swept eastwards and sought refuge in the open bays of Cherbourg and La Hogue.

There Russell found them on 22 May. He first attacked three large enemy ships stranded in Cherbourg Bay – Tourville's damaged flagship, the *Soleil Royal*, 106, *Admirable*, 90, and *Triomphant*, 74. After some resistance, supported by the batteries on shore, they were burnt and sunk. The last twelve French ships of the line retreated deep into Baie de la Hogue; there they were trapped, along with the transports assembling for King James III's invasion of England. Russell then received orders to destroy the enemy in the bay. By the skilful use of fireships and ships' boats, every one of the enemy battleships were destroyed during the night of 23/4 May or on the following morning. The same fate befell many of the transports and troopships, whose destruction was actually witnessed by James III. The Anglo-Dutch victory at La Hogue, so soon after the battle of Barfleur, was of decisive importance in the War of the English Succession.

LA PRAYA *see* PORTO PRAYA

LA HOGUE 22–4 May 1692 *Engraving by Romanus de Hooghe – the British and Dutch fleet defeat the French under Tourville*

LA ROCHELLE 22/3 June 1372

A severe English defeat during The Hundred Years' War. The young Earl of Pembroke took a fleet of armed merchantmen into the Bay of Biscay, carrying reinforcements to Aquitaine. While off La Rochelle, which was being besieged by the French, he was intercepted on 22 June by a strong fleet of Castilian galleys commanded by Ambrosio Bocanegra. The light galleys outmanoeuvred the English transports, heavily laden with soldiers, horses and stores. Some were set on fire and became unmanageable as the horses on board broke loose in panic. By the end of the second day's fighting, the entire British fleet had been captured or destroyed and Pembroke was taken prisoner to Santander.

LA ROCHELLE 22/3 June 1372 *The Earl of Pembroke's forty ships destroyed by the French and Spaniards*

LEGHORN   4 March 1653   *Oil painting by Renier Nooms*

LEGHORN   4 March 1653

Seven months after Badiley's action with Van Galen off ELBA (qv) the situation of the English and Dutch naval forces in the Mediterranean had changed little. Badiley remained at Elba, while Appleton was still bottled up in Leghorn by the Dutch. Early in 1653 the English commanders tried to join forces. They planned that as soon as Badiley arrived off Leghorn, Appleton would weigh to meet him and endeavour to pierce the Dutch blockade. However, the attempt miscarried. On 4 March Badiley duly appeared having sailed from Porto Longone. Van Galen feinted to attack him, inducing Appleton to weigh from the harbour too soon. When he came out with the *Leopard*, 50, and armed merchantmen *Bonaventure*, *Samson*, *Mary*, *Peregrine* and *Levant Merchant*, Van Galen turned to meet him with Badiley still some miles away. In the action which followed Appleton was overwhelmed. The *Bonaventure* received a shot in her magazine and blew up. Four of the squadron and Appleton himself were taken by the Dutch; only the *Mary* succeeded in fighting her way through to join Badiley.

LEMNOS   73 BC

A battle of the Third Mithridatic War (74–64 BC), between Rome and Mithridates, King of Pontus. The Roman commander, L. Licinius Lucullus, built up a formidable fleet with support from Rome's client states and eventually wrested command of the sea from the great fleet of Mithridates. In 73 Lucullus chased a smaller Pontic squadron from the Hellespont to the island of Lemnos, where they beached themselves. Landing some troops on the other side of the island, he attacked and defeated the enemy by land and sea.

LEPANTO   12 and 14 August 1499   *see* ZONCHIO

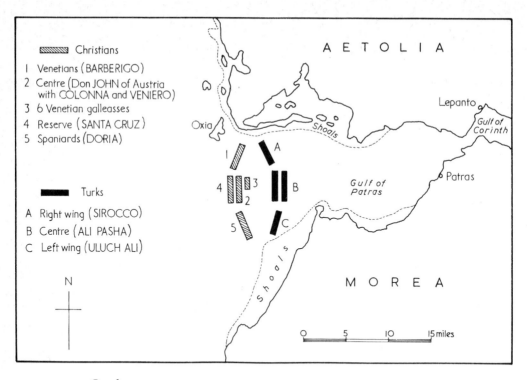

LEPANTO   7 October 1571

LEPANTO   7 October 1571

In the spring of 1570 the Ottoman sultan, Selim II, launched a large expeditionary force against Cyprus, then in the possession of Venice. Nicosia was sacked in August and a counter-attack by an allied fleet in the autumn was terminated by storms and disagreements. The following May, Spain, Venice and the Papacy pledged 300 ships and over 50,000 men for operations against the Turks. The Venetian galleys, normally manned by free-born citizens, now included impressed men, foreigners and even bandits. Pope Pius V hired twelve Tuscan ships, appointing Marc Antonio Colonna their commander. The Venetians under Sebastian Veniero were joined at Messina on 25 August by Don John of Austria, High Admiral of Spain.

Meanwhile the Turks had taken Famagusta on 4 August and were raiding the Eastern Adriatic. By September the Christians had assembled at Messina a large fleet – 208 galleys, six galleasses, twelve *nefs* and fifty other craft – carrying over 75,000 men. Under the supreme command of Don John of Austria, the ships belonged to many nations. There were Spanish, Neapolitan, Sicilian, Genoese, Maltese and a large contingent of 116 from Venice. On 16 September the papal nuncio blessed the departing fleet, which three weeks later reached the Curzolari Islands, 36 miles from Lepanto where the Turks had arrived on 27 September. Their fleet under Ali Pasha comprised 210 galleys, forty galliots, twenty small craft and 75,000 men. The strength of the Ottomans lay in their formidable reputation and the rapid rate of fire of their bowmen, whereas the Christian ships were superior in guns and protection. The Turks

LEPANTO   7 October 1571   *Engraving by Lambert Cornelisz, after a painting by I. Stradanus*

left harbour on 6 October and were sighted early next day by Doria as he passed Point Seropha. Don John formed line of battle at 9.30 am and long-range firing between the fleets began half an hour later. Ali Pasha commanded the Turkish centre, with his extended right and left wings under Mahomet Sirocco and Uluch Ali overlapping the Christians.

As the battle developed on the Turkish right, Sirocco tried to surround Barberigo but only a few of his ships got to westward and Quirini attacked the Turkish rear. Then Barberigo was mortally wounded by an arrow and Sirocco fled ashore and was killed, none of his squadron escaping capture. The two centres approached each other steadily; first bombarding, then grappling fiercely and boarding. Shortly before 1 o'clock Don John took the Turkish flagship in tow; Ali Pasha himself was killed and Turkish resistance began to crumble. Meanwhile, on the Turkish left, Uluch Ali's ninety ships had manoeuvred to outflank Andrea Doria's smaller squadron. The Turks quickly surrounded and took fifteen ships which had become separated but then Doria attacked and recaptured thirteen. Uluch Ali seized the *Capitana di Malta* but lost her again and late in the afternoon fled the field with eight ships. It was the Ottomans' final effort.

By dusk Don John had brought his victorious fleet to anchor. At a cost of twelve ships and 7,000 men he had taken 170 prizes, 7,000 prisoners and many more Turks had been killed. Lepanto was in every way a remarkable victory and one which permanently destroyed Ottoman naval power in the Mediterranean.

LEYTE GULF 23–6 October 1944

In their determination to retain the Philippines, the Japanese mounted a major fleet offensive to destroy the American beachhead established at Leyte Gulf on 20 October 1944. They evolved a clever three-pronged attack. Vice-Admiral Ozawa's Northern Force (four aircraft carriers with supporting warships) planned to approach the Philippines from the north, in order to decoy Admiral Halsey's Third Fleet away from Leyte Gulf and enable the other two Japanese groups to attack from the west. These were Centre Force (the most powerful group, comprising five battleships, twelve cruisers and fifteen destroyers under Vice-Admiral Kurita), which would enter Leyte Gulf from the north via the Sibuyan Sea and San Bernardino Strait. And

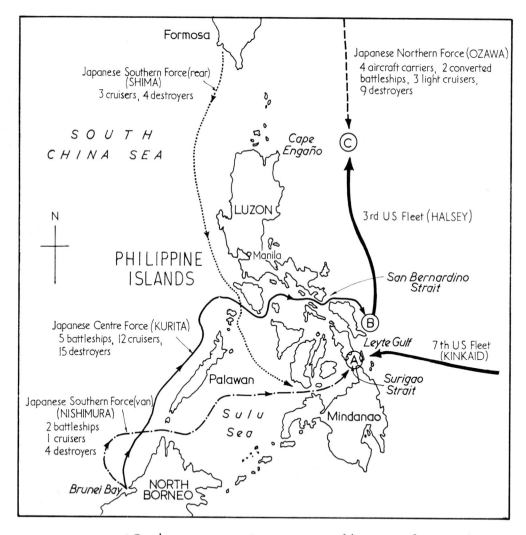

LEYTE GULF   23–6 October 1944 – *approximate movements of the opposing fleets – Battle Areas:* (A) *Surigao Strait,* (B) *Samar,* (C) *Cape Engaño*

Southern Force (in two divisions under Vice-Admirals Nishimura and Shima, with two battle-ships, four cruisers and eight destroyers), which would approach from the south via the Sulu and Mindanao Seas. Both these thrusts aimed to drive off Vice-Admiral Kinkaid's Seventh Fleet and then fall upon the unprotected invasion shipping lying in Leyte Gulf.

On 22 October both Kurita and Nishimura sailed from Brunei Bay, North Borneo and Shima's force lay in wait north of Palawan, preparatory to linking up with Nishimura. Mean-while Ozawa had left Japan and was approaching Luzon from the north as planned. The battle opened next day when the US submarines *Darter* and *Dace* torpedoed and sank off Palawan two of Kurita's heavy cruisers (including his flagship *Atago*) and damaged a third. Throughout 24 October Kurita was repeatedly attacked in the Sibuyan Sea by carrier aircraft from US Third Fleet. After taking heavy punishment the giant battleship *Musashi* (64,000 tons; nine 18.1in guns) capsized. Without air cover and under heavy attack, Centre Force temporarily reversed course that afternoon and awaited news of Ozawa's progress. This move strengthened Halsey's belief that the main threat lay in the north (an attack earlier by Ozawa's aircraft had sunk the light carrier *Princeton*). He thereupon sent his whole fleet in that direction, with orders to attack Ozawa next day, leaving the vital exit from San Bernardino Strait com-pletely unguarded. That same afternoon Kinkaid learned of the approach of the Japanese Southern Force and prepared to give battle in Surigao Strait.

Events reached a climax on 25 October, culminating in the three separate battles of Surigao Strait, Samar and Cape Engaño.

Rear-Admiral Oldendorf had been given command of the Seventh Fleet's fighting ships – six old battleships, eight cruisers and a large number of destroyers and PT boats. Acting on the latter's sighting reports, Oldendorf ambushed Nishimura in the darkness as he began to emerge from the northern exit of Surigao Strait. The American destroyers first delivered a series of torpedo attacks which sank the battleship *Fuso* and three destroyers. Then in the final gun action with Oldendorf's battleships, Nishimura's flagship, the battleship *Yamashiro*, was over-whelmed and the heavy cruiser *Mogami* crippled. Only the destroyer *Shigure* escaped in the darkness to join Shima and the rear division which, thirty miles behind, was just able to with-draw from the strait in time.

Meanwhile a dangerous situation had developed in the centre, where Kurita – still with four battleships and eleven cruisers – had emerged unchallenged from San Bernardino Strait in the early hours of the 25th and was steering SE for Leyte Gulf. Midway down the east coast of Samar Island, the Japanese admiral met a weak, mixed force of American escort carriers and destroyers. For the next three hours its commander, Rear-Admiral Clifton Sprague, was in a desperate situation. Heavily outnumbered, he called in vain for help from Halsey, who was 400 miles to the north harrying Ozawa. Kurita, however, completely failed to seize the great opportunity. Although his cruisers sank the escort carrier *Gambier Bay* and three American destroyers were lost in a gallant counter-attack, he suddenly broke off the action shortly after 9 am. Why he did so has never been fully explained; possibly it was on account of heavy losses (three more of his cruisers were sunk by air attack off Samar). More probably, faulty intelligence led him to believe a massive concentration of American ships was forming against him. In any event Kurita re-entered San Bernardino Strait that night and retired from the scene.

The third action of 25 October occurred far to the north. At dawn Halsey located the Japanese Northern Force off Cape Engaño, the NE point of Luzon. A succession of air strikes quickly sank all four of Ozawa's aircraft carriers, whose sacrifice was now in vain because the

Centre Force had failed. On the final day, 26 October, the Japanese endured further air attacks as they retired.

So ended one of the greatest naval battles of modern times, in which the United States gained a decisive victory. Not only was the fate of the Philippines decided; the Japanese loss of three battleships, four aircraft carriers, ten cruisers and nine destroyers marked the eclipse of their navy.

LIMAN   18 and 28 June 1788

An action during the Russo-Turkish War of 1787–91. In June 1788 Russian troops advanced down the northern bank of the Liman River towards the port of Ochakov in the Ukraine. They were supported by Prince Nassau-Siegen's river flotilla and several warships commanded by John Paul Jones, then in Russian service. On the morning of 18 June Turkish in-shore craft led by Hassan el Ghasi attacked but were easily driven off. Ten days later the Turks made another attempt but were heavily defeated, losing fifteen ships and some 3,000 men killed.

LIPARI ISLANDS   260 BC

At the outset of the First Punic War the Roman consul Cornelius Scipio took a small fleet to Messina in Sicily. Having established a base there he went on NW to Lipara, the chief town of the Aeolian or Lipari Islands. There, however, the Romans were suprised and heavily defeated by a much larger Carthaginian fleet which had sailed from Panormus (Palermo).

LISSA   13 March 1811

A remarkable action in which four English frigates defeated a much larger Franco-Venetian squadron in the Adriatic. In March 1811 Captain William Hoste, with the *Amphion*, *Active*, *Cerberus* and *Volage*, was using Lissa Island off the Dalmatian coast as his base and anchorage. At the same time Commodore Dubourdieu sailed from Ancona with a squadron comprising three 44-gun French frigates, three Venetian frigates and five smaller warships. On board were 500 troops for the occupation of Lissa. At dawn on 13 March Hoste sighted the enemy off the north coast of the island, the wind being from the NW. The French wasted no time and bore down to attack in two divisions. Hoste formed line in very close order and flew the signal: 'Remember Nelson!' Action was joined at 9 o'clock and a fierce mêlée continued until noon. By its end the French flagship, the *Favorite*, had been driven ashore and blew up, Dubourdieu himself being killed. Three more enemy frigates were captured and the remainder of the squadron fled.

LISSA   20 July 1866

Fought when ironclads were in their infancy, this battle has the distinction of being the first between armoured fleets in the open sea. When the Austro-Italian War began in June 1866, the Italian fleet lay at Ancona under the command of the sixty-year-old Admiral Carlo di Persano.

LISSA   20 July 1866   *Lithograph – Admiral Tegetthoff sinking the* Re d'Italia ▷

LISSA 13 March 1811 *Coloured aquatint by George Webster – Captain William Hoste's spirited
action in the Adriatic*

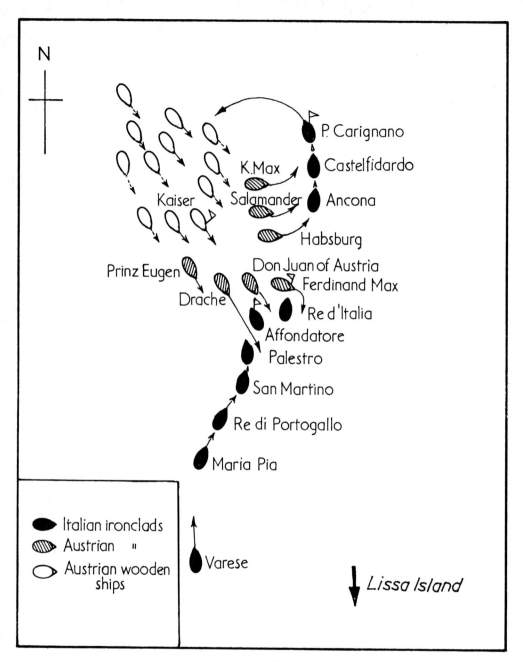

LISSA   20 July 1866   *the first clash of the ironclads*

The far younger Rear-Admiral von Tegetthoff commanded the Austrian imperial fleet based at Pola. Despite their considerable naval superiority, the Italians took no action for several weeks. At length on 16 July Persano sailed to attack Lissa Island off the Dalmatian coast. The operation was a failure, every attempt to force the harbour of Port S. Giorgio being repulsed by the local garrison. Early on 20 July Persano learned of the approach of the Austrian fleet and hurriedly assembled his ships north of the island.

Tegetthoff had left Pola on the afternoon of 19 July and approached Lissa with his fleet in three divisions. In the van were the ironclads *Erzherzog Ferdinand Max*, *Habsburg*, *Kaiser Max*, *Prinz Eugen*, *Don Juan de Austria*, *Drache* and *Salamander*. At 10 o'clock Tegetthoff sighted the enemy dead ahead and twenty-five minutes later made the stirring signal: '*Panzerschiffe den Feind anrennen und zum sinken bringen*!' ('Ironclads will dash at the enemy and sink him!'). Persano was steaming NNE with nine of his ironclads in single column line ahead and the tenth – the formidable ram *Affondatore* – on the starboard beam. At the last moment he shifted his flag from the *Re d'Italia* to the *Affondatore*.

Action began at 10.45 as the leading Austrian ironclads broke through the enemy column. A confused mêlée followed, made worse by the dense smoke which soon enveloped both fleets. After the first shock each ship manoeuvred independently, striving to ram or discharge broadsides. There was a duel between the Austrian wooden battleship *Kaiser* and the *Affondatore* and then the former rammed the *Re di Portogallo*. The climax came at 11.20 am after the Italian flagship *Re d'Italia* had been surrounded and disabled by four Austrian ironclads. Struck full amidships by the *Ferdinand Max*, she went down like a stone, taking 440 men with her. Later the Italian ironclad *Palestro* was set on fire and blew up. By late afternoon Tegetthoff had won a remarkable victory.

LOWESTOFT   3 June 1665

The opening naval battle of the Second Dutch War (1665–7). Obdam van Wassenaer in command of the Dutch fleet appeared off the Suffolk coast at the end of May 1665, having taken some English merchant ships near the Dogger Bank. Warned of the enemy's presence James, Duke of York, with the *Royal Charles*, 80, and the English fleet weighed from the Gunfleet and proceeded to Southwold Bay.

After two days of manoeuvring, action was joined off Lowestoft very early on 3 June. The wind was variable and the battle soon became a mêlée. In the centre Opdam's flagship the *Eendracht*, 76, fought a fierce duel with the *Royal Charles* but failed in an attempt to board her. During the exchange of broadsides a single chain-shot from the Dutchman killed several officers at the Duke of York's side. Then suddenly the *Eendracht* blew up from a hit in her powder-room, only five out of her complement of over 400 being saved. This severely demoralised the Dutch, many of whose ships began to give way. By 7 pm they were in full flight and complete disaster was averted only by the firmness of Cornelis Tromp and Jan Evertsen, who kept their squadrons together. Under their leadership the Dutch retired to the Texel and the Maas estuary, having lost more than thirty ships, against two on the English side. (*See map and illustration on pages 114 and 115.*)

LUNGA POINT   *see* TASSAFARONGA

LYCIA   AD 655

Known in Arabic as the battle of Dhat Al-Sawari. Muawiyah, the Islamic governor of Syria, planned to attack Byzantium with a combined Egypto-Syrian fleet. Off the coast of Lycia in Asia Minor he met a large Byzantine fleet commanded by the Emperor Constans II in person.

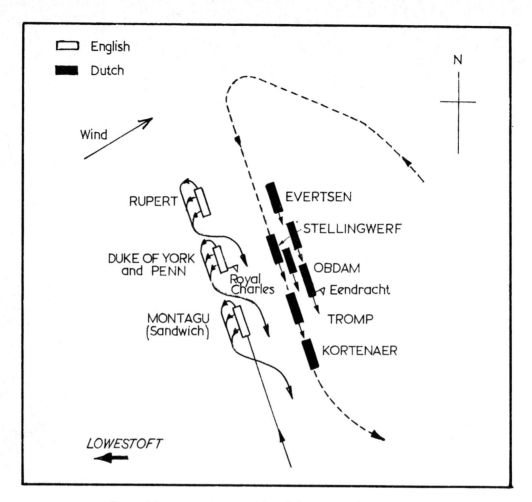

LEGEND:
English
Dutch

Wind

N

RUPERT

EVERTSEN

STELLINGWERF

DUKE OF YORK
and PENN

OBDAM

Royal
Charles

Eendracht

MONTAGU
(Sandwich)

TROMP

KORTENAER

LOWESTOFT

3 June 1665 – *approximate position of the opposing fleets,* 10 *am*

The emperor was decisively defeated and had to leave his flagship and escape in disguise aboard another vessel. Muawiyah's further plans, however, were unsuccessful and by the time of his death in 668, Constans had done much to rebuild Byzantine naval power and erase his defeat at Lycia.

MACASSAR STRAIT *see* BALIKPAPAN

MALACCA 1628

In 1628 the Sumatran King of Acheen sent 250 ships and 20,000 men to attack the Portuguese settlement at Malacca. Later that year Nuno Alvarez Botello came with his squadron to blockade the Sumatrans, who were lying up river some three miles from the town.

On the night of Botello's arrival the smaller Acheenese craft tried to escape but were driven

LOWESTOFT 3 June 1665 *Oil painting by H. van Minderhout*

back. Next morning the Sumatran fleet moved downstream and began a fierce engagement with the Portuguese. During the battle Botello was reinforced by the King of Pahang with 100 ships and by evening the entire Sumatran fleet had been taken or destroyed.

MALAGA 13 August 1704

A major battle between Anglo-Dutch and Franco-Spanish fleets in the Mediterranean during the War of the Spanish Succession. Three weeks after the Allies had captured Gibraltar, Comte de Toulouse sailed from Toulon with fifty ships of the line intending to defeat the allied fleet and retake the fortress. Admiral Sir George Rooke was in overall command of the Anglo-Dutch fleet, comprising fifty-three of the line, with Admiral Clowdisley Shovell leading the van division and the Dutch Admiral Callenburgh the rear. His ships were low in ammunition, much having been expended during the bombardment of Gibraltar.

MALAGA 13 August 1704 *Engraving after Isaac Sailmaker*

De Toulouse was sighted a few miles east of Gibraltar on 9 August and both fleets joined battle off Malaga four days later. The action developed into a hard cannonading duel, lasting many hours but devoid of decisive result. Although neither fleet lost a ship many were badly damaged and casualties were extremely heavy. Next day de Toulouse made no attempt to renew the action and Rooke got into Gibraltar unchallenged to repair damage. Then, having reinforced the garrison, he took the main body of the fleet home, leaving a small squadron under Sir John Leake to winter at Lisbon. Although a drawn battle, Malaga had real strategic significance. The Franco-Spanish attempt to recapture Gibraltar had failed and the Allies were not challenged again at sea for the rest of the war (*see also* MARBELLA).

MANILA BAY 1 May 1898

On the outbreak of war between Spain and America, Commodore George Dewey's Asiatic Squadron sailed from Hong Kong for the Philippines. During the night of 30 April it passed safely between the batteries of Corregidor and El Fraile and entered Manila Bay. Admiral Montojo's squadron of seven Spanish cruisers, three gunboats and two transports lay at anchor in the bay under the Cavite shore batteries. At daybreak on 1 May Dewey's flagship the *Olympia* led the cruisers *Raleigh*, *Petrel*, *Concord* and *Boston* towards the enemy. Montojo's ships opened fire at long range but the Americans did not reply until the range closed to 5,000 yards.

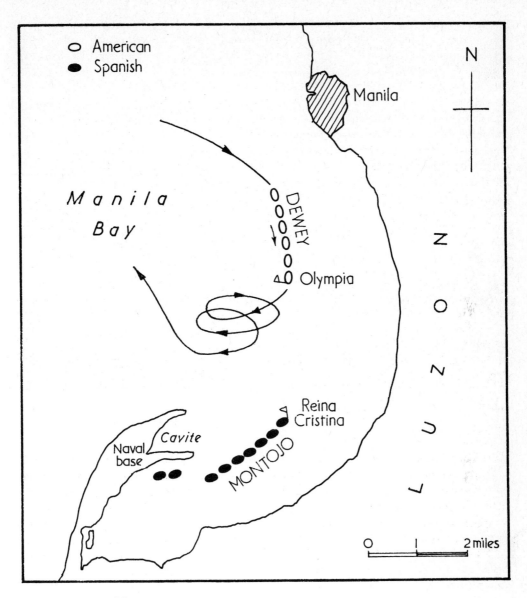

MANILA BAY   1 May 1898

They then steamed past the Spanish ships five times, subjecting them to a fierce bombardment. Montojo's flagship the *Reina Cristina* slipped her cable but was driven back by shell-fire. At 7.35 am Dewey was informed that the *Olympia's* ammunition was running low and he ordered a withdrawal. Discovering the report to be inaccurate, he sent his cruisers back into action with instructions to act independently. The battle ended at noon with the annihilation of the Spanish squadron, which lost seven ships sunk and the rest burned or captured.

MARBELLA 10 March 1705

Also known as the action of Cabrita or Cabareta Point. For many months after the capture of Gibraltar and the battle of VELEZ MALAGA (qv), the French and Spaniards made great efforts to regain the fortress. A French squadron under de Pointis tried to assist in the siege but was driven off by Sir John Leake's ships. The decisive engagement took place at the beginning of March 1705. De Pointis arrived in Gibraltar Bay with his squadron and prepared to land troops for the assault. However a westerly gale drove most of his force to leeward towards Marbella, where Leake lay off Cabrita Point with five of the line. At daybreak on 10 March Leake surprised the French and after a swift action defeated them. He took the *Ardent*, 66, *Marquis*, 66, and *Arrogant*, 60. De Pointis's flagship the *Magnanime*, 74, and the *Lys*, 66, were driven ashore near Marbella and burnt by the enemy to avoid capture.

MARTINIQUE 29 April 1781

Early in January 1781 Admiral Rodney, in command of British naval forces in the Caribbean, received a much-needed reinforcement from England – eight ships of the line and a large convoy under Rear-Admiral Samuel Hood. Next month Rodney captured the rich Dutch island of St Eustatius; his arbitrary seizure of its wealth, however, provoked a public outcry. While Rodney languished at St Eustatius, he learned that a large French convoy was en route to the West Indies. He ordered Hood with eleven of the line to join Rear-Admiral Drake's squadron off Fort Royal, Martinique, and then cruise to windward of the island in the hope of intercepting the enemy. Then, however, Rodney made the mistake of ordering Hood to reimpose the blockade of Fort Royal, as he wished to safeguard the passage of the homeward-bound convoy laden with the spoils taken from St Eustatius. Hood bitterly opposed the change of plan and was proved right. On 28 April he was off Fort Royal when a much larger French fleet of twenty of the line under Comte de Grasse, escorting a convoy of 150 sail, came in sight.

The British fleet was inferior in gun power and to leeward but during the night Hood skilfully manoeuvred for position. Next morning action was joined as the French came round the south coast of Martinique. In the course of the engagement, mainly fought at long range, the four French battleships in Fort Royal Bay got out and joined de Grasse to give him even greater numerical superiority. The *Russell*, *Centaur* and *Intrepid* of Hood's fleet were badly damaged and eventually de Grasse succeeded in getting his convoy into Fort Royal unharmed. Although Hood fought well against a superior fleet, the French had achieved their main objective. (*See map on pages 190–191.*)

MATAPAN 19 July 1717

While on passage between Marathonisi and Cape Matapan, a mixed force of fifty-seven ships and galleys – Spanish, Portuguese, Venetian and Papal – was attacked by a Turkish squadron of approximately the same strength. The action began at 6 am and soon became general. Eventually after heavy fighting, in which many ships were damaged on both sides, the Turks withdrew. This was one of the last occasions in which Mediterranean galleys were used in a fleet action.

MATAPAN 28 March 1941 *Oil painting by Norman Wilkinson – the Italian heavy cruisers* Zara *and* Fiume *caught by searchlight and gunfire*

MATAPAN 28/9 March 1941

Increased Italian naval activity towards the end of March 1941 convinced Admiral Sir Andrew Cunningham, commander-in-chief of the Mediterranean fleet, that the enemy was preparing to attack Greek-bound convoys. On the afternoon of 27 March three Italian cruisers were sighted 320 miles west of Crete steaming SE. Having warned convoys in the area, Cunningham then ordered Vice-Admiral Pridham-Wippell to proceed with four cruisers and four destroyers to a position thirty miles west of Gavdos (an islet off Crete). That evening Cunningham sailed from Alexandria with the battleships *Warspite*, *Barham*, *Valiant*, the aircraft carrier *Formidable* and nine destroyers to rendezvous with the cruisers.

Early next morning reconnaissance aircraft from the *Formidable* and Pridham-Wippell's cruisers made contact with the enemy force. After a brief engagement the Italians broke off and headed NW, recalled by Admiral Iachino who was rapidly coming up on the British squadron's port quarter with the battleship *Vittorio Veneto*, five heavy cruisers and screening destroyers. At 11 o'clock the *Vittorio Veneto* sighted the British light forces and opened fire.

Half an hour later aircraft from the *Formidable* carried out an unsuccessful attack but it was sufficient to persuade Iachino to return to Taranto.

When the British cruisers had joined the main fleet, Cunningham set off in pursuit of the enemy sixty-five miles ahead. Further aerial attacks were launched and one torpedo hit was obtained on the *Vittorio Veneto*, which reduced her speed to 19 knots. During a later strike by *Formidable*'s torpedo-bombers, delivered half an hour after sunset, the heavy cruiser *Pola* was hit and disabled. Still unaware of the close proximity of Cunningham's fleet, Iachino then ordered the heavy cruisers *Zara* and *Fiume*, together with four destroyers, to turn back and take the *Pola* in tow. Radar contact having been established with the crippled cruiser, the crews of the British battleships went to action stations. Just before 10.30 pm the returning Italian division suddenly appeared across their bows at close range. The British 15in guns immediately trained on the new targets and searchlights illuminated the *Zara* and *Fiume*. Both Italian cruisers were totally unprepared for action, with their guns trained fore and aft. The devastating fire of the battleships' main armament at a range of 3,500 yards soon reduced both to blazing wrecks. After attempting a torpedo attack the Italian destroyer *Vittorio Alfieri* was sunk by the *Barham*'s gunfire and later another – the *Giosue Carducci* – was destroyed. In the early hours of 29 March the crippled *Pola* was found by two British destroyers and sunk after her crew had been taken off.

MELORIA   6 August 1284

The decisive sea battle in the war between Pisa and Genoa (1282–4). At the end of July 1284 a large Pisan fleet of seventy-two galleys led by Morosini and della Gherardesca unexpectedly appeared off Genoa. The Genoese naval commander Oberto Doria at once manned all available ships – about sixty-five galleys – and left port to do battle. After several days' manoeuvring, both fleets came into action on 6 August off Meloria Island, not far from Leghorn. There was a bitter struggle before the Pisans were defeated, with the loss of their flagship, thirty ships taken and seven sunk.

MERS EL-KEBIR   *see* ORAN

MIDWAY   4–6 June 1942

This battle marked a turning-point in the Pacific naval war, as it broke the ascendancy which the Japanese had gained in the first six months of 1942. The Japanese commander-in-chief, Admiral Yamamoto, launched an invasion fleet, heavily supported by warships, against Midway Island in the central Pacific, as the stepping-stone for an attack on Hawaii. Admiral Nagumo's experienced carrier strike group (*Akagi, Kaga, Hiryu, Soryu*) formed the spearhead. Aware of the impending operation, two US taskforces under Admirals Spruance and Fletcher (including carriers *Enterprise, Hornet* and *Yorktown*) were formed east of Midway.

On 3 June American aircraft based on Midway attacked the approaching enemy without success. The decisive battle was fought next day. Early that morning Japanese carrier planes heavily bombed the island and inflicted considerable damage. After they had returned, Nagumo altered course and began refuelling and rearming his planes for a second strike, unaware that he was about to be attacked. While this was being done the Japanese carriers were extremely vulnerable, their flight decks crowded with heavily laden aircraft. The first American strikes by the torpedo-bombers failed, many being shot down by fighters and the group from the *Hornet* did not reach the target. However the next attack by fifty-seven Dauntless dive-bombers from *Enterprise* and *Yorktown* was devastating; between 10.25 and 10.30 am the *Akagi*, *Kaga* and *Soryu* were crippled in succession and sank later. Only the *Hiryu* managed to launch her planes and they so damaged the *Yorktown* that she was sunk by the Japanese submarine *I-168* two days later. But the *Hiryu* did not escape. During the afternoon of 4 June she was attacked by dive-bombers from *Enterprise* and succumbed after repeated hits. Next day the heavy cruiser *Mikuma* was also bombed and sunk.

Thereafter the Japanese abandoned their whole operation against Midway Island. The destruction of Nagumo's force proved an irreparable loss – altogether four large fleet carriers with 250 naval aircraft and their experienced crews.

MINORCA   20 May 1756

A British reverse in the Mediterranean at the opening of the Seven Years' War with France, which resulted in the loss of Minorca and its valuable naval base at Port Mahon. In April 1756 a French squadron of twelve of the line under de la Galissonnière escorted transports with 15,000 troops on board, which were disembarked at Minorca, and blockaded Port Mahon. With resources strained elsewhere the Admiralty could only raise a force of ten ships of the line under Vice-Admiral John Byng, who left England at the beginning of April and reached Minorca on 19 May. Next day de la Galissonnière came out to meet him and a confused, indecisive engagement took place off Port Mahon. Throughout, Byng weakly refrained from making any positive attack. Worse was to follow. Instead of remaining near Minorca, he decided to retire to Gibraltar; the French seized the opportunity and compelled the British garrison at Port Mahon to surrender on 29 June.

Faced by a furious public outcry in England, the Newcastle ministry sacrificed the unfortunate admiral. Brought back to England for court martial, he was condemned for neglect of duty and shot at Portsmouth on 14 March 1757. Byng's fate aroused widespread feeling, including Voltaire's famous comment: '*Dans ce pays-ci il est bon de tuer de temps en temps un amiral pour encourager les autres.*'

MOBILE BAY   5 August 1864

The remarkable victory by the Federal commander Rear-Admiral David Farragut during the American Civil War, which deprived the Confederacy of one of its few remaining ports. The only entrance into Mobile Bay, Alabama, was a narrow channel through a minefield protected by the defences of Fort Morgan. Within the anchorage lay the Confederate ironclad *Tennessee* and three gunboats under the command of Admiral Franklin Buchanan. Early on 5 August Farragut approached the channel with his squadron in two columns – one of fourteen wooden steamers lashed together in pairs, the other of four monitors led by the *Tecumseh*. Soon after the beginning of the action, the *Tecumseh* hit a mine and rapidly sank with heavy loss of life. In the ensuing confusion the leading Federal steamers at first hesitated until Farragut urged them on with the cry: 'Damn the torpedoes! Full steam ahead!' His ships then passed successfully through the minefield, although several were hit by the guns of Fort Morgan and the *Oneida* had to be towed away. After two of the Confederate gunboats had been accounted for,

MOBILE BAY 5 August 1864 *Lithograph published by Currier and Ives – Farragut forces the mined passage with the loss of* Tecumseh

fierce fighting continued as Farragut's ships tried to sink the ironclad *Tennessee* by ramming and shellfire. Eventually she struck her colours and Farragut obtained the surrender of the defending forts. With his squadron inside the bay, it could no longer be used by the Confederate blockade-runners.

MONTE CHRISTI 20 March and 20 June 1780

The name of two Anglo-French actions, fought off the north coast of San Domingo in the West Indies in 1780. On both occasions the British commander was Captain William Cornwallis. In the first – on 20 March – Cornwallis was cruising off Monte Christi with three small ships of the line, when he met a French convoy on its way from Martinique to Cap François. It was heavily escorted by four of the line and a frigate under La Motte-Picquet. A running fight ensued which continued through the night and the British frigate *Janus* was badly damaged. Next day Cornwallis was reinforced and the French withdrew.

Exactly three months later, Cornwallis was again off Monte Christi – with the *Lion*, 64, and four ships in support – when he sighted Commodore de Ternay with seven ships of the line. The latter was escorting an important convoy of transports carrying French troops to Rhode Island. Although in superior force, de Ternay hesitated to attack and Cornwallis skilfully rescued the *Ruby*, 64, which had become cut off from the rest of the squadron. (*See map on pages 190–191.*)

MORBIHAN GULF 56 BC

From Morbihan in Brittany, the tribe of the Veneti led the resistance of north-western Gaul to Julius Caesar's efforts to gather grain supplies. Decimus Brutus commanded the Roman fleet and the ships of its Gaulish allies from the Loire region.

In the Gulf of Morbihan on an unknown date in 56 BC Brutus encountered a Veneti fleet of 220 galleys. He neutralised his opponent's sailing qualities by having his men cut the enemy's halyards with hooks on the end of long poles. Helped by a sudden dead calm, the Romans were then able to board. The Veneti were eventually crushed after a prolonged battle, which Caesar watched from a neighbouring hill. The surrender of all Brittany soon followed.

MOUNT ECNOME see ECNOMUS

MYCALE 479 BC

This Greek victory against the Persians is said to have been won on the same day as that of Plataea on land. A fleet of 250 ships from Athens, Sparta and Delos induced the Persians to abandon Samos and retreat to Mycale on the mainland of Asia Minor. The Persians beached their ships and surrounded them with a garrisoned stockade. The Greek commander Leotychides, a Spartan, urged Persia's Ionian allies to desert and when battle commenced they did so. After a stiff shore action, the Persians fled and their ships were destroyed. The Greek fleet then sailed for Samos. Athens and her allies planned to establish a base on the Hellespont to dominate the Aegean trade but the Spartans were not interested and sailed home.

MYLAE 260 BC

Hannibal's Carthaginian fleet of some 120 ships raided the Italian coast at Mylae and then met the Roman fleet under consul Caius Duilius. The Romans had fitted spiked boarding planks called *corvi* to the bows of their ships. When the overconfident Carthaginians moved into the attack without much order, they found themselves boarded and overpowered by the Roman legionaries. Thirty ships were lost in the Carthaginian van and Hannibal escaped in a small boat. The Romans then captured twenty more ships before the Carthaginians withdrew in disorder.

MYLAE 13 August 36 BC

During the struggle between Octavian and Pompey for mastery of Sicily, Agrippa – Octavian's admiral – undertook to engage Pompey's fleet while Octavian ferried his army across the Straits of Messina. After Agrippa had sailed from Hiera in the Lipari Islands he discovered Pompey's fleet lying off Mylae on the north coast of Sicily. Agrippa's ships were generally heavier; at close quarters their higher decks gave them the advantage in hurling missiles and securing grappling irons. Watching from a neighbouring hill, Pompey saw his ships defeated but they were able to retire in good order.

MYONNESUS 190 BC

Fought off the coast of Asia Minor during the war between Rome and King Antiochus of Syria, which began in 192 BC. The Roman fleet of fifty-eight ships under Aemilius, supported by a Rhodian squadron, sailed from Teos on the Erythraean peninsula. Proceeding south, it met the Syrian fleet of ninety ships under Polyxenides off Myonnesus. Using his lighter Levantine craft, Polyxenides attempted to envelop the Roman fleet but the Rhodian squadron prevented this with rams, archery and fire baskets. Eventually the Asians broke and the victorious Romans and Rhodians went on to the Hellespont.

MYTILENE 406 BC

In the last years of the Peloponnesian War, a Spartan fleet under Callicratidas blockaded a smaller Athenian force in the harbour of Mytilene on Lesbos. In the ensuing battle thirty of Conon's vessels were captured but one broke through the blockade to bring the news to Athens. As a result the Athenians and their allies sent a large relief fleet against Callicratidas, who left fifty ships under Eteonicus to maintain the blockade of Mytilene while he sailed out to do battle. The outcome was the great Athenian victory off the ARGINUSAE ISLANDS (qv).

The second battle of NARVIK 13 April 1940 *Oil painting by Norman Wilkinson* – Warspite *and destroyers entering Narvik Fjord*

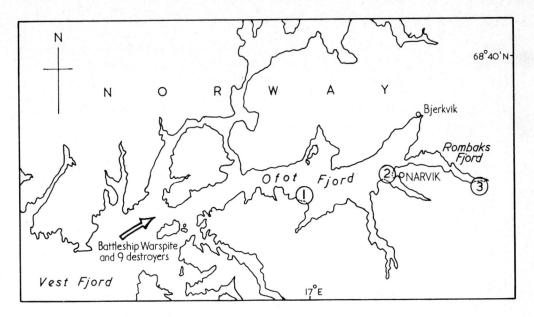

The second battle of NARVIK 13 April 1940

1 *Destroyer* Erich Koellner *lurking in a narrow inlet*
2 *Main destroyer action:* Erich Giese, Diether von Röder, Hermann Künne *sunk*
3 *Last 4 destroyers* – Wolfgang Zenker, Bernd von Arnim, Hans Lüdemann *and* Georg Thiele *seek refuge in Rombaks Fjord but are sunk or scuttled*

NARVIK 10 and 13 April 1940

When Germany invaded Norway on 9 April 1940, ten large German destroyers were sent far north and disembarked troops to seize Narvik. The port's importance lay in the fact that during the winter months it handled the bulk of the vital traffic of Swedish iron ore to Germany, when Luleå in the Gulf of Bothnia was ice-bound.

At dawn on 10 April the 2nd British Destroyer Flotilla under Captain Warburton-Lee – *Hardy, Hunter, Havock, Hotspur* and *Hostile* – entered Ofot Fjord to attack the enemy forces at Narvik. Despite the odds, the attack was initially successful and the German destroyers *Wilhelm Heidkamp* and *Anton Schmidt* were sunk. However five more enemy destroyers suddenly appeared. The *Hunter* was torpedoed and the *Hardy* disabled and beached, Warburton-Lee being fatally wounded when a shell struck the wheelhouse. The action ceased about 6.30 am as the rest of the British flotilla withdrew.

The second battle of Narvik occurred three days later when Vice-Admiral Whitworth, with a strong force comprising the battleship *Warspite* and nine destroyers, was ordered to destroy the enemy. In poor visibility the *Icarus* led the destroyers in, with the *Warspite* in support $2\frac{1}{2}$ miles astern. First the *Erich Koellner* was discovered lurking in a narrow inlet and destroyed; then a fierce battle was fought outside Narvik harbour and three more German destroyers were sunk. Finally the survivors were pursued right to the head of the very narrow Rombaks Fjord, where they scuttled themselves or were sunk. Altogether the Germans lost eight large modern destroyers and one submarine in the battle of 13 April.

NAULOCHUS 29/30 August 36 BC

The third naval battle between the forces of Octavian and Pompey for control of Sicily in 36 BC (*see also* MYLAE and TAUROMENIUM). On this occasion the opposing fleets met off the NE coast of Sicily near Naulochus. Agrippa, Octavian's admiral, made decisive use of the *harpago* (grappling hooks at the end of a long rope), which enabled his soldiers to board. Pompey's ships turned in flight and, although seventeen escaped with him to Messina, the rest were captured or burnt. Agrippa lost only three ships.

NAUPACTUS 429 BC

Fought in the narrows at the entrance to the Gulf of Corinth during the first years of the Peloponnesian War and sometimes known as the battle of Panormus. The contestants were an Athenian squadron commanded by Phormio and a much larger Peloponnesian fleet under the Spartan admiral Cnemus. After the first engagement nine Athenian ships were forced to run ashore but then Cnemus, despite his numerical superiority, allowed the remainder to escape into Naupactus. Subsequently several Peloponnesian ships grounded on shoals in the Narrows. When the Athenians came out again and took six prizes, Cnemus retreated to Panormus.

NAVARINO 20 October 1827

As a result of the prolonged Greek War of Independence, a treaty was signed between Russia, France and Great Britain in July 1827 with the aim of securing an armistice between Turkey and Greece. In September Vice-Admiral Sir Henry Codrington, commander-in-chief in the Mediterranean, was instructed to prevent further reinforcements reaching Ibrahim Pasha, the Turkish commander in the Morea, but to use force only as a last resort. Codrington with a small squadron (battleships *Asia, Genoa, Albion* and two frigates) then sailed to Navarino Bay on the SW coast of the Peloponnese, where the combined Turco-Egyptian fleet of sixty-five ships (including three battleships and forty armed transports) lay at anchor. There Codrington was later joined by a French and a Russian squadron, so that by the middle of October the combined allied fleet comprised twenty-seven warships, including eleven of the line, under his overall command.

Realising that a lengthy blockade was impracticable, Codrington decided to take the fleet right into Navarino Bay to ensure that Ibrahim Pasha did not break the truce. As he entered the bay on the morning of 20 October, the Turkish ships lay moored in an extended horseshoe formation with their guns trained on the entrance. There was some parleying and Ibrahim sent a message that the Allies had entered the bay without permission. By 2.30 pm the leading allied ships were anchored alongside the Turks but then a boat from the *Dartmouth* was fired on as it approached a group of fireships. The situation became increasingly tense until some Egyptian warships opened fire with a broadside. Action rapidly became general, with the shore batteries and the allied ships still entering the bay joining in. There followed a murderous bombardment at close range, which continued for three hours until nightfall. During the furious fighting a large number of Ibrahim's ships were sunk and many more, which had been disabled, were burnt by their crews during the night. By the following dawn only fifteen Turkish ships remained afloat and the total Muslim casualties exceeded 4,000. Although no allied ships were sunk many were severely damaged.

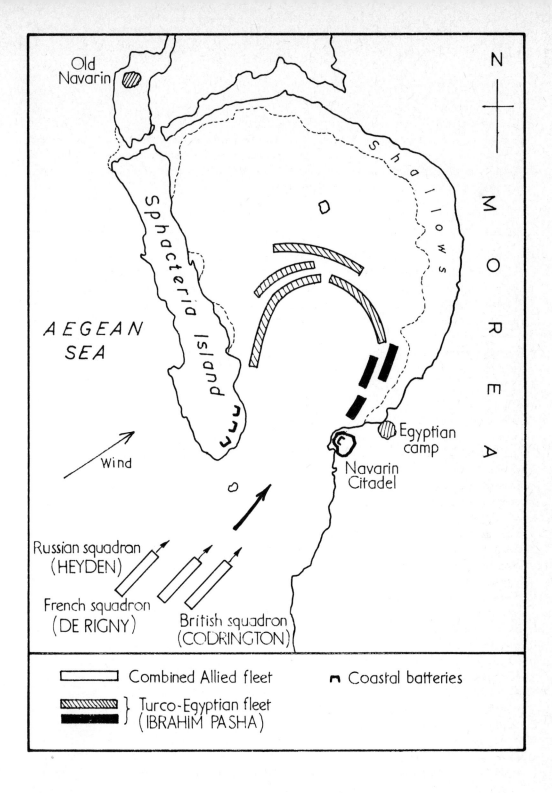

NAVARINO   20 October 1827 – *the opening of the battle*

NAVARINO   20 October 1827   *Oil painting by Thomas Luny*

Navarino was the last major fleet action to be fought under sail; its outcome greatly contributed towards Greece's finally gaining her independence two years later.

NAXOS   September 376 BC

Pollio's Spartan fleet of sixty ships, based on Aegina, was blockading the approaches to the Saronic Gulf to intercept Athenian grain ships, when it encountered eighty Athenian triremes under Chabrias off Naxos. The Spartans were decisively defeated, losing forty-nine triremes, and most of the Cyclades Islands went over to the Athenian alliance.

NEGAPATAM   25 June 1746   *see* FORT ST DAVID

NEGAPATAM   3 August 1758

An indecisive action between British and French squadrons in the Indian Ocean during the Seven Years' War, three months after their first encounter off CUDDALORE (qv). On 27 July 1758 Vice-Admiral George Pocock appeared off French-held Pondicherry, with the *Yarmouth*,

64, and six of the line. Next morning Comte d'Aché put to sea from there with his squadron of nine of the line. After pursuing south for several days. Pocock finally brought the enemy to action off Negapatam at noon on 3 August. There was a sharp fight, during which d'Aché's flagship the *Zodiaque*, 74, had her wheel carried away by a shot from the *Yarmouth*; as a result she collided with the *Duc d'Orléans* but eventually got free. The French tactics were purely defensive and using their superior speed they broke off action and retired north. Pocock pursuing in vain until nightfall. Although inconclusive, the action caused heavy casualties, particularly on the French side.

NEGAPATAM 6 July 1782

The third encounter between English and French squadrons under Admiral Hughes and Suffren in the Indian Ocean during 1782 (*see also* SADRAS and PROVIDIEN). After the battle of Providien, Hughes stayed two months at Trincomalee with his squadron, strengthening the defences there. Suffren returned to the Coromandel coast and embarked troops at Cuddalore, with the intention of recapturing British-held Negapatam sixty miles to the south. Hughes sailed to prevent him and both squadrons – equally matched with eleven ships of the line – clashed off Negapatam on 6 July. The action followed a familiar pattern, fiercely fought but indecisive. At one stage the French *Sévère*, 64, struck to the *Sultan*, 74, but her men refused to obey Captain de Cillart's orders and continued to resist capture. Eventually the *Sévère* was able to rejoin her squadron. Action ceased about 6 pm as both squadrons stood in shore and anchored. While Hughes went into Negapatam, Suffren retired north to Cuddalore, his mission unaccomplished.

NEGAPATAM 6 July 1782 *Oil painting by Dominic Serres*

NEVIS 20 May 1667

During the Second Dutch War, a combined Franco-Dutch squadron began to threaten some of the English possessions in the West Indies. On 18 May 1667 the squadron – comprising seventeen men-of-war under de la Barre and Crijnssen – sailed from Guadeloupe, with 1,100 troops embarked, to attack Nevis in the Leeward Islands. Two days later it met off Nevis Point a British squadron of twelve ships commanded by Captain John Berry in the *Coronation*, 56. In the ensuing action Berry was beaten and lost three ships. However he still remained in possession of Nevis and the enemy retired to Martinique.

NILE, THE 1 August 1798

For three long frustrating months, between early May and the end of July 1798, Rear-Admiral Horatio Nelson and his squadron had searched the Mediterranean in vain for sight of the enemy. His quarry was the French Toulon fleet under Admiral Brueys and the great convoy carrying Napoleon and the Army of Egypt to their destination. But Napoleon completely eluded him and after a few days in Malta, the expeditionary fleet arrived on 1 July at Aboukir Bay, where the French army quickly disembarked to conquer Egypt. Eventually Nelson arrived off Alexandria and in the early afternoon of 1 August the enemy fleet was sighted at anchor in Aboukir Bay, fifteen miles to the east. The chase was finally over but Brueys had chosen an apparently strong position. His ships lay at anchor in line ahead within the bay, protected by off-shore shoals and a battery mounted on Aboukir Island. Moreover, although the opposing forces were nearly equal in numbers – fourteen of the line against thirteen – the French ships were larger and heavier gunned.

Nevertheless, Nelson had the advantage of surprise and when he appeared at 6 pm many of Brueys's men were on shore and his ships were not cleared for action on the landward side. Nelson quickly saw that, even so late in the day, a sudden attack on the enemy's blind side – using the narrow gap between the ships at anchor and the coastal shoals – might be successful. Until it was too late Brueys never believed he would be attacked that day.

With two hours of daylight remaining, Nelson entered Aboukir Bay with the NNW breeze at his back and steered for the French line. Action began about 6.30 pm as the leading ship, Captain Foley's *Goliath*, crossed the enemy's van and came into action with the *Guerrier* and *Conquerant*. One by one the British ships either passed inside the French line in the wake of the *Goliath* or engaged from the seaward side, led by Nelson with the *Vanguard*. Concentrated fire was thus brought to bear on the enemy van and centre. Within two hours the first five ships in the line – *Guerrier*, *Conquerant*, *Spartiate*, *Aquilon*, *Peuple Souverain* – had been overwhelmed and struck their colours. During this period Nelson was struck in the forehead by a flying splinter but the wound did not prove serious. In the centre where Brueys lay with his greatest ships – the giant three-decker *L'Orient*, 120, the *Franklin*, 80, and the *Tonnant*, 80 – there was a tremendous struggle in the darkness before the issue was decided. Dragging her anchor, the *Bellerophon*, 74, was met by the full force of *L'Orient's* broadside; dismasted and almost wrecked, she fell away with over 200 killed and wounded. The *Majestic*, too, suffered severely in a duel with the *Heureux* and Captain Westcott was killed. Only the opportune arrival of the last English ships – *Swiftsure*, *Alexander*, *Leander* (the *Culloden* had run aground on the Aboukir Island shoals and took no part in the battle) – redressed the balance. During the fierce conflict in the centre Admiral Brueys was struck by a cannon-ball from the *Swiftsure* and killed. Then *L'Orient*

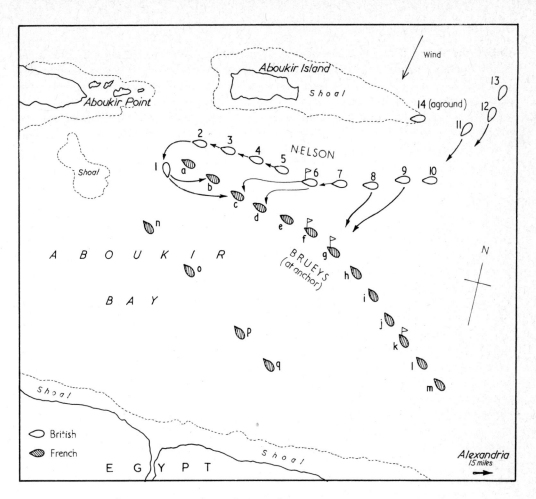

THE NILE   1 August 1798 – *the opening attack at sunset*

BRITISH	FRENCH
1 Goliath, *74*	a Guerrier, *74**
2 Zealous, *74*	b Conquérant, *74**
3 Orion, *74*	c Spartiate, *74**
4 Audacious, *74*	d Aquilon, *74**
5 Theseus, *74*	e Peuple Souverain, *74**
6 Vanguard, *74* (*Nelson*)	f Franklin, *80** (*Blanquet du Chayla*)
7 Minotaur, *74*	g L'Orient, *120*** (*Brueys*)
8 Bellerophon, *74*	h Tonnant, *80**
9 Defence, *74*	i Heureux, *74**
10 Majestic, *74*	j Timoléon, *74***
11 Alexander, *74*	k Guillaume Tell, *80* (*Villeneuve*)
12 Swiftsure, *74*	l Mercure, *74**
13 Leander, *50*	m Généreux, *74*
14 Culloden, *74*	n, o, p, q *the frigates* Sérieuse**,
	Artémise**, Diane
* *captured*	*and* Justice
** *burnt or destroyed*	

THE NILE   1 August 1798   *Oil painting by Nicholas Pocock*

was seen to be on fire; soon after 10 pm she blew up with a tremendous explosion which lit up the whole bay.

The destruction of the French flagship was the decisive moment of the battle. Although both Blanquet du Chayla and Duguay-Trouin, in command of the *Franklin* and *Tonnant*, continued to fight with great heroism, the French were beaten. With the collapse of the centre, the English ships passed down the line to engage the enemy's rear but by then their crews were exhausted. Towards dawn three more enemy 74s were taken or burnt.

Altogether the French lost eleven ships of the line and two frigates in the battle. Only Rear-Admiral Villeneuve with his flagship the *Guillaume Tell*, 80, the *Généreux*, 74, and two frigates managed to leave the anchorage and escape. And they too were all captured in the Mediterranean within eighteen months.

The Nile was a glorious British victory, due in the main to Nelson's audacity and the superb discipline of his fleet; but partly, also, to the mistakes made by the French admiral. The virtual annihilation of Brueys's fleet had the most widespread consequences. Strategically British naval supremacy in the Mediterranean was established and the return of the Army of Egypt to France made impossible. Politically Napoleon's reputation for invincibility received its first check.

NORTH CAPE   26 December 1943   *Oil painting by C. E. Turner – the sinking of the* Scharnhorst

NORTH CAPE   26 December 1943

In view of the reduced threat by German warships based in north Norway and persistent Russian demands for more allied aid, the British Admiralty agreed in the autumn of 1943 to resume Arctic convoys. Thereafter the first five convoys got through without loss. In mid-December a plan put forward by Rear-Admiral Bey, commander-in-chief Northern Squadron, to use the battlecruiser *Scharnhorst* and supporting destroyers against the next convoy to Russia, was approved by the German High Command. On 20 December east-bound convoy JW 55B (nineteen ships) sailed from Loch Ewe and west-bound RA 55A (twenty-two ships) left Kola inlet two days later – both under heavy destroyer escort. For their further protection the commander-in-chief Home Fleet, Admiral Sir Bruce Fraser, made available the battleship *Duke of York* (flag), cruiser *Jamaica* and four destroyers (Force 2); and 10th Cruiser Squadron under Vice-Admiral Burnett (Force 1). Fraser left Reykjavik at midnight on 23 December and by noon next day convoy JW 55B was only 400 miles from Alten Fjord, constantly shadowed

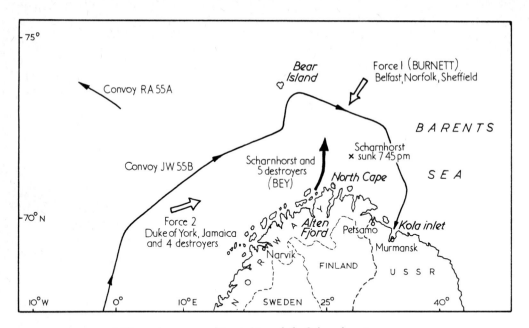

NORTH CAPE   26 December 1943   *the sinking of the* Scharnhorst

by German long-range aircraft. Homeward-bound RA 55A played no part in the forthcoming battle.

At 7 pm on the 25th, Bey sailed from Alten Fjord with *Scharnhorst* and five destroyers under orders to attack JW 55B at first light. The weather was appalling with such heavy seas running that early next morning the destroyers parted company from the flagship and never rejoined. At 4 am on the 26th the convoy was 50 miles south of Bear Island, proceeding ENE; 150 miles to the east were Burnett's cruisers and, approximately 200 miles to the south-west, Fraser and Force 2. When he learned *Scharnhorst* was at sea, Fraser increased to 24 knots and broke wireless silence to ascertain Burnett's position. About 8.30 am heavy cruiser *Norfolk* picked up the German battleship by radar and an hour later Burnett's cruisers were in action. *Scharnhorst* did not at first reply but turned sharply south and drew away at 30 knots. Contact was then lost for three hours until *Scharnhorst* renewed her attempt to reach the convoy. There followed the second cruiser action between 12.20 and 12.40 pm, in which *Norfolk* was struck by two 11in shells, losing one turret and her radar. Minor damage was caused to the *Scharnhorst* but, with her speed unimpaired, she set course south for home, unaware that this led straight into the path of the approaching Force 1.

Shortly after 4.15 pm the *Duke of York*'s radar located the enemy 22 miles away to NNE and Fraser altered course to bring all his guns to bear. When first illuminated by starshell the *Scharnhorst* was taken completely by surprise, proceeding at full speed with her guns trained fore and aft. By 6.20 her main armament had been silenced and speed reduced. Fraser's destroyers then attacked and obtained four torpedo hits. In the final gun action *Scharnhorst* was reduced to a shambles before she finally sank at 7.45 pm in a position approximately 100 miles NNE of North Cape. Only thirty-six men out of her complement of more than 1,800 were rescued from the darkness and the icy sea.

NORTH FORELAND 2/3 June 1653 *see* THE GABBARD

NORTH FORELAND 25/6 July 1666 *see* ST JAMES'S DAY

NOTIUM spring 407 BC

A combined Sparto-Rhodian fleet under the command of Lysander sailed to Ephesus in the spring of 407. Twenty miles away at Samos, the Athenian admiral Alcibiades, thinking Lysander would not stir, detached part of his fleet to raid Cyme. The remainder was left in Antiochus' charge at Notium, a few miles west of Ephesus, with orders to await Alcibiades' return. However Antiochus used two of his ships to provoke Lysander to battle with disastrous consequences. The Athenians lost twenty ships, Antiochus himself was killed and Alcibiades returned too late to affect the outcome.

ÖLAND 1 June 1676

Fought during the war between Sweden and Denmark (1674–6), only a week after the battle of JASMUND (qv). On 1 June off Öland Island the Swedes under Admiral Creutz sighted a combined Danish and Dutch fleet commanded by the famous Dutch Admiral Cornelis Tromp. Before battle was joined Creutz's flagship the *Krona* was struck by a sudden squall. As she heeled over, water poured into her lower gun ports and she quickly sank with heavy loss of life. The disaster threw the Swedish fleet into confusion and Tromp took full advantage of the situation. After two hours fighting the Swedish second-in-command Vice-Admiral Uggla struck but his ship the *Svard* was then destroyed by a Dutch fireship. By the end of the day the Swedes had been utterly defeated, losing three of their largest ships.

ÖLAND 26 July 1789

During the winter of 1788–9 ice in the Baltic prevented further naval activity in the Russo-Swedish War. The Swedish fleet remained at Karlskrona and the Russian ships wintered in three groups at Copenhagen, Reval and Kronstadt. Although Karlskrona became ice-free first, Duke Carl's twenty-nine ships remained in harbour until the summer. In July twenty Russian ships under Tchitchagov sailed from Reval for the southern Baltic. Simultaneously Koslanianov's squadron was ordered from Copenhagen to rendevous with Tchitchagov in order to combine against the Swedes. However Duke Carl's fleet left Karlskrona before the Russians united and on 25 July it was sighted off Öland by Tchitchagov's squadron. An indecisive six-hour battle was fought next day. It was the Swedes last opportunity to break Russian dominance in the Baltic.

ORAN 3 July 1940

After the fall of France in June 1940, the British government's fear that her fleet might pass into enemy hands compelled the use of drastic measures. The bulk of the French fleet lay at the naval base of Mers El-Kebir, near Oran in Algeria. It comprised the *Dunkerque* and *Strasbourg*, the

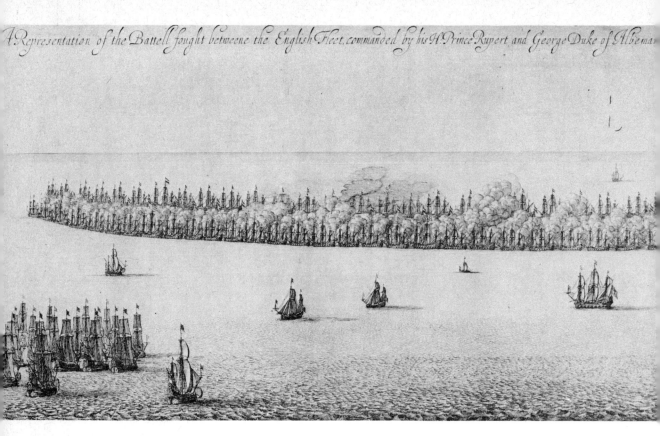

old battleships *Bretagne* and *Provence*, eleven destroyers and five submarines – under the overall command of Admiral Gensoul. In a very difficult situation Admiral Somerville was despatched from Gibraltar with 'Force H' on 2 July with orders to offer Gensoul three alternatives. He could join the British forces; sail to a British port or the French West Indies under escort; or scuttle his ships within six hours. Otherwise force would be used. Throughout most of 3 July fruitless negotiations continued off Oran until Gensoul finally rejected the ultimatum. Shortly before 6 pm Somerville's ships opened fire and after a brief action the *Bretagne* blew up and sank with over 950 lives lost; the *Dunkerque* and *Provence* were seriously damaged and beached. Only the *Strasbourg* and six destroyers got out of harbour and managed to reach Toulon or Algiers safely. Oran was a melancholy and tragic event which aroused the deepest antagonism in the French navy.

ORFORDNESS   25/26 July 1666

A great English victory during the Second Dutch War (1665–7), particularly important as it was achieved soon after the defeat in the FOUR DAYS' BATTLE (qv). Also named the battle of St James's Day or North Foreland.

The Dutch fleet, again under the command of de Ruyter, was ready for sea by 15 July and reached the English coast a week later. On the evening of 22 July the English fleet – under the joint command of Prince Rupert and the Duke of Albemarle (formerly General Monk) –

ST JAMES'S DAY *Etching by Wenceslaus Hollar*

anchored in the Gunfleet, with the enemy 18 miles away to the NE. After two days' manoeuvring for position in the outer reaches of the Thames estuary between North Foreland and Orfordness, action was joined at 10 am on 25 July (St James's Day). The opposing van and centre divisions were locked in combat as they proceeded due east. After Jan Evertsen and two other flag-officers had been killed, the Dutch van retreated. In the centre de Ruyter's ships fought with great stubbornness; his flagship *De Zeven Provincien* was completely dismasted and two English ships were disabled. About 4 o'clock the Dutch gave way and both divisions drifted apart, heavily damaged. Towards dusk de Ruyter managed to re-form and then conducted a masterly retreat.

Meanwhile the two rear divisions were separately engaged – far to the west. Early in the battle, Cornelis Tromp had taken his ships right out of the Dutch line quite independently and turned to attack the English rear division under Admiral Jeremy Smyth. He was initially successful and burnt the *Resolution*, 64, but later in the day Smyth gained the upper hand and by next morning Tromp was being hotly pursued towards the Dutch coast. Although both fleets renewed action for a time on the 26th, the Dutch finally took refuge amidst the shoals off Flushing. Altogether de Ruyter lost twenty ships and suffered over 7,000 casualties. Victory gave the English command of the sea – at least for 1666 – and Rupert and Albemarle cruised triumphantly along the Dutch coast. One immediate result was the massive destruction of over 160 Dutch merchantmen in the Vlie on 8 August, an action known as 'Holme's Bonfire'.

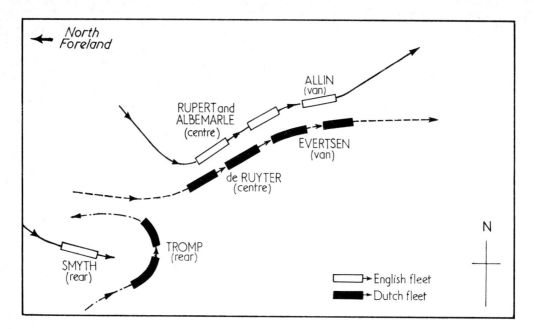

ORFORDNESS or ST JAMES'S DAY   25 July 1666 – *Tromp's breakaway at about noon*

PALERMO   12 June 1676   *Lithograph by P. Schotel*

ORTEGAL *see* CAPE ORTEGAL

PALERMO 12 June 1676

Two months after the battle of AUGUSTA (qv), the French finally triumphed over the combined Hispano-Dutch fleet in Sicilian waters. The death of de Ruyter had been a severe blow to the Allies and his successor, Rear-Admiral Haan, could not match his ability. Disgusted at the incompetence of the Spanish squadron, de Haan withdrew into Palermo to refit. There on 12 June the French fleet under Comte de Vivonne, with Duquesne as his second-in-command, caught up with him. A squadron of nine ships under the Marquis de Preuilly led the attack upon the allied fleet, anchored in a crescent along the coast in front of the town. Then fireships, driven by the NE wind, were sent in. In the resulting chaos, three Dutch and five Spanish ships of the line were burnt or blown up and Haan himself was killed. The destruction ceased only when the French had expended their fireships; the surviving allied ships took refuge behind the mole or ran themselves aground out of reach of the enemy guns. This action firmly established the French fleet in the Mediterranean; shortly afterwards the Dutch squadron was recalled and the Spaniards did not show themselves again at sea.

PANORMUS *see* NAUPACTUS

PATRAS 429 BC

A battle between Athenian and Corinthian squadrons during the early part of the Peloponnesian War. Twenty Athenian ships under Phormio attacked forty-seven Corinthian *trieres* on their way to Chalcis, as they were crossing from the south to the north side of the Gulf of Patras. The heavier Corinthian ships formed a complete circle, their bows facing outwards ready to ram, with the rest of the *trieres* and small craft in the centre. Phormio encircled them, awaiting the arrival of the regular easterly morning breeze, which would cause the Corinthians to drift foul of each other. As soon as this happened, he gave the signal to attack and the Corinthians were routed. Afterwards the Athenians returned to Naupactus with twelve prizes.

PHILIPPINE SEA 19/20 June 1944

The American invasion of the Mariana Islands in the central Pacific, early in June 1944, induced the Japanese Combined Fleet under Vice-Admiral Ozawa to seek a decisive battle with the US Fifth Fleet. Land-based planes from Guam and Truk and aircraft from Ozawa's nine carriers on 19 June launched four massive attacks on the American carrier task force in the Philippine Sea. They were a complete failure. After an eight-hour battle – known as 'The Great Marianas Turkey Shoot' – Admirals Spruance and Mitscher's ships and fighter pilots had destroyed over 300 Japanese planes. Moreover the submarines *Albacore* and *Cavalla* penetrated the Japanese destroyer screen and torpedoed and sank their two largest aircraft carriers, *Taiho* and *Shokaku*. The battle continued next day as American carrier planes attacked the retiring enemy at long range. One more Japanese carrier, the *Hiyo*, was sunk, although many American aircraft were lost in trying to regain their carriers in the darkness. The severity of the Japanese losses in carriers, aircraft and trained crews – which they could not replace – made the Philippine Sea the decisive carrier battle of the Pacific War.

PLYMOUTH 16 August 1652

An indecisive engagement at the outset of the First Anglo-Dutch War and fought three months after the battle of DOVER (qv). On 3 August the Dutch admiral Michiel de Ruyter arrived off Calais with thirty men-of-war, preparatory to escorting an important outward-bound convoy down Channel. He sailed a week later and on 16 August met an English fleet of thirty-eight warships under Admiral Sir George Ayscue off Plymouth.

Reliable details of the battle are lacking, except that it was stubbornly fought and continued from early afternoon until nightfall. Ayscue had the wind advantage which prevented the Dutch from using their fireships. Both sides claimed victory but afterwards de Ruyter was able to continue on his course and proceed down Channel with the convoy.

POLA 7 May 1379

Fought during the bitter maritime struggle between Venice and Genoa, known as the War of Chioggia (1378–81). The Venetian fleet under Vittore Pisani lay at anchor in Pola harbour, when early on 7 May 1379 Luciano Doria suddenly appeared with a force of twenty-three Genoese galleys. Pisani would gladly have refused action; he had fewer ships and many of their crews were sick. But he was chided by his officers and so came out to do battle with sixteen galleys. Although the Genoese lost their flagship and Doria was killed by a stray arrow, they completely routed the Venetians. Pisani got back to Pola with only six galleys and 2,000 of his men taken prisoner. News of the disaster spread consternation in Venice, which continued until the triumph at CHIOGGIA (qv) the following year.

PONDICHERRY 10 September 1759

The third and final action between Vice-Admiral Pocock and Comte d'Aché's squadrons in the Indian Ocean during the Seven Years' War (*see also* CUDDALORE and NEGAPATAM). By the summer of 1759 the fate of the important French base at Pondicherry depended on d'Aché. He had been reinforced at Mauritius – to eleven of the line and two frigates – but long delayed his return to the Coromandel coast. For many weeks Pocock cruised with his squadron off Pondicherry, hoping to intercept, and his patience was finally rewarded on 10 September. Both squadrons formed into line ahead on parallel course and a fierce running battle ensued, with Pocock fighting at odds of seven against eleven. The British gunnery was most effective; after the enemy flagship *Zodiaque*, 74, had hauled out of line, with her captain killed and d'Aché himself wounded, the French retired. Their fire, however, had shattered the rigging of the English ships and they could not pursue. So next morning the French were able to work round Pocock and got safely into Pondicherry. D'Aché thus achieved his object but at the cost of 1,500 casualties. Soon afterwards he left India with his squadron, which was a severe blow to the French cause.

PORTLAND 18–20 February 1653

A protracted engagement of the First Anglo-Dutch War, also known as 'The Three Days' Battle'. After the Dutch victory off DUNGENESS (qv) in December 1652, great efforts were made to strengthen the Commonwealth fleet. By the following February, eighty sail had as-

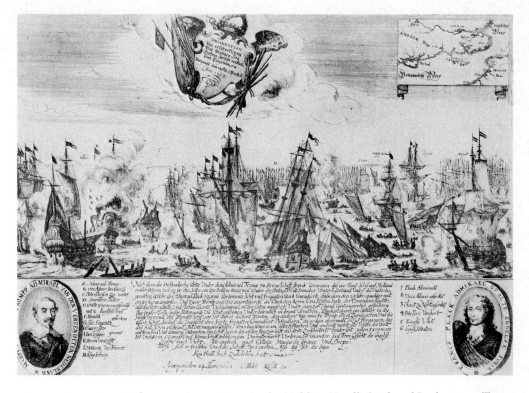

PORTLAND   18–20 February 1653   *Engraving by Melchior Kusell, dated 24 March 1653 – Tromp against Blake*

sembled at Portsmouth under the command of General-at-Sea Robert Blake, supported by Monk and Deane, and with William Penn as vice-admiral. Blake's task was to intercept the Dutch fleet of equal strength under Tromp, which was proceeding up the English Channel bringing home a large convoy of over 150 merchantmen.

Action was joined off Portland Bill on 18 February and a long running battle ensued. Tromp was hampered throughout by the need to protect the convoy, by poor support from several of his captains and a severe shortage of ammunition in the fleet. Nevertheless his opening attack discomfited Blake, who had only a few ships around him to meet it and the rest of the English fleet were slow to join. Several of Blake's squadron were badly damaged and he himself was wounded in the thigh. After a stubborn fight the Dutch withdrew about 4 pm. During the night Tromp slipped past the English and rejoined the convoy, which had been proceeding steadily up Channel. With great skill Tromp followed closely in its wake, stationing his ships as a fighting rearguard. Blake pursued for the next two days and there were several partial engagements. The crisis came on 20 February as the Dutch got desperately short of gunpowder and the convoy began to fall into confusion. Gradually the English ships overcame the rearguard and captured a number of merchantmen.

Only Tromp's superb seamanship prevented disaster. That evening, with the wind NW, he approached Cap Gris Nez – a lee shore, with the enemy to windward. Certain that he was

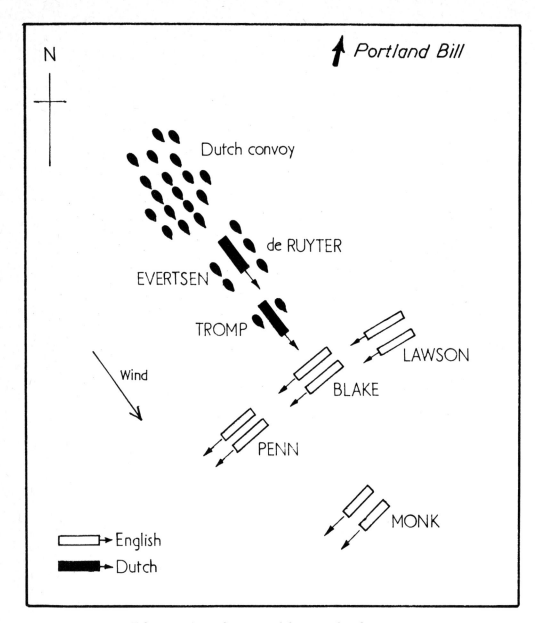

N

Portland Bill

Dutch convoy

de RUYTER

EVERTSEN

TROMP

LAWSON

Wind

BLAKE

PENN

MONK

English
Dutch

PORTLAND 18–20 February 1653 – *the opening of the action, first day*

trapped, Blake did not press home the attack and came to anchor. But that night Tromp with great skill weathered the headland and brought his fleet and the remainder of the convoy safely to Gravelines. Nonetheless the Dutch had been defeated, losing eight warships (against one English ship sunk) and at least thirty merchantmen. The battle was a turning-point of the war and henceforth the Channel was closed to all Dutch seaborne trade.

PORTO FARINA   4 April 1655

A successful operation by General-at-Sea Robert Blake in the Mediterranean against a Tunisian corsair squadron. The action took place in the harbour of Porto Farina, twenty miles east of Bizerta. On 4 April Blake ran his squadron into the harbour with the aid of a gentle breeze off the sea. Having silenced the shore batteries, he proceeded to burn every one of the nine Tunisian corsairs at anchor in the harbour and then withdrew without loss.

PORTO NOVO   *see* PONDICHERRY

PORTO PRAYA   16 April 1781

The first success gained by the French admiral Pierre André de Suffren and a fitting prelude to his later battles with Admiral Hughes in the Indian Ocean during 1782–3. Having sailed from Brest with five ships of the line, Suffren on 16 April 1781 surprised a larger British squadron at anchor in Porto Praya roads, on the south coast of St Jago in the Cape Verde Islands. Commodore George Johnstone with five of the line, many smaller warships and a number of troop transports was en route to seize the Dutch colony at the Cape of Good Hope. The arrival of the French caught him completely unprepared; the squadron was provisioning and over 1,500 of his men were ashore. Fortunately for him Suffren's attack was less effective than it might have been; his flagship *Héros*, 74, was assisted only by the *Annibal*, 74, and the others gave no support. Some of the British transports were damaged and then Suffren left the anchorage. While Johnstone remained at Porto Praya for two weeks, Suffren hurried on to the Cape and took possession of the Dutch colony.

PREVEZA   26–8 September 1538

On 25 September 1538 the combined Christian fleet commanded by the famous Andrea Doria reached Preveza on the coast of Epirus. The town commands the narrow straits at the entrance to the Ambracian Gulf. Inside the straits lay the Turkish fleet of 150 galleys under Khair-ed-Din Barbarossa. After an inconclusive long-range action fought on the 26th, both sides withdrew. That night Doria decided to seek a safer anchorage, fearing that his ships would be driven ashore if a storm arose. By the morning of the 28th his whole fleet was strung out for some ten miles along the coast of Leukas. Seeing his opportunity, Barbarossa emerged to fall upon the stragglers. His galleys made repeated attacks on the *Galleon of Venice*, the largest ship in the fleet but her commander Alessandro Condalmiero repulsed each one. Late in the afternoon Doria reassembled his fleet but the Turks refrained from further action. Next day Doria quitted Preveza, leaving Barbarossa in complete command of the Ionian sea.

PROVIDIEN   12 April 1782

The second duel between Admirals Suffren and Hughes, as their squadrons fought for maritime supremacy in the Indian Ocean during 1782–3. After the engagement off SADRAS (qv) on 17 February 1782, Hughes refitted his squadron at Madras and then embarked troops for the reinforcement of Trincomalee in Ceylon. This fine anchorage had been captured in January but was only lightly garrisoned and vulnerable to French attack. Hearing of Hughes's movements,

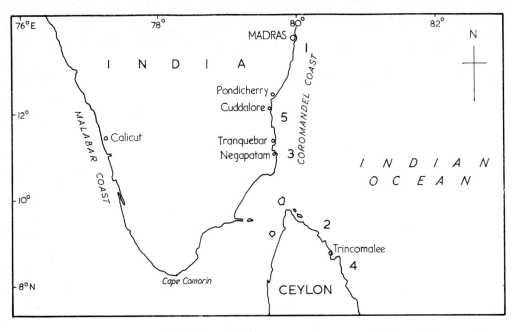

INDIAN OCEAN 1782–3 – *The Suffren–Hughes engagements*

1 *Sadras, 17 February 1782*
2 *Providien, 12 April 1782*
3 *Negapatam, 5/6 July 1782*
4 *Trincomalee, 3 September 1782*
5 *Cuddalore, 20 June 1783*

Suffren sailed from Cuddalore and followed him south. On 12 April both squadrons met off Providien on the NW coast of Ceylon.

The eleven English ships of the line were at a disadvantage when sighted – close in shore with little room to manoeuvre and to leeward of the French. Suffren concentrated his attack on the centre and a tremendous fight developed between his flagship *Héros*, 74, *Orient*, 74, and *Brillant*, 64, against Hughes's flagship *Superb*, 74, and *Monmouth*, 64. The *Monmouth* was battered almost to a wreck but fought back magnificently and refused to surrender. Fierce fighting continued until both sides drew aside in exhaustion and anchored for the night. They remained in sight of each other for over a week, repairing their damage. At last the French withdrew to the north and Hughes reached Trincomalee with his troops and stores on 22 April.

PULA AOR 15 February 1804

Vice-Admiral Linois – with the *Marengo*, 74, and frigates *Belle Poule*, 40, *Sémillante*, 36, and *Berceau*, 32 – was cruising in the Straits of Malacca, when on 14 February 1804 he intercepted the East India Company tea fleet, homeward-bound from Canton to England. The convoy was both large and valuable: 31 merchant ships, including 16 East Indiamen, under Captain Nathaniel Dance as senior naval officer in the *Earl Camden*. Although the East Indiamen were armed, the convoy had no warship escort of any kind.

For the next two days Linois acted with the utmost irresolution, hesitating to attack in the

PROVIDIEN   12 April 1782   *Engraving by Dominic Serres – the* Monmouth *reduced almost to a wreck but refusing to surrender*

PULA AOR   15 February 1804   *Aquatint by Thomas Buttersworth*

belief that there were warships in the convoy. Dance on the other hand shewed great boldness. He formed his East Indiamen into line and after shots had been exchanged off Pula Aor, an island in the Malacca Straits, he actually chased the French warships and forced them to retire. On bringing the convoy safely back to England, Dance received a great ovation; by contrast Linois's timidity was severely condemned in France.

PYLOS autumn 427 BC

An engagement during the Peloponnesian War between Athens and Sparta. The Athenian fleet of seventy ships was recalled from Zacynthus (Zante) by Demosthenes to raise the blockade of Pylos. It suddenly appeared at both entrances to the harbour and surprised the besieging Spartans under Brasidas. Five Spartan vessels were captured and others towed away from the beach. Marooned on nearby Sphacteria Island, the Spartan troops capitulated a few weeks later.

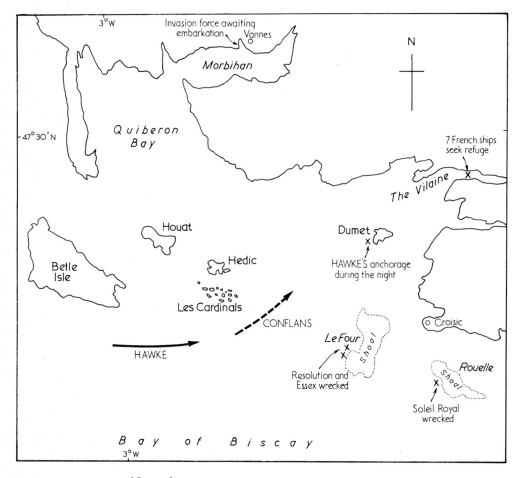

QUIBERON BAY 20 November 1759

QUIBERON BAY   20 November 1759   *Oil painting by Thomas Luny*

QUIBERON BAY   20 November 1759

Throughout the summer and autumn of 1759, Admiral Sir Edward Hawke and the Western Squadron had maintained a close blockade of the French fleet at Brest and thwarted the enemy's invasion plans. With the approach of winter and westerly gales, however, the task became very arduous. On 9 November Hawke was forced to return to Plymouth; the same day a French squadron from the West Indies got into Brest unchallenged. Conflans, commander of the Brest fleet, realised the blockading squadron was no longer there. Hawke got back to his station off Ushant five days later but by then Conflans had escaped with twenty-one of the line and two frigates, steering south for Vannes to embark the invasion force. En route he was delayed by gales and at daybreak on 20 November his fleet lay hove-to west of Belleisle.

Hawke learned of the enemy's course and set off in pursuit with twenty-three of the line in worsening weather. Early on the 20th the *Magnanime* sighted the French off Belleisle and by noon Hawke's leading ships were close upon their rear division. In a rising gale Conflans, who had local pilots on board, led his ships towards the narrow southern entrance into Quiberon Bay (guarded by the Scylla of the Grands Cardinals rocks to port and the Charybdis of the treacherous Four Shoal to starboard). He did not believe Hawke would force action in such confined waters and bad weather; but he was wrong.

Soon after 2.30 pm Conflans's rear ships were engaged and the division's flagship – *Formidable*, 80 – struck after a fierce fight. The French line then fell into utter disorder and three 74s – *Thesée, Superbe, Héros* – were lost, the former foundering with over 700 men on board. In the crisis the French admiral tried to lead his fleet out to sea again. But Hawke with the *Royal George*, 100, attacked him as he steered for the entrance of the bay and drove him back. Fighting continued in heavy seas and appalling weather until nightfall, when Hawke signalled his fleet to anchor off Dumet Island. During the night some of the French ships beat out the of bay and escaped south to Rochefort; others sought refuge in the estuary of the Vilaine but broke their backs on the bar or were trapped inside. On the British side the *Resolution*, 74, and *Essex*, 64, ran aground on Four Shoal and were wrecked. Next morning Conflans's flagship the *Soleil Royal*, 80, struck the Rouelle Shoal and had to be burnt; later the *Juste*, 70, foundered at the mouth of the Loire. Altogether the French lost seven battleships and over 2,500 men killed or drowned.

At Quiberon Bay, Hawke not only put an end to the threat of invasion but also triumphed in his main objective – the destruction of the enemy fleet. By fine seamanship and leadership, a brilliant victory had been won under the most adverse conditions of wind and weather and upon the enemy's shore.

RENNELL ISLAND   29/30 January 1943

The last of the seven bitterly fought naval battles of the GUADALCANAL campaign (qv). It occurred shortly before the Japanese finally evacuated the island and resistance there ceased. On 29 January a US task force of six cruisers and eight destroyers under Rear-Admiral Giffen was near Rennell Island in the southern Solomons, escorting troop transports to Guadalcanal. At dusk it was attacked by Japanese torpedo-bombers operating from Munda. The heavy cruiser *Chicago* was hit and stopped and the destroyer *La Vallette* damaged. Although taken in tow, the *Chicago* was attacked again next day. Hit by four torpedoes she sank some miles east of Rennell Island.

RIVER PLATE, THE   13 December 1939

On 21 August 1939 the German pocket-battleship *Admiral Graf Spee* (12,100 tons; six 11in and eight 5.9in guns), under the command of Captain Langsdorff, sailed from Wilhelmshaven on a commerce-raiding cruise. In just over two months she sank nine British merchant ships in the South Atlantic and then early in December set course for the River Plate estuary. Alerted by one of her victims, Commodore Henry Harwood, in command of the South American division, concentrated his immediately available forces – the heavy cruiser *Exeter* and light cruisers *Ajax* and *Achilles* (Royal New Zealand Navy) – in that area.

Early on 13 December smoke was sighted and, on being sent to investigate, the *Exeter* reported the approach of a pocket-battleship. The main gun action lasted from approximately 6.20 to 7.30 am and occurred some 300 miles east of the Plate estuary. As the *Graf Spee* steamed straight towards the British squadron, rapidly closing the range, Harwood wisely divided his forces to minimise the effect of the enemy's main armament. Nevertheless the German shooting was very accurate and after a few minutes Langsdorff concentrated all his fire upon the *Exeter*. By 7 am she had been struck by four 11in shells and lost two turrets. Half an hour later her last turret went out of action and she limped away severely damaged. Meanwhile the light cruisers, though also under heavy fire, continued to fight and their tenacity saved the crippled *Exeter*. Although the *Ajax* was damaged, losing both her after-turrets, Langsdorff decided to break off the action and make for the River Plate, fearing that other British warships were closing in on him. Pursued due west for twelve hours by the light cruisers, the *Graf Spee* finally anchored in the neutral port of Montevideo that evening. By international law the Uruguayan Government limited her stay there to seventy-two hours, which expired at 8 pm on 17 December. At 6.15 pm that evening *Graf Spee* left the harbour and shortly afterwards blew herself up in Montevideo Roads, rather than renew action with the British forces waiting outside. Langsdorff himself committed suicide two days later.

RIVER PLATE 13 December 1939 *Oil painting by Norman Wilkinson, showing* Ajax *and* Achilles *in pursuit of* Admiral Graf Spee

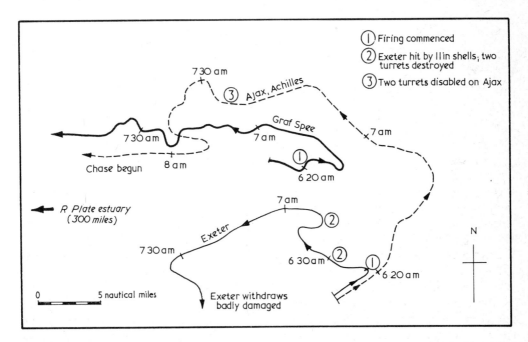

THE RIVER PLATE 13 December 1939 – *the main gun action about 6.20 to 7.30 am*

ROMERSWAEL   29 January 1574

At the time of the Revolt of the Netherlands the Spaniards raised two fleets to relieve Middelburg, which was being besieged by the Zeelanders in January 1574. Seventy ships under Admiral Glimes lay at Bergen-op-Zoom; a smaller squadron commanded by Sancho d'Avila reached Flushing towards the end of the month. Meanwhile Boisot in command of the Dutch 'Gueux de Mer' (Sea Beggars) had moved up the Scheldt and anchored his fleet opposite Bergen. On the 29th Glimes weighed from his anchorage and soon both forces were engaged in fierce hand-to-hand combat off Romerswael. Eventually the Spaniards retired, having lost fifteen ships and 1,200 men and soon afterwards Middelburg capitulated to the Zeelanders.

SADRAS   29 April 1758   *see* CUDDALORE

SADRAS   17 February 1782

The first of five Anglo-French engagements fought in the Indian Ocean during 1782–3 (*see also* PROVIDIEN, NEGAPATAM, TRINCOMALEE and CUDDALORE). On 9 February 1782 Comte d'Orves died and command of the French squadron on the Coromandel coast was assumed by the brilliant Admiral Pierre André de Suffren. A week later he had his first encounter with Vice-Admiral Sir Edward Hughes in command of the English squadron.

Having failed to surprise Hughes off Madras – finding his ships well protected by the shore batteries – Suffren took his squadron south towards Pondicherry and Hughes followed. The French force included a convoy of transports and during the night of 15/16 February, Hughes captured six of them. Next day both fleets came into action off Sadras. Although quite evenly matched – Suffren had eleven ships of the line, Hughes nine – the French had the wind advantage. By late afternoon Suffren succeeded in concentrating his attack upon the last five of the English line. In the partial but fierce action that followed, the *Exeter*, 64, was severely damaged and almost taken and Hughes's flagship, the *Superb*, also suffered. About 6 pm, however, the wind shifted to SE, enabling the British van to come up and rescue the *Exeter*. The battle ended indecisively and Suffren would have achieved greater success if his captains had given him better support.

SAINTES, LES   12 April 1782

At the beginning of 1782 British naval forces in the Caribbean faced a serious situation. Despite Rear-Admiral Samuel Hood's brilliant exploit at ST KITTS (qv) in January, the island colonies were gradually being overrun by the French. The climax was reached when a combined Franco-Spanish expeditionary force, supported by thirty-five ships of the line under the Comte de Grasse, planned a joint attack upon Jamaica. Admiral Rodney, having returned with reinforcements from England at the end of February, lay at St Lucia keeping a close watch on the French preparations at Fort Royal, Martinique. With thirty-six of the line under his command, he intended to intercept de Grasse before he could join forces with the Spanish squadron off San Domingo. On 8 April Rodney's frigates reported that the French had weighed from Fort Royal and he at once sailed from his anchorage to give chase. Next morning both fleets came into partial action off DOMINICA (qv), during which de Grasse missed a great opportunity

of defeating Hood's van division which became separated from the main body of the English fleet. The French admiral never got a second chance. There followed three days of pursuit, with Rodney gradually gaining upon the enemy; on 11 April the *Zélé*, 74, collided with de Grasse's flagship the *Ville de Paris*, 104, which caused further delay.

On the morning of 12 April the French fleet, encumbered by its large convoy, was finally brought to action by Rodney near Les Saintes, a group of small islands in the channel between Guadeloupe and Dominica. At first the battle followed the traditional pattern as the opposing lines slowly passed each other on opposite courses exchanging broadsides. Then about 9.15 am the wind veered SE and de Grasse found himself approaching the becalmed area under the lee of Dominica. With its freedom of movement hampered, the French line became ragged and gaps began to appear between the individual ships. Rodney quickly seized the great opportunity presented. In a series of brilliant manoeuvres, first his flagship the *Formidable*, then the *Duke* and the *Bedford*, formed the spearheads which pierced the enemy line in two places. All twelve ships of Hood's rear division followed the *Bedford* through the gap. The French line was thrown into utter confusion and the 74s *Glorieux*, *César* and *Hector* were crippled and later struck. About noon the wind freshened from the east and the enemy strove to escape westwards. The *Ardent*, 64, which had dropped astern, was captured and de Grasse's huge flagship the *Ville de Paris*, 104, was surrounded. After a hard fight, she eventually hauled down her colours at sunset. But by then de Vaudreuil, who had taken over the command, had got away with the rest of the French fleet. Rodney pursued very half-heartedly and gave it up about 6.45 pm. Next day Hood complained bitterly that many more enemy ships would have been

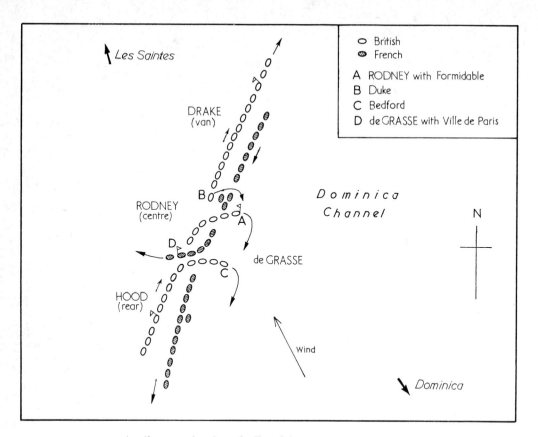

LES SAINTES   12 April 1782 – *breaking the French line*

taken had the pursuit been conducted with greater vigour. Nevertheless the English fleet had gained a remarkable victory, breaking the enemy line for the first time. (*See map on pages 190–191.*)

ST JAMES'S DAY *see* ORFORDNESS

ST KITTS   25/6 January 1782

Fought in the final phase of the Anglo-French naval struggle in the West Indies during the American War of Independence. At the end of 1781 Rear-Admiral Sir Samuel Hood assumed temporary command of the station during Admiral Rodney's absence in England, just when the French began a major offensive against the British West Indian islands. On 9 January 1728 Comte de Grasse, with twenty-four ships of the line and a large fleet of transports, arrived off Basseterre, St Kitts, and landed 8,000 troops. As soon as he learned of the French attack, Hood sailed from St John's, Antigua, with twenty-two of the line, intending to surprise the enemy at their anchorage at daybreak on the 24th. However the French lookouts on St Kitts observed his approach and de Grasse immediately put to sea. Hood then made a bold decision: he de-

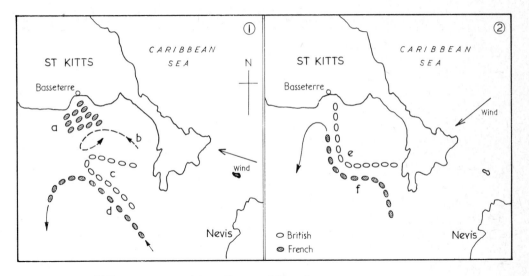

ST KITTS   25/6 January 1782   (1) *25 January*, (2) *26 January*

a	*de Grasse at anchor*	d	*de Grasse's first attack*
b	*Hood's plan of attack*	e	*Hood at anchor*
c	*Hood at anchor*	f	*de Grasse's second attack*

termined to seize the Basseterre anchorage and repulse every effort to dislodge him. On the afternoon of 25 January the French endeavoured to force action and de Grasse's flagship *Ville de Paris*, 110, led an attack on the British rear. Undeterred, Hood took his ships into the roadstead under fire and in succession they took up their berths and dropped anchor. Having completed this masterly manoeuvre, Hood beat off a series of French attacks that day and the next. Finally de Grasse gave up and retired. Although St Kitts fell into French hands three weeks later, the naval operations had been dominated by Hood's brilliant defence. (*See map on pages 190–191.*)

ST LUCIA   15 December 1778   *Painting by Dominic Serres*

ST LUCIA   15 December 1778

When France entered the American War of Independence in February 1778, the British West Indian islands were weakly protected. The only naval force on station comprised two ships of the line and thirteen smaller warships under Rear-Admiral Samuel Barrington. The French took advantage of the situation to seize Dominica in September.

Two months later Barrington was reinforced from North America but at the same time a French fleet of twelve of the line commanded by Admiral d'Estaing arrived upon the scene. On 14 December a British expeditionary force, supported by Barrington's squadron, was disembarking at Castries to take possession of St Lucia, when news was received of the approach of the French fleet.

Next morning d'Estaing in the *Languedoc*, 90, led his ships towards the entrance to the Carenage but was repulsed by the harbour batteries. He then turned south to the bay of Grand Cul de Sac, where Barrington's squadron lay at anchor, its guns trained out to sea. Two determined French attacks were driven off and finally d'Estaing went north and that night landed 7,000 troops in Anse du Choc Bay. By the end of the month the French had abandoned the operation and the occupation of St Lucia was completed. (*See map on pages 190–191.*)

ST VINCENT   *see*   CAPE ST VINCENT

SALAMIS   September 480 BC

The Greek defeat at Thermopylae in the summer of 480 exposed the whole of Attica to the Persian invaders. Before proceeding further on land, however, King Xerxes was determined to strike at the Greek fleet in order to effect a complete conquest.

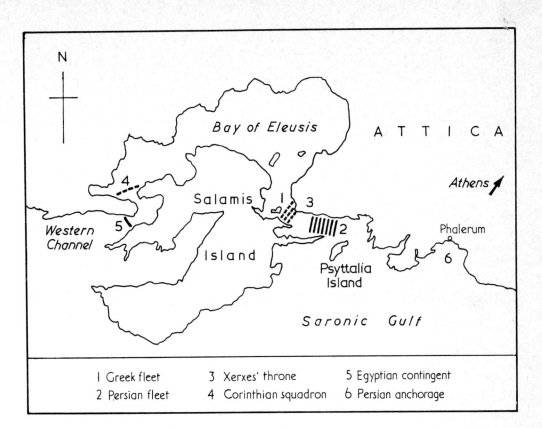

1 Greek fleet	3 Xerxes' throne	5 Egyptian contingent
2 Persian fleet	4 Corinthian squadron	6 Persian anchorage

SALAMIS   480 BC

After the combined Greek fleet had sailed from Artemisium to Salamis there was dissension among its leaders, some of whom felt withdrawal to the isthmus of Corinth was essential to protect the Peloponnese. The wisdom of Themistocles, the Athenian commander, prevailed however. He realised that the fleet's resolute defence of the narrow straits near Salamis Island would minimise the Persians' superiority in numbers.

Xerxes accepted the challenge and brought his fleet to Phalerum, sending an Egyptian contingent to block the western channel of Salamis. The Greeks countered by sending a small Corinthian squadron there to prevent an attack on their rear and withdrew the rest of their fleet, which numbered 380 ships, into the Bay of Eleusis. Having established a base on Psyttalia, the Persians massed their fleet south of the island. While Xerxes watched from his throne near the Heracleum shore, the Persians began to sail north in search of the Greek fleet. On Themistocles' orders the Greeks waited for the wind to rise, knowing it would affect the manoeuvrability of the higher-decked Persian galleys. Then they came down the channel and the Greek right wing swung round to ram the enemy's centre at an angle. Because of the wind or sudden panic among their crews, the Persians became disordered and collided with each other in the narrow straits. In the vast mêlée which followed, the Greek hoplites triumphed in the fierce hand-to-hand fighting. After Athenian and Aeginetan squadrons had threatened encirclement, the Persian left wing broke. The enemy then fled out to sea beyond Psyttalia and the Greeks seized the island as a haven for their damaged ships. While he gazed upon the destruction of his fleet, Xerxes became so incensed that he ordered his sailors to be killed as they scrambled ashore. The fighting did not continue beyond the straits, Themistocles wisely deciding not to risk his ships in the open sea. After the battle, which lasted eight hours, the Persians retreated to Phalerum having lost more than one-third of their original fleet of 600 ships. The cost to the Greeks was forty ships. In every way Salamis was a remarkable victory against the might of Persia and one which compelled Xerxes' ultimate withdrawal to Asia.

SALAMIS 306 BC

In the summer of 306, Ptolemy of Egypt brought his fleet to Cyprus to aid his brother Menelaus, blockaded in the harbour of Salamis by an Athenian fleet under Demetrius. Leaving a guard under Antisthenes, Demetrius intercepted Ptolemy as he sailed from Citium. In the close fighting the higher decks of the Athenian vessels gave them the advantage. Demetrius broke the enemy's right wing and turned on the centre. At the same time Ptolemy overcame the Athenian squadron commanded by Plistias; but, having given chase, he returned to find the rest of his fleet defeated and had to retire to Citium.

SAMAR *see* LEYTE GULF

SAN DOMINGO 6 February 1806

A highly successful British naval action in the Caribbean during the Napoleonic Wars. Two months after Trafalgar, part of the French fleet remaining at Brest broke out into the Atlantic. One squadron under Rear-Admiral Leissègues – *Imperial*, 120 (flagship), *Alexandre*, 80, *Jupiter*, 74, *Diomède*, 74, and two frigates – proceeded to the West Indies. Vice-Admiral Sir John Duckworth, then cruising off Cadiz, went in pursuit and reached Barbados on 12 January 1806. There he was joined by the commander-in-chief Leeward Islands station, Rear-Admiral Cochrane, with news that the enemy squadron lay off San Domingo. At daybreak on 6 February Duckworth in the *Superb*, 74, with five of the line and two frigates in support, found the enemy anchored in Occa Bay at the eastern end of the island. Leissègues, who was engaged in landing troops and stores for the French garrison, tried to get away but was intercepted. Action began at 10 am and continued for $1\frac{1}{2}$ hours, after which the huge *Imperial* and the *Diomède* were driven ashore and later burnt. Duckworth then captured the three remaining French ships of the line and only the frigates escaped. (*See map on pages 190–191*.)

SANDWICH *see* DOVER 24 August 1217

SANTA CRUZ 20 April 1657

In the spring of 1657 General-at-Sea Robert Blake was blockading Cadiz with a Commonwealth squadron, when he received news of the Spanish plate fleet from the West Indies. He at once weighed with twenty-three men-of-war and on 20 April arrived off Santa Cruz de Tenerife in the Canary Islands. Within the strongly fortified harbour lay the sixteen Spanish treasure galleons. In a brilliant exploit Blake's ships penetrated the defences and after a fierce fight, both

SAN DOMINGO   6 February 1806   *Oil painting by Nicholas Pocock of Duckworth's victory in the Caribbean*

with the galleons and the harbour forts, destroyed the Spanish fleet. By skilful seamanship the English squadron regained the open sea, having lost sixty men killed and with severe damage to the *Speaker*, 64, which was taken in tow. It was Blake's last action. He became very ill on the voyage home and died on 7 August as his flagship the *George*, 60, was entering Plymouth Sound.

SANTA CRUZ ISLANDS   26 October 1942

A battle between United States and Japanese carrier fleets north of the Santa Cruz Islands, which lie 250 miles east of the Lower Solomons in the Western Pacific. The main participants were four Japanese aircraft carriers under Admiral Kondo against Admiral Kinkaid's task force, which included the carriers *Enterprise* and *Hornet* and the battleship *South Dakota*. During 26 October both sides launched a succession of attacks with their carrier planes. Materially the Japanese were more successful: they sank the *Hornet* and badly damaged the *Enterprise*. For a time the Americans were without any operational aircraft carriers in the Pacific. Casualties in combat crews and planes were severe on both sides, a loss which the Japanese in particular could ill afford.

SANTA MARTA 20–4 August 1702

An action in the West Indies during the War of the Spanish Succession, memorable for the courage shown by the English squadron commander and the disgraceful conduct of most of his subordinates. On 20 August Vice-Admiral John Benbow with six of the line met a smaller French squadron under Monsieur Ducasse off Santa Marta on the coast of the Spanish Main. A running fight continued for the next four days, with Benbow leading his flagship *Breda*, 70, many times against the enemy. He was supported only by the 48s *Ruby* and *Falmouth*, the rest of the squadron completely ignoring his signals. On the last day Benbow's right leg was smashed by a chain-shot but he refused to leave the quarterdeck. Eventually, with his ship seriously damaged, he broke off action and returned to Jamaica. There the captains of the *Defiance*, *Greenwich*, *Pendennis* and *Windsor* were court-martialled for cowardice and the two former sentenced to death. Benbow himself later died of his wounds. (*See map on pages 190–191.*)

SANTIAGO DE CUBA 3 July 1898

Spain's second naval defeat in the Spanish-American War of 1898 (*see also* MANILA BAY). Rear-Admiral Cervera's squadron – cruisers *Maria Teresa* (flag), *Vizcaya*, *Cristobal Colon* and *Almirante Oquendo*; destroyers *Pluton* and *Furor* – reached Cuba from the Cape Verdes and on 19 May entered the port of Santiago. After being blockaded in harbour for six weeks by a United States squadron, Cervera determined to break out. Soon after leaving harbour on the morning of 3 July, he was engaged by the battleships *Oregon*, *Iowa*, *Indiana*, *Texas* and the cruiser *Brooklyn*. The unequal contest did not last long. Both Spanish destroyers were crippled, as Cervera's cruisers steamed westwards at their best speed with the American ships in hot pursuit. The *Maria Teresa* and *Oquendo* were set on fire and ran aground; soon after 11 o'clock the *Vizcaya* suffered the same fate off Aserraderos. The last Spanish cruiser, *Cristobal Colon*, was caught some 48 miles west of Santiago and surrendered after beaching herself. The American squadron suffered superficial damage and a single casualty.

'SAUMAREZ'S ACTION' *see* ALGECIRAS

SAVO ISLAND 9 August 1942

Two days after the American landings on Guadalcanal, a powerful Japanese squadron under Admiral Mikawa was despatched from Rabaul to attack the anchorage. His force comprised the heavy cruisers *Chokai*, *Aoba*, *Kako*, *Kinugasa* and *Furutaka*, with two light cruisers and one destroyer. Having proceeded down the Slot in broad daylight on 8 August, Mikawa approached Savo Island from the NW, undetected. The American force on patrol in the area – five heavy cruisers (including HMAS *Canberra*) and six destroyers – was quite unaware of the impending danger. In darkness Mikawa catapulted reconnaissance planes from his cruisers and they provided exact information of the American movements. Shortly before 2 am the Japanese heavy cruisers opened fire on their opponents, illuminated by flares and their guns still trained fore and aft. The result was a massacre. Within half an hour heavy cruisers *Astoria*, *Quincy*, *Vincennes* and HMAS *Canberra* had been sunk or so crippled that they foundered later. This remarkable victory was achieved with negligible damage to the Japanese squadron. Afterwards Mikawa decided not to carry out his proposed attack on the anchorage and returned to Rabaul.

'SCHARNHORST' ACTION *see* NORTH CAPE

SCHEVENINGEN 31 July 1653

The final fleet action of the First Anglo-Dutch War and one of the hardest fought. After the Dutch defeat at THE GABBARD in June 1653 (qv), the Commonwealth fleet maintained a close commercial blockade of the Dutch ports, bringing their trade to a standstill. So serious were the effects that the Dutch had to do everything possible to break its hold. At the beginning of August Maarten Tromp with eighty-five men-of-war lay in the Maas, while a smaller squadron of thirty-one ships under de Witt was at the Texel. To prevent their junction, General-at-Sea Robert Monk (commander-in-chief in the absence of Blake who was ill) cruised off the Texel with the English fleet.

On 24 July Tromp brought his fleet out of the Maas. By a brilliant manoeuvre he succeeded three days later in luring Monk away from his watch over the Texel. As the English fleet followed him south in hot pursuit, de Witt was able to come out unchallenged. There was a partial but severe engagement between Monk and Tromp off Katwijk late on 29 July. Then having altered course under cover of night, the Dutch commander-in-chief was joined next day by de Witt's squadron off Scheveningen.

Here Monk joined battle with the combined fleet at 7 am on 31 July. Shortly after it had begun, Tromp's flagship *Brederode* led the attack on the English ships. There was little wind and the combatants were soon enshrouded in dense smoke by the fury of the cannonade. In its midst Tromp was struck and killed by a musket-ball – an irreparable loss to the Dutch. Command of the fleet passed to Jan Evertsen and every effort was made to conceal the admiral's death in case the Dutch should lose heart. The battle raged fiercely for many hours, with severe casualties and damage on both sides. Eventually around 8 pm the Dutch gave way and retreated north towards the Texel, having lost nine ships. Although damage to the English fleet was extensive, the Dutch suffered even more heavily. They were unable to raise another fleet and mourned the death of their greatest admiral.

SCHEVENINGEN 31 July 1653 *Grisaille by Willem Van de Velde*

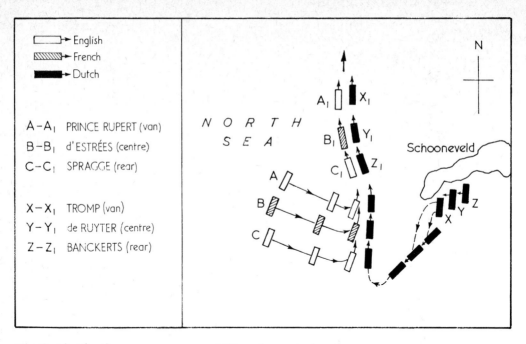

The legend contained in the image:

English
French
Dutch

A–A₁ PRINCE RUPERT (van)
B–B₁ d'ESTRÉES (centre)
C–C₁ SPRAGGE (rear)

X–X₁ TROMP (van)
Y–Y₁ de RUYTER (centre)
Z–Z₁ BANCKERTS (rear)

NORTH SEA

Schooneveld

N

The first battle of SCHOONEVELD   28 May 1673 – *opening stages*

SCHOONEVELD   28 May and 4 June 1673

Two fierce but indecisive actions of the Third Dutch War (1672–4). In the campaign of 1673 the combined forces of England and France sought to crush the Dutch Republic by land and sea. Their strategy at sea aimed at blockading the coast, defeating the smaller Dutch fleet and then landing an expeditionary force. But they were met by a resolute defence, in which the Dutch fleet was brilliantly led by Admiral de Ruyter.

On 20 May the English fleet weighed from the Gunfleet, under Prince Rupert in the *Royal Charles*, with Admiral Sir Edward Spragge as his second-in-command. The French squadron under d'Estrées joined in the Channel, bringing the strength of the combined fleet to over eighty ships of the line. Five days later the Allies sighted the Dutch fleet lying at its anchorage in the Schooneveld – a long, narrow basin guarding the entrance to the Scheldt estuary. De Ruyter with fifty-two ships of the line had positioned himself ideally amidst the maze of shoals and sandbanks and the Allies hesitated for three days. Eventually on 28 May Rupert decided to attack but before he could do so the Dutch fleet suddenly emerged with the wind in their favour and action was joined at noon. A fierce running fight ensued which lasted for nine hours and ended with the Allies extricating themselves with difficulty and anchoring off the Oster Bank. The French lost two ships and the Dutch 70-gun *Deventer* foundered during the night.

For the next five days the opposing fleets repaired their damage, with the Dutch having the great advantage of being in home waters. The second battle of Schooneveld took place on 4 June, when de Ruyter attacked with the wind again in his favour. The struggle was as fierce as before but inconclusive, no ships being lost on either side. Nevertheless the allied fleet was compelled to leave the Dutch coast to repair and refit and de Ruyter's defensive battles had thwarted the Anglo-French plans.

First battle of SCHOONEVELD   28 May 1673   *Grisaille by Van de Velde the Elder*

Second battle of SCHOONEVELD   4 June 1673   *Oil painting by Van de Velde the Elder*

SETTEPOZZI spring 1263

A battle which arose out of the intense rivalry between the maritime republics of Genoa and Venice in the thirteenth century. In 1261 the former made an alliance with the Byzantine Emperor Michael Paleologus against Venice. The following year Venetian squadrons were operating in the Levant. In the spring of 1263, thirty-two of the doge's galleys commanded by Giberto Dandolo met a Graeco-Genoese fleet of thirty-nine galleys and ten pinnaces led by the Genoese admiral Pietro Avvocato. The encounter took place near the island of Settepozzi (the Seven Wells) off the coast of Nauplia. After a desperate struggle the Venetians triumphed and Avvocato was killed.

SIDE July 190 BC

A battle between the fleets of Rhodes and Phoenicia, the allies of Rome and the Seleucid Emperor Antiochus respectively, who were struggling for mastery of Asia Minor. In command of forty-two Rhodian ships, Eudamas met the slightly larger Phoenician fleet off Side on the Pamphylian coast of Asia Minor. Despite the Phoenicians' numerical superiority, Eudamas emerged victorious, although the exhausted Rhodian rowers were unable to pursue and the Phoenicians lost only two *hepteres*.

SINIGAGLIA summer AD 551

An important battle fought in the Adriatic at a time when the Byzantine Emperor Justinian the Great (527–65) was striving to reassert Roman power in Italy, after it had been shattered by the Gothic invasions. Between 545 and 549 Totila, King of the Ostrogoths, had retaken Rome and most of Italy. In the summer of 557 he began a land and sea blockade of Ravenna and Ancona, the last two Italian cities still in Byzantine hands. A battle between a Gothic fleet of forty-seven ships and fifty Byzantines then took place off Sinigaglia (Sena Gallica in Latin), about twenty miles NW of Ancona. The Goths were heavily defeated and fled after losing thirty-six ships. Their naval operations in the Adriatic ceased and the blockade of Ravenna was abandoned.

SINOPE 30 November 1853

The practical annihilation of the Turkish squadron in this battle revealed for the first time the devastating effect of shell-fire upon wooden-hulled ships. On the outbreak of the Russo-Turkish War, Osman Pasha's squadron lay at anchor in the Black Sea port of Sinope. Early on 30 November it was attacked by a Russian squadron under Admiral Nakhimoff, whose six battleships were armed with 68-pounders firing smooth-bore shells. Having called on the Turks to surrender and received a broadside in reply, the Russians began shelling with deadly effect. Osman Pasha's ships fought back bravely but in a hopeless cause. Within a matter of hours the entire Turkish squadron, with the exception of a steamer which escaped through the smoke, had been destroyed and most of their crews perished.

SIRTE 17 December 1941

A brief and indecisive engagement in the Gulf of Sirte between units of the British Mediter-

SINOPE   30 November 1853   *Watercolour by Captain W. Hyde Parker*

ranean and Italian fleets. Admiral Iachino with two battleships supported by light forces was covering the passage of an Italian convoy from Taranto to North Africa. At dusk on 17 December he met a force of light cruisers and destroyers under Rear-Admiral Vian, proceeding on convoy duty from Alexandria to Malta. The Italians opened fire but broke off action as soon as Vian showed his intention to attack.

SIRTE   22 March 1942

The second battle of Sirte arose out of the desperate need to get supplies to beleaguered Malta in the spring of 1942. On 20 March four fast merchant ships sailed from Alexandria, escorted by Rear-Admiral Vian with light cruisers *Cleopatra*, *Dido*, *Euryalus* and *Carlisle* and ten destroyers. Two days later he was joined by the cruiser *Penelope* and destroyer *Legion* from Malta. On receiving intelligence of the convoy's passage, Admiral Iachino left Taranto just after midnight 21/2 March with the battleship *Littorio* and four destroyers; proceeding due south to intercept, he was reinforced en route by three heavy cruisers and four destroyers from Messina.

That afternoon between approximately 2.30 and 7 pm four separate engagements took place in heavy seas. By determination, brilliant tactics and the skilful use of smoke, Vian's force succeeded in driving off the *Littorio* and the enemy cruisers and preventing their reaching the convoy. The destroyers *Havock*, *Kingston* and *Lively* were hit by 15in shells but survived. After

Second battle of SIRTE   22 March 1942   *Oil painting by Norman Wilkinson, showing Admiral Vian's flagship, the light cruiser* Cleopatra, *emerging from a smokescreen to engage the Italian battleship* Littorio

the 1st destroyer division had delivered a torpedo attack, Iachino turned away to the north and the battle was over. Next day two of the convoy reached Malta safely but *Breconshire* and *Clan Campbell* were bombed and sunk very close to their destination.

SKAGERRAK   *see*   JUTLAND

SLAAK, THE   12 September 1631

In September 1631 a Spanish convoy carrying Duke John of Nassau's invasion force sailed from Antwerp for Zealand. Its escort comprised a flotilla of flat-bottomed boats commanded by Marquis d'Aytona. On the night of 12 September the Spaniards met a small Dutch fleet under Vice-Admiral Marinus Hollare. The encounter took place in The Slaak channel between Tholen and St Philipslaand, near the Eastern Scheldt estuary. In a desperate battle all but nine of the Spanish ships were taken or destroyed. Hundreds of soldiers were drowned and some 4,000 made prisoner.

SLUYS 24 June 1340

A great English naval victory at the beginning of The Hundred Years' War. After many delays King Edward III embarked his expeditionary force in the Orwell and on 22 June 1340 set sail for Flanders with a fleet of 200 ships. The wind was favourable and the fleet arrived off Blankenberghe next day. There the king learned that a formidable French fleet lay at anchor in the mouth of the Zwyn, guarding the approaches to Bruges. It was clear the enemy had to be dislodged in order to secure the passage of the expeditionary force. The French fleet was strong: 200 ships under the joint command of Hugh Quieret and Nicholas Béhuchet, including a force of Genoese galleys commanded by Egidio Bocanegra (Barbavera) and some Spanish ships.

In those days the estuary of the Zwyn formed a large open roadstead with the town of Sluys at its head. The English fleet arrived there on 23 June and sighted the enemy moored in the harbour. Edward chose to anchor at sea for the night but next afternoon bore down upon the French with the sun, tide and wind in his favour. On his approach, Bocanegra urged the French to take to the open sea but Quieret and Béhuchet preferred to fight within the narrow confines of the harbour. They ordered their ships to be lashed together with iron chains and cables and awaited the attack. As both fleets grappled together, a desperate hand-to-hand struggle ensued, which lasted for many hours and ceased only with nightfall. The English archery was deadly at close quarters and in the end Edward won an overwhelming victory. Although the Genoese galleys escaped during the night, the French fleet was almost totally destroyed. Casualties were heavy on both sides. Quieret was killed, Béhuchet captured unhurt and Edward himself wounded in the thigh. After the battle the English expeditionary force landed and laid siege to Tournai. The subsequent military campaign, however, was a failure and a truce was signed in September.

SOLEBAY 28 May 1672

The opening sea battle of the Third Dutch War (1672–4), also known as the action of Southwold Bay. Having joined with the French fleet from Brest under d'Estrées on 21 May, the Duke of York took the combined fleet to Southwold Bay on the Suffolk coast to revictual. Meanwhile the Dutch commander-in-chief Admiral de Ruyter had sailed from the Maas; on 28 May, with the wind in his favour, he suddenly attacked the allied ships as they lay at anchor in the bay.

Action began about 3 pm, with the Allies caught unawares and going into battle in some disorder. The English centre and rear divisions under the Duke of York and the Earl of Sandwich kept together as they stood to the north; but the inexperienced French ships failed to follow and, cut off by the Zealand squadron under Banckerts, took no part in the main battle. This enabled de Ruyter to concentrate his attack – especially with the fireships – upon the English line. A fierce action ensued at close quarters, which continued until dusk and caused heavy casualties on both sides. The Dutch fireships in particular wrought great havoc. At the height of the struggle the *Royal James*, 100 – flagship of the rear division – was beset by two fireships and then about noon by a third, which set her ablaze. The Earl of Sandwich tried to save his ship but eventually had to get away in a boat. The boat became so overcrowded that she sank and all on board were drowned. So fierce was the battle that the Duke of York was forced to shift his flag three times. The Dutch lost the *Jozua*, 60, and *Stavoren*, 48, and another warship which blew up during the night.

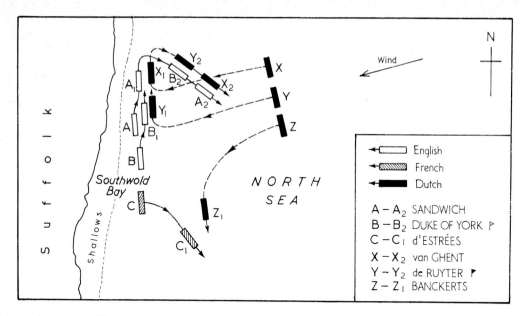

N

Wind

S u f f o l k

Southwold Bay

Shallows

N O R T H
S E A

English
French
Dutch

A – A₂ SANDWICH
B – B₂ DUKE OF YORK ⚑
C – C₁ d'ESTRÉES
X – X₂ van GHENT
Y – Y₂ de RUYTER ⚑
Z – Z₁ BANCKERTS

SOLEBAY   28 May 1672

SOLEBAY   28 May 1672   *Oil painting by Peter Monamy – the burning of the* Royal James

Eventually de Ruyter retired and the allied fleet returned to port to refit, not being ready for sea again until the end of June. For the time being de Ruyter's sudden and skilful attack had disrupted Anglo-French plans to invade Holland by sea.

SOLOMON ISLANDS 1942–1943

The scene of two years bitter fighting between United States and Japanese forces in World War II, including no fewer than thirteen separate naval engagements. For the possession of Guadalacanal in 1942 were fought the actions of: SAVO ISLAND (9 August); EASTERN SOLOMONS (24/5 August); CAPE ESPERANCE (11/12 October); SANTA CRUZ ISLANDS (26 October); GUADALCANAL (12–15 November) and TASSAFARONGA (30 November) (qqv). As the Americans gradually regained command of the Solomon Islands in 1943, there occurred the actions of: RENNELL ISLAND (29/30 January); KULA GULF (6 July); KOLOMBANGARA (12/13 July); VELLA GULF (6/7 August); VELLA LAVELLA (6/7 October); EMPRESS AUGUSTA BAY (2 November) and CAPE ST GEORGE (25 November) (qqv). (*See also* Guadalcanal and accompanying map.)

SOUND, THE 29 October 1658

This battle arose out of the ambitions of King Charles X of Sweden to dominate the Baltic and

THE SOUND 29 October 1658 *Grisaille by Van de Velde the Elder*

subjugate Denmark and Poland. With important trade in the Baltic, the Dutch allied with Denmark to restrain Swedish aggression. Having defeated the Danes in the War of 1657–8, Charles X tried to force them to close The Sound (the vital channel leading from the Kattegat into the Baltic) to all foreign vessels. When they refused he invaded Denmark, besieged Copenhagen and seized Elsinore and Kronborg, the key points commanding The Sound.

The Dutch at once came to the Danes' aid. In October 1658 a force of thirty-five ships under Admiral Obdam carrying 4,000 troops sailed for Denmark with orders to defeat the Swedes and relieve Copenhagen. On 29 October Obdam met the numerically stronger Swedish fleet under Wrangel at the northern entrance to The Sound. A fierce and prolonged mêlée ensued. In the struggle the Dutch Vice-Admiral de Witt in the *Brederode* fought against the *Drake* until both went ashore together on the Danish side of The Sound. Held fast, the *Brederode* was attacked and boarded by the *Wismar*; de Witt was killed and his flagship sunk. Elsewhere the Swedish flagship *Victoria* was severely damaged and had to make for Helsingor; Obdam's *Eendracht*, too, was hard pressed for a time. Gradually the Dutch gained the upper hand and in the end took or sank five Swedish ships of the line, against the loss of the *Brederode*. In the late afternoon Obdam set course for Copenhagen, with the Swedes unable to follow, and there disembarked his troops.

SOUTH FORELAND *see* DOVER 24 August 1217

SOUTHWOLD BAY *see* SOLEBAY

SPADA 19 July 1940

The first major success gained by British naval forces in the Mediterranean during 1940. While on passage from Tripoli to Leros, the Italian light cruisers *Giovanni delle Bande Nere* and *Bartolomeo Colleoni* were first located by air reconnaissance and then brought to action by the cruiser HMAS *Sydney* and five destroyers *Hasty*, *Havock*, *Hero*, *Hyperion* and *Ilex*. During the action off the north coast of Crete, the *Bartolomeo Colleoni* was hit, rendered unmanoeuvrable and finally sunk.

SPANISH ARMADA, THE July and August 1588

After many months of frustration and delay, the Spanish Armada under the Duke of Medina Sidonia set sail from Corunna and on 19 July sighted the Lizard. It comprised approximately 130 ships including thirty-three fighting galleons and four galleasses. In Plymouth Sound lay the main English fleet under Lord Howard of Effingham, with Drake as vice-admiral. Unless compelled to do so, Sidonia did not intend to fight a sea battle: his main purpose was to take the Armada up the English Channel and join with Parma's army of invasion encamped at Calais.

Having come out of Plymouth with great difficulty on the night of 19/20 July as the wind was dead against, the English ships began to attack the Armada's rear the morning of the day after. There followed a series of running engagements over the next nine days; the Armada slowly proceeding up Channel in crescent formation with the nimbler English ships like terriers at its heels. On 21 July the Spaniards lost the *Nuestra Senhora del Rosario* and the *San Salvador*;

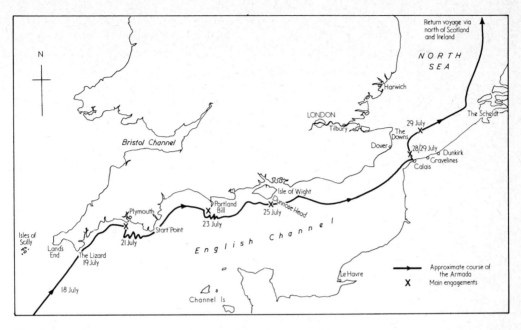

The defeat of THE SPANISH ARMADA   July–August 1588

SPANISH ARMADA   25 July 1588   *Engraving by J. Pine, after painting by Lemprière, showing the action off the Isle of Wight*

two days later there was a sharp engagement off Portland Bill between the galleasses and a squadron led by Martin Frobisher. A fierce fight off Dunnose Head, Isle of Wight, on the 25th went in favour of the English ships but the wind dropped during the afternoon and the fleets drifted apart.

In spite of the engagements in the Channel, Sidonia brought the Armada to anchor off Calais on 27 July in good order and virtually intact. At this juncture the English fleet was reinforced by squadrons under Lord Henry Seymour and Sir William Winter, which were in the Downs guarding the mouth of the Thames. It was evident to Effingham and Drake that drastic action would have to be taken against the Armada to prevent the embarkation of Parma's army. During the night of 28/9 July, eight fireships were sent against Sidonia's anchorage with complete success. In the ensuing panic the Spaniards cut their cables and the fleet fell into complete confusion. The decisive battle was fought next day off Gravelines. After eight hours' struggle four Spanish galleons were lost and many more seriously damaged. In late afternoon the Armada was in imminent danger of destruction, as wind and current drove it towards the lee shore of the Flemish shoals. But at the last moment the wind suddenly changed from NW to WSW and it got away.

Anxious to avoid further action, Sidonia then took the fateful decision of attempting to return home via the north of Scotland and Ireland. For three days the English fleet continued the pursuit in the North Sea and then desisted, because of lack of ammunition, in the latitude of the Firth of Forth. Thereafter the Spaniards were on their own and, as is well known, they fared disastrously. Many Armada ships were shipwrecked on the coast of Scotland and Ireland during the voyage home. The state of the survivors, when they reached Spain from September onwards, bore testimony to their experiences. So ended the 'Great Enterprise of England'.

SPITHEAD   18/19 July 1545

In July 1545 Lord Lisle's fleet was anchored behind the sandbanks off Portsmouth anticipating an attack from the French who were cruising in the Channel. On the 18th d'Annebault arrived off the Isle of Wight and sent four galleys ahead to reconnoitre. The English fleet then weighed and an indecisive action followed at long range, during which Lisle unsuccessfully attempted to entice the French towards Spit Sand shoal, within range of the shore batteries. At nightfall d'Annebault withdrew to St Helen's Road. Action was resumed next morning, during which the heavily laden *Mary Rose* heeled over when her helm was put about. Water poured through the open gun ports and she quickly sank with heavy loss of life. Lack of wind hampered the movements of the English ships and Lisle's flagship *Henry Grace à Dieu* in particular was harassed by the French galleys. The battle ended without decision and d'Annebault withdrew next day.

'STRACHAN'S ACTION'   *see* CAPE ORTEGAL

STROMBOLI   8 January 1676

Also known as the battle of Alicudi and the first of three actions between the French fleet and combined Dutch and Spanish squadrons in Sicilian waters during 1676 (*see also* AUGUSTA and

PALERMO). When Louis XIV intervened to support the Sicilians in revolt against their Spanish masters, Spain obtained help from the Dutch who despatched a squadron to the Mediterranean under the veteran Admiral de Ruyter.

At the beginning of January 1676 de Ruyter cruised with his squadron between the Lipari Islands and Sicily, in the hope of intercepting a large French convoy and its protecting fleet under the Marquis Duquesne. This area was the key to the situation as it lay in the direct course from Toulon to the French garrison at Messina. On 5 January de Ruyter learned the French fleet had been sighted off Alicudi, the most westerly of the Liparis. Two days later he met the enemy off Stromboli but refrained from action, because they were in greater strength and his allies, the Spanish squadron, were still at Palermo and not yet ready for sea. Action was finally joined on 8 January, when the wind shifted in Duquesne's favour and he bore down to attack. In a furious three-hour battle Duqesne attempted unsuccessfully to isolate part of the Dutch squadron, while de Ruyter skilfully avoided encirclement. The result was indecisive in that neither side lost a major warship. However, de Ruyter with an inferior force had prevented the French getting through to Messina and next day he was reinforced by the Spanish admiral from Palermo.

STYRSUDDEN   3/4 June 1790

In her war against Russia, 1788–90, Sweden made a bold attempt to attack St Petersburg in the final campaign. Under the command of Carl, Duke of Södermanland, her fleet proceeded up the Gulf of Finland supporting the operations of the army and coastal flotilla. The Russian Vice-Admiral Kruse sailed from Kronstadt and early on 3 June both fleets met off Styrsudden, a cape on the south Finnish coast towards the eastern end of the gulf. On that day and the next, two inconclusive actions were fought. Thwarted of his intentions, Duke Carl then took his fleet north-west and entered VIBORG BAY (qv).

SUNDA STRAIT   28 February/1 March 1942

The sequel to the battle of the JAVA SEA (qv). The sole allied survivors of that action – the American heavy cruiser *Houston* and Australian light cruiser *Perth* – had arrived damaged at Batavia in the early hours of 28 February. The same afternoon, however, they sailed for Banten Bay and Sunda Strait on learning that large Japanese forces had landed in the area. Four enemy transports were accounted for, but shortly before midnight both allied warships were ambushed in the narrow Sunda Strait by a squadron under Admiral Kurita which included four heavy cruisers. There could be only one outcome and *Houston* and *Perth* sank after being repeatedly hit by torpedoes.

Meanwhile the damaged cruiser *Exeter* and destroyer *Encounter*, accompanied by the old US destroyer *Pope*, had left Soerabaya and proceeded due west. They too tried to escape through Sunda Strait. But on the morning of 1 March they were discovered by Kurita's force and Japanese dive-bombers and overwhelmed. So ended the disastrous allied attempts to withstand the enemy's invasion of the Dutch East Indies.

SURIGAO STRAIT   *see* LEYTE GULF

SVENSKUND 9/10 July 1790

The final naval battle of the Russo-Swedish War of 1788–90. After escaping from VIBORG (qv), the Swedish fleet was reinforced in Svenskund Fjord, bringing its total strength to more than 200 ships. At their anchorage the Swedish ships took up strong defensive positions, their guns trained towards the entrance of the fjord. On the morning of 9 July the Russian inshore fleet of some 140 ships, commanded by Prince Nassau-Siegen, came into the attack. It was met by devastating gunfire from the Swedes and withdrew with heavy losses after ten hours' bitter fighting. At dawn next morning the Swedes counter-attacked and Nassau-Siegen fled in disorder to Aspo. The Russians lost 64 ships and more than 7,000 men at a cost of only four Swedish ships and minor casualties. Shortly after the battle the Treaty of Verela concluded the war.

SYBOTA ISLANDS September 433 and spring 427 BC

The Sybota Islands, situated between the southern tip of Corcyra (Corfu) and mainland Epirus, were the scene of two naval battles in the Peloponnesian War. In the first a Corinthian fleet supported by ships from Megara, Elis, Leukas and elsewhere fought a Corcyrean fleet, which was aided by an Athenian squadron. Both sides claimed the victory but the Corcyreans lost many more ships. Nearly six years later an Athenian squadron was attacked by Corinthian ships, while en route from Naupactus to quell the revolt on Corcyra. After the battle the Corinthians retired to Sybota with thirteen prizes.

SYRACUSE 413 BC

Four naval engagements took place within the confines of the Great Harbour of Syracuse during the ill-omened Athenian expedition to Sicily at the height of the Peloponnesian War. In the spring of 413 the Syracusans under the Spartan Gylippus attacked the Athenian fleet but were routed, although they captured the Plemmyrium forts at the southern entrance to the harbour. A surprise attack by the Syracusans soon afterwards caused much damage. In July reinforcements reached Nicias, the commander of the Athenian forces. The decisive battle occurred on 7 September, when seventy-six Syracusan ships attacked the slightly larger Athenian fleet in the harbour. After a desperate struggle the Athenian centre and right wing were crushed and their ships driven back to the shore. Seeing the Syracusans blockading the entrance to the harbour, the Athenians tried in vain to break through to the sea. After this defeat the Athenians finally withdrew from Syracuse.

TAMATAVE 20 May 1811

A spirited Anglo-French action in the Indian Ocean during the Napoleonic Wars. Three large French frigates under the overall command of Commodore Roquebert – *Renommée*, 40, *Clorinde*, 40, and *Nereide*, 40 – sailed from Brest on 2 February 1811 en route for Mauritius. They arrived off the island on 6 May, only to find it was in British occupation. Roquebert then went south to Madagascar, whence he was pursued by the British naval force stationed at Port Louis, Mauritius – Captain Charles Schomberg with the 36-gun frigates *Astraea*, *Phoebe* and *Galatea* and the sloop *Racehorse*. The French frigates temporarily gained control of the port of Tamatave on the east coast of Madagascar. At dawn on 20 May, however, Schomberg encountered Roquebert off Foul Point, north of Tamatave, and brought him to action. At first

TAMATAVE 20 May 1811 *Aquatint by Lieutenant F. W. Beechey*

the French got the upper hand and the *Galatea* was badly damaged; but after a long fight the *Renommée* struck when Roquebert himself was killed. The *Nereide* fled into Tamatave and surrendered there a few days later. Only the *Clorinde*, which took little part in the battle, escaped and reached Brest on 16 September.

TARENTUM 212 BC

An action during the Second Punic War, in which twenty Carthagian ships attacked and defeated a Roman squadron, which was escorting a supply convoy to the garrison at Tarentum (Taranto). The Roman commander was killed in hand-to-hand fighting. His flagship and most of the rest of the squadron were captured, though the supply ships escaped.

TASSAFARONGA 30 November/1 December 1942

Also known as the Lunga Point action and fought soon after the great naval battle of GUADALCANAL, 12–15 November (qv). Under cover of night Rear-Admiral Tanaka led six Japanese destroyers, heavily laden with troops and supplies, towards Tassafaronga on the north coast of Guadalcanal. Just before midnight on 30 November he was surprised by a superior American force of five cruisers and six destroyers under Rear-Admiral Wright. Undeterred, Tanaka reacted violently and the 'long-lance' torpedoes launched by his destroyers took a heavy toll. Within a few minutes all four American heavy cruisers – *Pensacola, Northampton, New Orleans, Minneapolis* – had been hit and severely damaged and the *Northampton* sank next day. The sole Japanese loss was the destroyer *Takanami* sunk by gunfire. Although a sharp American defeat, the engagement did not affect the final Japanese withdrawal from Guadalcanal.

TAUROMENIUM 15 August 36 BC

The second naval battle between the forces of Pompey and Octavian during their struggle for control of Sicily in 36 BC (*see also* MYLAE and NAULOCHUS). Two days after the inconclusive engagement off Mylae, Pompey's fleet arrived at Tauromenium (Taormina). There it found Octavian's army pitching camp, having been successfully transported across the Straits of Messina by his fleet. Next day there were two separate naval actions in which Pompey was victorious and Octavian lost sixty ships.

TCHESME 5/6 July 1770

A crucial battle of the Russo-Turkish War of 1768–74. During 1769 a Russian fleet was established in the Mediterranean under Admiral Orlov, with Admiral Spiridov and Rear-Admiral John Elphinston (who had entered Russian service from the Royal Navy) as his subordinates. At the end of June 1770, Orlov learned that the Turkish fleet was off Chios and sailed with nine of the line and three frigates to intercept. Early on 5 July he discovered Hosameddin Pasha in strength with twenty battleships and three frigates, at anchor off Tchesme on the coast of Asia Minor opposite Chios. The Russians attacked at once. After a fierce action between the *Real Mustafa*, 84, and Spiridov's flagship the *Sveti Eustafi*, 64, in which both blew up, the Turks retreated into the harbour of Tchesme. That evening the Russian fleet blockaded the harbour entrance and next day Orlov sent in a squadron, including a bomb-vessel and several fireships. The attack was led by his flag-captain, Samuel Greig, a Scotsman in Russian service. The effect of the fireships in the crowded anchorage was devastating. By the end of the day the Turkish fleet had been practically destroyed – losing twelve battleships burnt or taken and many smaller vessels.

TCHESME 5/6 July 1770 *Engraving by P. C. Canot, after Richard Paton, showing the annihilation of the Turkish fleet*

THE TEXEL 11 August 1673 *Oil painting by Abraham Storck*

TENDRA 8 September 1790

Control of the Black Sea was one of the main issues of the Russo-Turkish War of 1787–91. At that time the Russian Black Sea fleet was commanded by the able Admiral Ushakov. On 5 September 1790 – nearly two months after his action with a Turkish squadron off Kertch in the Crimea – Ushakov sailed from Sevastopol with his fleet of ten of the line and six frigates. Three days later he found the Turkish fleet at anchor off Tendra Island, forty miles east of Odessa. Hussein Pasha with fourteen of the line and eight frigates weighed anchor and formed into line of battle. In early afternoon a running battle developed which continued until 8 pm, with the Turks in full retreat. Two of their damaged battleships were taken next day and a third foundered on its way back to Constantinople.

TEXEL, THE 11 August 1673

The last naval battle of the Third Dutch War (1672–4) and the most fiercely fought. It also marked the final Anglo-French attempt to defeat the Dutch fleet and then effect a landing on the coast of Holland. After the first and second battles of SCHOONEVELD (qv) earlier in the

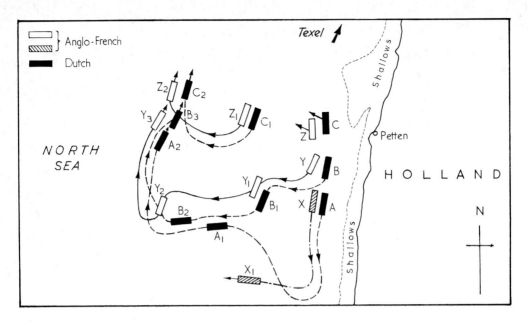

THE TEXEL   11 August 1673

X–X$_1$	*Anglo-French van (d'Estrées)*		A–A$_2$	*Dutch van (Banckerts)*
Y–Y$_3$	*centre (Rupert)*		B–B$_3$	*centre (de Ruyter)*
Z–Z$_2$	*rear (Spragge)*		C–C$_2$	*rear (Tromp)*

summer, the Allies were not ready to put to sea until mid-July. Having joined with the French squadron under d'Estrées, Prince Rupert reached the Dutch coast on 25 July with the combined fleet of ninety-two warships. Three days later de Ruyter weighed from the Schooneveld with the smaller Dutch fleet and his approach forestalled the Allies' threat against Scheveningen. Bad weather then kept both fleets at anchor for several days. Action was finally joined off the Texel on 11 August, the Dutch having the weather-gage.

With the same skill which he had shown at Solebay, de Ruyter succeeded in making a concentrated attack despite being in inferior force. The whole allied van, d'Estrées's division of thirty ships, was contained by Banckerts's squadron and the French took little part in the battle. As a result, the brunt of the enemy attack fell upon the English centre and rear divisions. Prince Rupert's ships in the centre were beset for many hours and suffered heavy casualties before eventually breaking free. A tremendous duel developed between the opposing rear divisions under Sir Edward Spragge and Cornelis Tromp. So desperate was the struggle that both admirals had to shift their flags three times. Spragge's flagship, the *Prince Royal*, 100, was disabled but survived after a magnificent defence. Unhappily, Spragge himself was drowned after a shot struck and sank the boat in which he was transferring.

Eventually both fleets drew apart exhausted and in the gathering darkness de Ruyter withdrew towards the coast. Despite the heavy casualties, no ships were lost on either side. Although Prince Rupert later complained he would have won if the French had participated, the real triumph lay with de Ruyter. His brilliant tactics with an inferior fleet ensured that the allied invasion attempt came to nought.

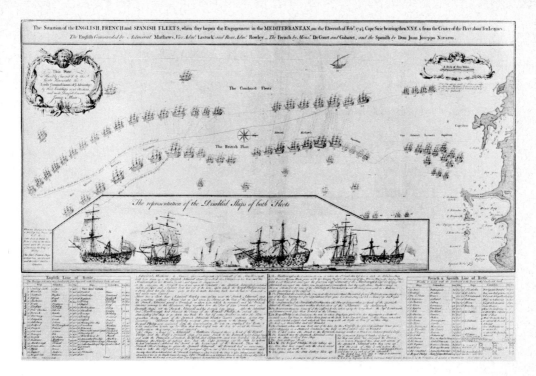

TOULON 11 February 1744 *Engraving by W. H. Toms, after J. Main*

TOULON 11 February 1744

Late in 1743 the British Mediterranean fleet, commanded by Admiral Thomas Mathews, chased a Spanish squadron of twelve of the line under Don José Navarro into Toulon and blockaded it there. At that time England was at war with Spain alone but there was a growing threat that France might join forces with her adversary. And so it proved. On 8 February 1744 the French fleet of fifteen of the line under Admiral de Court came out of Toulon with the Spanish squadron in company. Mathews was off Hyères with the *Namur*, 90, and twenty-eight ships of the line; he himself was leading the centre division, Rear-Admiral Rowley the van and Vice-Admiral Lestock (who was on notoriously bad terms with his commander-in-chief) the rear.

After three days' pursuit on a southerly course, Mathews began action with the enemy on the morning of 11 February. Both fleets were evenly matched; the English had the wind advantage but there was a heavy swell running and only a light breeze. Moreover Mathews's initiative was fatally handicapped by the fact that Lestock and the rear division were miles astern, quite out of supporting distance. There followed six hours of inconclusive action, during which Mathews attacked the Spanish squadron in the enemy's rear, leaving the line with the *Namur* to do so. Some of the centre division followed his example. Navarro's flagship the *Real Felipe*, 14, was disabled and in a brilliant episode Captain Edward Hawke of future fame took the *Poder*, 60. The rest of the British fleet, however, fell into utter confusion and completely failed to support their admiral.

Although desultory fighting continued for the next two days as the fleets stayed in contact,

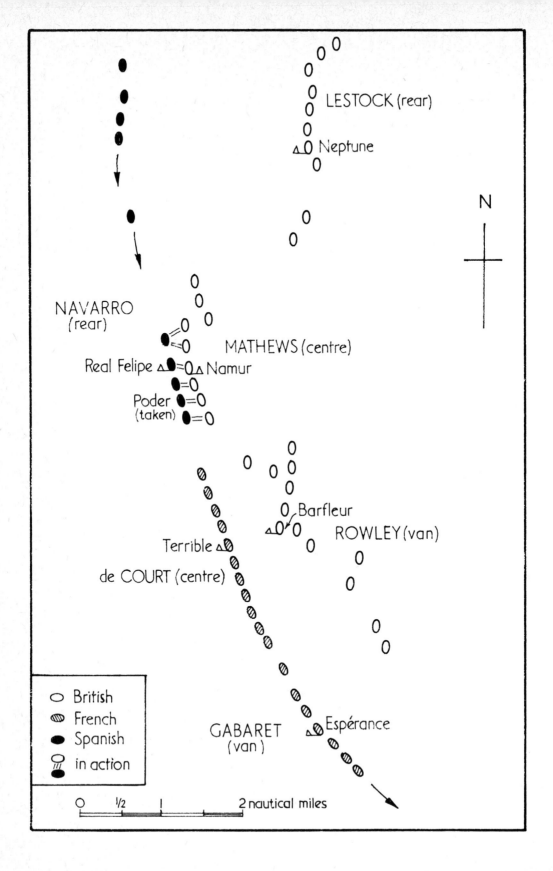

LESTOCK (rear)

Neptune

N

NAVARRO
(rear)

MATHEWS (centre)

Real Felipe △●=○△ Namur

Poder
(taken)

Barfleur

Terrible △

ROWLEY (van)

de COURT (centre)

GABARET
(van)

Espérance

○ British
French
● Spanish
in action

○ ½ 1 2 nautical miles

Mathews finally relinquished the pursuit and returned to Port Mahon. The negative result of the battle created anger on both sides. On their return to England Mathews, Lestock and a number of their subordinates were court-martialled for neglect of duty. Mathews was condemned and dismissed the service, but Lestock received an acquittal. The verdicts aroused a storm of criticism in England.

TRAFALGAR   21 October 1805

The crux of Napoleon's invasion plans against England in the summer of 1805 centred on the Straits of Dover. Naval command of those waters, however temporary or brief, would enable the Grande Armée encamped at Boulogne to cross. To achieve his purpose Napoleon ordered the blockaded French squadrons to break out of Brest, Toulon and the Biscay ports, join with the Spanish ships at Ferrol and Cadiz and proceed to the West Indies. Having combined with Missiessy's squadron already there, they would then return to Europe in great strength to win control of the straits. The grandiose plan, however, took insufficient account of the realities of naval strategy and the strength of British counter-measures.

In the event the main French squadron under Ganteaume failed to break out of Brest and Missiessy departed from the Caribbean independently. Only Villeneuve managed to escape from Toulon with eleven of the line and, having linked up with the Spanish squadron at Cadiz, he reached Martinique on 14 May. After a long and fruitless pursuit of Villeneuve to the West Indies and back, Nelson came back to Gibraltar empty-handed in the middle of July. Furthermore, the Admiralty's efforts to defeat Villeneuve on his return to Europe were nullified by Calder's unsatisfactory action off FINISTERRE on 22 July (qv). As a result the French admiral got into Vigo and then joined with the Spanish squadron at Ferrol, to bring the strength of the Combined Fleet up to twenty-nine ships of the line. However the original project of concentrating the Franco-Spanish squadrons for the invasion attempt could no longer be maintained and in the middle of August Villeneuve took the fleet south to Cadiz, where he was blockaded by the English squadrons. Napoleon had to acknowledge the failure of his invasion plans; the Grande Armée broke camp at Boulogne and marched across Europe to the field of Austerlitz. Nevertheless the problem of inflicting a decisive defeat on the Combined Fleet remained and its solution lay in the hands of one man. At the end of August the Admiralty appointed Nelson to the command of the Mediterranean fleet with the specific task of destroying Villeneuve.

Nelson spent only twenty-five days in England and early on 15 September sailed from Portsmouth for the last time on board his flagship the *Victory*, 100. Two weeks later he joined the fleet off Cadiz. By the beginning of October he had twenty-seven ships of the line to oppose the Combined Fleet. With his flag in the *Bucentaure*, 80, Villeneuve had thirty-three – eighteen French and fifteen Spanish under Admiral Gravina in the *Principe de Asturias*, 112.

From the outset Nelson sought to ensure the annihilation of the enemy. By dividing his fleet into two attacking columns, he aimed to pierce the enemy line and bring overwhelming force to bear on the centre and rear divisions before the van could intervene. But before this could happen, the reluctant Villeneuve had to come out of Cadiz and two steps taken by the Emperor forced him to do so. The unhappy admiral was ordered to take his fleet into the Mediterranean;

◁ TOULON   11 February 1744 – *situation about 1 pm*

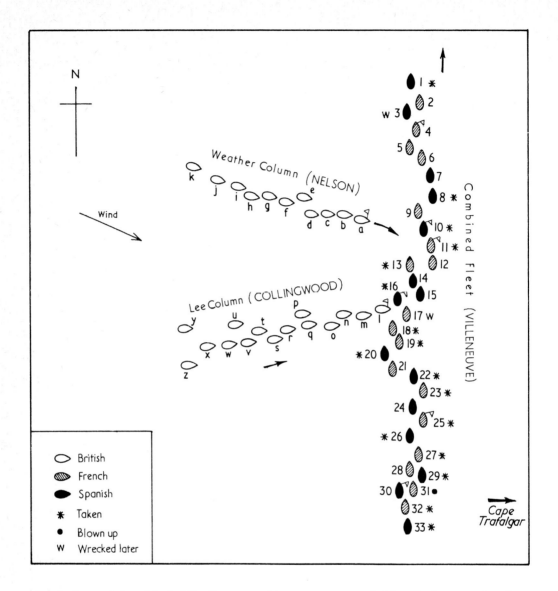

then he learned that Admiral Rosily was on his way to supersede him. Early on 19 October the frigate *Sirius* on patrol outside Cadiz reported the enemy to be on the move and slowly the Combined Fleet cleared harbour and set course south for the Straits of Gibraltar. For the next two days both fleets manoeuvred. As Nelson's frigates kept close watch on the enemy's movements, he remained over the horizon with the main fleet to ensure that Villeneuve was not frightened into returning to Cadiz.

At daybreak on 21 October both fleets were in sight of each other off Cape Trafalgar, with Villeneuve still steering south. The weather was clear with a slight breeze blowing from WNW and an Atlantic swell. About 6 o'clock Nelson, as he had previously decided, divided the fleet into two columns: the van or weather division of twelve of the line led by himself in the *Victory*; the rear or lee division of fifteen of the line under Vice-Admiral Collingwood with the

TRAFALGAR 21 October 1805 – *the situation at noon: the attack of the British columns*

BRITISH FLEET		COMBINED FLEET	
a	Victory (*Nelson*)	1	Neptuno
b	Téméraire	2	Scipion
c	Neptune	3	Rayo
d	Leviathan	4	Formidable (*Rear-Admiral Dumanoir*)
e	Conqueror	5	Duguay-Trouin
f	Britannia	6	Mont Blanc
g	Agamemnon	7	San Francisco de Asis
h	Ajax	8	San Agustin
i	Orion	9	Héros
j	Minotaur	10	Santissima Trinidad (*Rear-Admiral de Cisneros*)
k	Spartiate	11	Bucentaure (*Villeneuve*)
l	Royal Sovereign (*Collingwood*)	12	Neptune
m	Belleisle	13	Redoutable
n	Mars	14	San Leandro
o	Tonnant	15	San Justo
p	Colossus	16	Santa Ana (*Vice-Admiral de Alava*)
q	Bellerophon	17	Indomptable
r	Achilles	18	Fougueux
s	Revenge	19	Intrépide
t	Polyphemus	20	Monarca
u	Dreadnought	21	Pluton
v	Swiftsure	22	Bahama
w	Defiance	23	Aigle
x	Thunderer	24	Montañes
y	Prince	25	Algésiras (*Rear-Admiral Magon*)
z	Defence	26	Argonauta
		27	Swiftsure
		28	Argonaute
		29	San Ildefonso
		30	Principe de Asturias (*Admiral Gravina*)
		31	Achille
		32	Berwick
		33	San Juan Nepomuceno

Royal Sovereign. The Combined Fleet was proceeding in a huge straggling formation slightly crescent-shaped, with French and Spanish ships intermingled. Shortly after 8 o'clock Villeneuve reversed course and stood to the north for Cadiz but it was too late to avoid battle. Three hours later both British columns began their final approach, moving slowly but inexorably towards the enemy line. At 11.45 am Nelson made his famous 'England expects . . .' signal.

The battle began at noon when the *Fougueux* opened fire on the *Royal Sovereign* as the lee division came into action first. Collingwood's flagship had to endure the heavy fire of seven enemy ships for several minutes before she broke the line between the *Fougueux* and the Spanish

Santa Ana, severely damaging the latter. Through the gap which had been torn came the *Belleisle* and the rest of the column. Within half an hour the first eight ships of the lee division were in close action, during which *Belleisle*, *Mars* and *Bellerophon* were badly damaged, the two latter having their captains killed. Meanwhile Nelson, with the weather division, skilfully disguised until the last moment the point at which he would strike the enemy line. After feinting to attack the van – which caused its commander Rear-Admiral Dumanoir great uncertainty – Nelson suddenly headed straight for the centre and Villeneuve's flagship *Bucentaure*. As the *Victory* bore on towards the heart of the enemy defence, she faced a withering fire for over half an hour before being able to reply and suffered heavy casualties. At last about 12.30 pm she struck the line between the *Bucentaure* and the *Redoutable*, being closely followed by the *Téméraire*. A tremendous struggle then ensued between *Victory*, *Téméraire*, *Bucentaure* and *Redoutable*, during which Captain Lucas's *Redoutable* in particular fought with the utmost heroism. Although only a 74, she prolonged her resistance against both the British first-rates at the cost of appalling casualties. About 1.15 pm Nelson fell; a bullet fired by a marksmen in the mizzentop of the *Redoutable* had entered his left shoulder and lodged in the spine. Carried below, he died three hours later but not before learning he had won a glorious victory.

Very heavy fighting continued in the centre and rear throughout the afternoon, the battle reaching its height between 1 and 2 pm. The Combined Fleet's resistance then began to crumble as the weight of the British broadsides at close range became overwhelming. Too late Villeneuve tried to signal the van division to come to his aid but Dumanoir could only participate in the final withdrawal. At 1.45 pm the *Bucentaure* struck and Villeneuve surrendered with his flagship; soon afterwards the giant Spanish *Santissima Trinidad*, the *Fougueux* and the *Redoutable* were taken.

Meanwhile Collingwood's success against the enemy's rear had been even greater. By half-past three eleven enemy ships of the line had struck and the *Achille*, 74, blew up after being burnt to the water's edge. Partial firing continued for another hour but by then the Combined Fleet had been completely shattered. In the final phase Collingwood, who had assumed overall command of the fleet, fought a number of separate engagements with Dumanoir's van division and during this period three more enemy ships were dismasted and taken. Eventually the survivors under Dumanoir broke away north and retreated towards Cadiz. Altogether the Combined Fleet lost eighteen ships of the line taken or destroyed in the battle and over 6,000 men killed or wounded.

During the evening a storm blew up which continued for the next three days and only four of the enemy prizes reached Gibraltar safely. Although not a single British ship was sunk, many were severely damaged and survived the gales with difficulty.

Nelson obtained a decisive and complete victory at Trafalgar at the cost of his own life. The destruction of the Combined Fleet terminated Napoleon's bid for maritime ascendancy; for the remainder of the war French naval effort was mainly restricted to commerce raiding.

TRAPANI 249 BC

A resounding defeat for the Romans during the First Punic War. Their fleet under Gnaeus Claudius sailed from Lilybaeum with inexperienced crews to attack the Carthaginians in harbour at Trapani (Drepanum) on the NW coast of Sicily. Just before their arrival, Adherbal got his ships out of the harbour and turned to scatter the Romans, who were close off shore.

TRAFALGAR   21 October 1805   *Oil painting by Nicholas Pocock*

TRAPANI   June 1266

Another of the many battles between Venice and Genoa during the thirteenth century, as they struggled for naval supremacy in the Mediterranean. In June 1266, Giacomo Dandolo with twenty-five Venetian galleys met a Genoese fleet at Trapani on the NW coast of Sicily. The Genoese admiral Lanfranco Barbarino refused action, entrenching himself behind a fortification of linked galleys. Three times the Venetians tried to break through the line and at the third attempt they succeeded. Panic then ensued among the Genoese galleys and many of them were captured or sunk.

TRINCOMALEE   12 April 1782   *see* PROVIDIEN

TRINCOMALEE   3 September 1782

Nearly two months after his action with Admiral Hughes at NEGAPATAM (qv), the brilliant French Admiral Suffren achieved his greatest success in Indian waters. On 22 August he sailed from Cuddalore with his squadron, escorting transports, and six days later forced the capitulation of the important British base at Trincomalee in Ceylon. Too late Hughes at Madras realised the danger; when he arrived with twelve ships of the line off Trincomalee on 2 September, it was already in enemy hands. Next morning Suffren came out of harbour with fourteen of the line and battle was joined twenty-five miles SE of Trincomalee at 2 o'clock that afternoon. A three-hour action ensued in which Suffren was poorly supported by his captains. Upon his flagship, *Héros*, 74, the *Illustre*, 74, and the *Ajax*, 64, fell the brunt of the fighting with the British centre, during which the *Héros* lost her mainmast. As darkness fell both squadrons drew apart and the action ceased. Suffren withdrew into Trincomalee but on the way in, the *L'Orient*, 74, grounded on a reef at the harbour entrance and was wrecked. With no other safe anchorage on the Ceylon coast in the monsoon season, Hughes took his squadron north to Madras and anchored there on 9 September.

TSUSHIMA 27/8 May 1905

Crushing Russian naval defeats by Japan in 1904 induced the Czar to order the Baltic Fleet to the Far East. On 13 October 1904 Admiral Rojhestvensky sailed from Libau with four battleships and a motley collection of old ironclads, cruisers, destroyers and auxiliaries. After a historic 17,000 miles voyage half way round the world, he reached Kamranh Bay, Indo-China

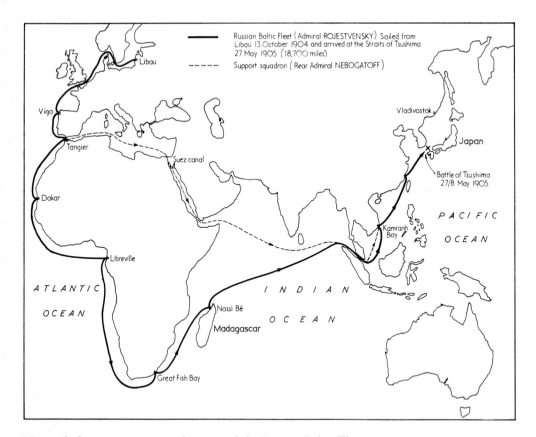

The prelude to TSUSHIMA – *the voyage of the Russian Baltic Fleet*

in April 1905. While coaling at Nossi Bé, Madagascar, en route, Rojhestvensky had learned of the fall of Port Arthur but decided to continue. Reinforced by a squadron under Rear-Admiral Nebogatoff, the combined fleet left Kamranh Bay on 14 May, bound for the Straits of Tsushima on its way to Vladivostok. Shortage of fuel prevented the choice of a more circuitous route.

Meanwhile Admiral Togo in command of the Japanese fleet carefully made preparations for the enemy's arrival. Anticipating that the Baltic Fleet would proceed via Tsushima, he had sent scouts to patrol its approaches while he waited with the main fleet in Masampo Bay, a fine anchorage on the south coast of Korea. In the early hours of 27 May the auxiliary cruiser *Shinano Maru* sighted the enemy steering through the mist towards the straits. Alerted by wireless message, Togo immediately put to sea with three battleships and eight armoured cruisers and at 1.45 pm came upon the Russian fleet in close cruising formation, steaming NNE in two columns. Having boldly crossed the enemy's bows to bring his ships on parallel course, Togo engaged. Rapid and accurate Japanese fire soon caused heavy damage and by 3 pm the Russian battleship *Osliabia* had been sunk and the flagship *Suvaroff* disabled and set on fire. Rojhestvensky himself was injured and the command passed to Nebogatoff, with orders to attempt to reach Vladivostok. By that time, however, the Russian fleet was in utter disorder; despite desperate manoeuvres to escape, its fate was sealed. At dusk Togo's heavy ships withdrew having sunk three battleships. During the night Japanese torpedo boats swarmed over the area inflicting further losses. At 10 o'clock next morning Nebogatoff surrendered with the battleships *Nikolai I* and *Orel* and the surviving remnants of the fleet. Among the later prizes was the destroyer *Biedovy* with Rojhestvensky and his staff on board.

The victory achieved at Tsushima by Togo and the Japanese fleet was shattering in its completeness. The Russian Baltic Fleet had been practically annihilated. Of its thirty-eight warships, twenty-nine – including the eight battleships – were either sunk, captured or destroyed. Six others reached Shanghai or Manila, where they were interned; only the cruiser *Almaz* and two destroyers succeeded in reaching Vladivostok. The casualties were in proportion: 117 Japanese killed against 4,830 Russians. Under humiliating terms for Russia, the peace treaty was signed three months after the battle.

USHANT   27 July 1778

The first Anglo-French fleet action of the American War of Independence, fought three months after France had entered the struggle. Admiral Augustus Keppel, in command of the Channel Fleet, sailed from Portsmouth on 9 July, having assembled twenty-six of the line with the greatest difficulty. No such problems beset the French and the day before Comte d'Orvilliers had weighed from Brest with thirty-two of the line. Both fleets sighted each other off Ushant on 23 July and after much manoeuvring came into action four days later some seventy miles west of the island. The battle which followed was inconclusive. During the afternoon the fleets passed each other on opposite tacks and exchanged broadsides. Later Keppel sought to renew action but several of his ships had been disabled. Worst of all, he was quite unsupported by his rear division. Vice-Admiral Hugh Palliser had dropped far astern and ignored urgent signals to rejoin. By the time he had come up it was too late. Although Keppel tried to reform his line, d'Orvilliers retired in the gathering dusk, altered course during the night and regained Brest. The unsatisfactory outcome of the battle gave rise to a bitter and prolonged dispute between Keppel and Palliser, during which both were court-martialled but acquitted.

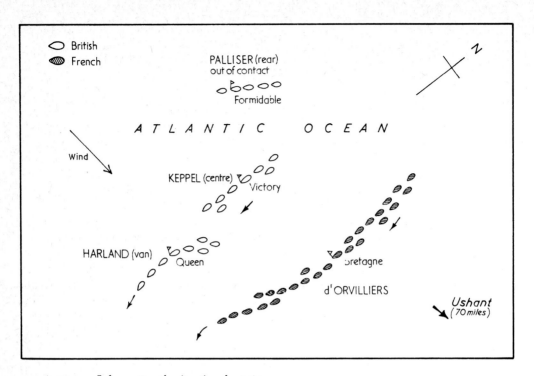

USHANT   27 July 1778 – *the situation about 6 pm*

USHANT   12 December 1781

On 10 December 1781 a large French convoy, carrying important reinforcements and supplies for the West Indies, set sail from Brest. It was powerfully escorted by nineteen ships of the line under Admiral de Guichen. Two days later a detachment of the Channel Fleet – twelve of the line under Rear-Admiral Kempenfelt – sighted the enemy 150 miles west of Ushant. Kempenfelt at once ordered his ships to chase. He then observed that, though the French squadron was too strong for him, it was sailing well ahead and to lee of the convoy. With great skill he interposed himself between de Guichen and his charges and succeeded in taking fifteen valuable prizes. Kempenfelt's achievement was recognised on his return to Spithead but the Admiralty was severely criticised for not providing him with a stronger force.

VELEZ MALAGA   *see* MALAGA

VELLA GULF   6/7 August 1943

The fourth of seven naval engagements between United States and Japanese forces during the Solomon Islands campaign in 1943. Four Japanese destroyers under Captain Sugiura were attempting to bring troops and supplies to Kolombangara Island in the New Georgia group. Just before midnight on 6/7 August they were surprised by six American destroyers (Com-

mander Moosbrugger) in Vella Gulf. In a half-hour battle the *Kawakaze*, *Hagikaze* and *Arashi* were torpedoed and sunk, only the *Shigure* escaping. The American victory was achieved without loss or damage.

VELLA LAVELLA   6/7 October 1943

Fought two months after VELLA GULF (qv), as the Americans gradually gained command of the Solomon Islands, despite desperate efforts by the Japanese not to give ground. Nine Japanese destroyers under Rear-Admiral Ijuin were evacuating troops from Vella Lavella Island in the New Georgia group. During the night of 6/7 October they were intercepted by three American destroyers led by Captain Walker. The Americans gallantly pressed home their attack but suffered severely. The *Chevalier* was torpedoed and later had to be sunk; *O'Bannon* (having collided with the stricken *Chevalier*) and *Selfridge* were badly damaged. The Japanese lost the destroyer *Yugumo* but were able next day to complete the evacuation of Vella Lavella.

VIBORG BAY   3/4 July 1790

A crucial action in the final phase of the Russo-Swedish War, 1788–90. On 2 June 1790 a large Swedish fleet – 280 galleys, transports and gunboats – anchored in Viborg Bay on the south coast of Finland, in preparation for a combined assault against St Petersburg. After enduring a month's blockade by the Russian fleet, it became imperative for the Swedes to break out of Viborg as their supplies were dwindling. Early on 3 July the Swedish sailing ships, followed by the galleys, weighed anchor and four fireships were sent towards the Russian fleet. However the fireships ran foul of each other and three blew up, spreading confusion throughout the Swedish fleet. As a result seven of their ships ran aground and were taken. After further losses, the remainder fought their way out of the bay and escaped (*see also* STYRSUDDEN and SVENSKUND).

VIGO BAY 12 October 1702

A major Anglo-Dutch victory at the beginning of the War of the Spanish Succession; particularly important as it occurred soon after the Allies' disastrous failure at Cadiz. On the voyage home Admiral Sir George Rooke, commanding the Allied fleet, learned that the Spanish treasure ships had arrived in Vigo Bay on the west coast of Galicia. They had left Havana for Europe early in July, powerfully escorted by a French squadron under M. de Châteaurenault. On reaching Vigo, the French admiral strengthened the local defences and a strong boom was laid across the entrance to Redondela harbour. However, less than half the treasure had been put on shore when the allied fleet appeared on 11 October.

Rooke decided to attack next morning with all his fireships but only some of the battle line, since there was no room for the whole fleet to work in those restricted waters. The assault, led by Vice-Admirals Hopsonn in the *Torbay*, 80, and Van der Goes in the *Zeven Provincien*, 90, was brilliantly successful. After the boom had been pierced and troops landed to carry the batteries, a fierce action took place in the bay. By sunset Châteaurenault's fleet had ceased to exist; ten French ships of the line were burnt or taken and the rest driven ashore. The same fate befell the Spanish ships, from which much treasure and booty was taken or sunk in Vigo Bay.

'WAGER'S ACTION' *see* CARTAGENA

'WARREN'S ACTION' *see* DONEGAL

WINCHELSEA *see* 'LES ESPAGNOLS SUR MER'

YALU RIVER 17 September 1894

An important naval battle of the Sino-Japanese War, 1894–5. On 16 September 1894 Admiral Ting put to sea from Talien Bay, Port Arthur with the Chinese fleet – ten warships including the heavy armoured ships *Ting Yuen* and *Chen Yuen*. His purpose was to escort troop transports to the mouth of the Yalu River 200 miles to the east, in an effort to stem the rapid advance of the Japanese Army in Korea. By coincidence Admiral Ito with ten Japanese warships was then steaming towards Port Arthur. Both forces met next morning in the Gulf of Korea, between Talu Island and the Yalu estuary.

The action was fierce and continued until 5.30 pm; but at an early stage the Chinese line had lost all cohesion and control. Ultimately Admiral Ting lost five ships sunk or driven

VIGO BAY 12 October 1702 *Oil painting by Ludolf Bakhuizen*

ashore, although both his armoured cruisers survived, heavily damaged. On the Japanese side only the flagship the *Matsushima* was badly hit. Ito intended to renew battle next day but Ting, after steering first for Wei-hai-wei, altered course during the night and got his battered survivors into Port Arthur.

YELLOW SEA 9 July 1592

Fought two months after the Japanese invasion of Korea in May 1592. The redoubtable Yi Sun-Sin commanded the Korean fleet, which included *kwi-suns*, ironclad galleys of his own design. Having moved his fleet to the SW coast, Yi Sun-Sin sighted on 9 July a large convoy of Japanese transports, strongly escorted. After feigning retreat, which caused the Japanese admiral to order a general chase, Yi Sun-Sin suddenly turned on his pursuers. The battle became a rout and over 120 Japanese warships were destroyed as well as most of the convoy (*see also* FUSAN).

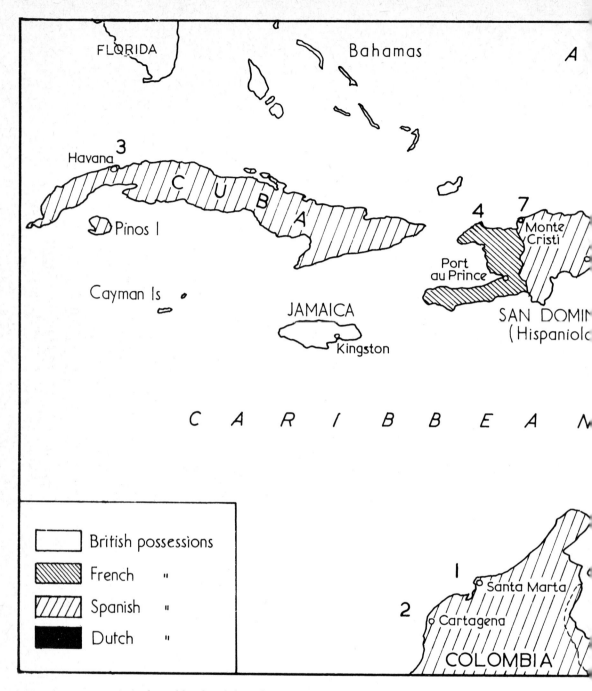

WEST INDIES *principal naval battles of the eighteenth century*

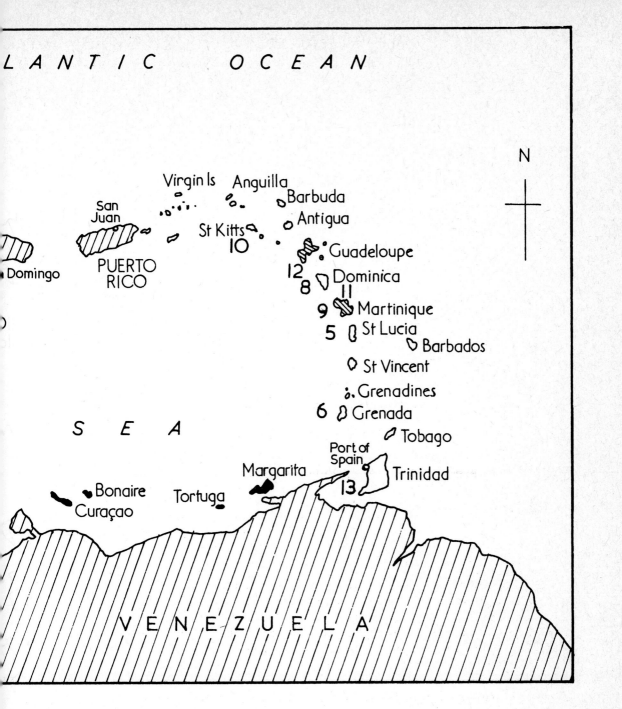

ATLANTIC OCEAN

N

Virgin Is
Anguilla
San Juan
Barbuda
Domingo
Antigua
St Kitts
10
Guadeloupe
PUERTO RICO
12
Dominica
8
11
9
Martinique
5
St Lucia
Barbados
St Vincent
Grenadines
6
Grenada
Tobago
SEA
Port of Spain
Margarita
13
Trinidad
Bonaire
Tortuga
Curaçao

VENEZUELA

7   *Monte Christi, 20 March and 20 June 1780*
8   *Dominica, 17 April 1780*
9   *Martinique, 29 April 1781*
10   *St Kitts, 25–26 January 1782*
11   *Dominica, 9 April 1782*
12   *Les Saintes, 12 April 1782*

REVOLUTIONARY AND NAPOLEONIC WARS 1793–1815

13   *Shaggaramus Bay, 17 February 1797*
     (very small engagement)
14   *San Domingo, 6 February 1806*

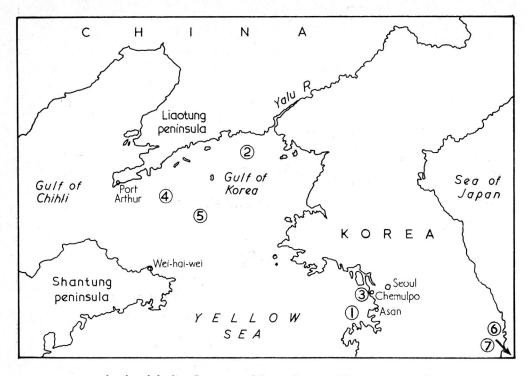

YELLOW SEA *battles of the Sino-Japanese and Russo-Japanese Wars, 1894–5 and 1904–5*

SINO-JAPANESE WAR 1894–5	RUSSO-JAPANESE WAR 1904–5
1 *Asan, 25 July 1894*	3 *Chemulpo, 9 February 1904*
2 *Yalu, 17 September 1894*	4–5 *Yellow Sea, 10 August 1904*
	6 *Japan Sea, 14 August 1904*
	7 *Tsushima, 27/28 May 1905*

YELLOW SEA 10 August 1904

By the end of July 1904 it was imperative for the Russian fleet blockaded in Port Arthur to break out, as Japanese troops had advanced to positions whence they could shell the anchorage. Early on 10 August Admiral Vitgeft weighed and with his flagship *Tsarevich*, five battleships, four light cruisers and eight destroyers, steamed out into the Yellow Sea in an attempt to reach Vladivostok. News of their departure was radioed to Admiral Togo, who with four battle-ships, six cruisers and numerous destroyers, changed course to intercept. Contact between both fleets was made at 12.30 pm. In the preliminary two-hour engagement Vitgeft outmanoeuvred his opponent and pressed on at speed to the SE.

Action was resumed at 5.30 pm north of the Shantung peninsula, both fleets on parallel courses exchanging fire at gradually decreasing range. As the fighting became fiercer Togo's flagship the *Mikasa* was repeatedly hit. Then two 12in shells struck the *Tsarevich*, one killing Vitgeft and most of his staff on the bridge, the other jamming her steering gear. As the *Tsarevich* veered out of control towards the rear of her own line, the Russian ships were thrown into confusion. From the bridge of the *Peresviet*, Prince Uktomsky, the second-in-command, tried to signal a return to Port Arthur but by then the battle had been lost. Next day some of the Russian ships did regain Port Arthur, where they were scuttled six months later; others reached neutral ports and were interned. The battle was a striking victory for Togo and the Japanese fleet (*see also* JAPAN SEA).

ZIERIKZEE   18 August 1304

When Guy, Count of Flanders and the Count of Holland were struggling for control of the Scheldt estuary, a Flemish fleet blockaded Zierikzee on the island of Schouwen. The Count of Holland appealed for help to France, Flanders' inveterate enemy. Philip the Fair duly sent a large fleet under Raigner de Grimaldi, which included a squadron of Genoese galleys. On 18 August a fierce battle was fought off Zierikzee, during which the Flemish unsuccessfully used fireships. Eventually Grimaldi triumphed; the Count of Flanders and his flagship were taken and the blockade raised.

ZONCHIO   12 and 14 August 1499

In an attempt to check the rising Ottoman naval power in the Mediterranean, a fleet was assembled at Venice in the summer of 1499. Commanded by Antonio Grimani, it included fifty galleys gathered from Candia, Corfu and Dalmatia. Meanwhile the Turks under Borrak Raïs had sailed through the Dardanelles and reached Lepanto at the narrow entrance to the Gulf of Corinth. Thence Grimani proceeded. The strength of the opposing forces was about equal; for while the Venetian galleys mounted heavy artillery, the Turkish fleet included numerous *palanderie*, well-armed light craft of great speed. In two successive engagements off Zonchio and Lepanto, Grimani was severely defeated and the outcome marked a further stage in the decline of Venice as a naval power.

ZUYDER ZEE   11 October 1573

Also known as the battle of Enkhuizen, in which the Frisian 'Gueux de Mer' (sea beggars) inflicted a severe defeat on the Spaniards during the Revolt of the Netherlands. During the year 1573 the sea beggars had liberated ports on the coast of Zeeland and Holland and the terrible siege of Haarlem had taken place. Both events showed that the Duke of Alva's brutal efforts to crush the revolt had failed. On 3 October a Spanish fleet of 30 ships under Maximilien de Hennin, Count of Bossu, sailed from Amsterdam to sweep the Zuyder Zee. Off Enkhuizen a week later it met the Frisian fleet under Cornelius Dirksson. After a prolonged struggle, the sea beggars emerged victorious. Six Spanish ships were taken including the flagship, the *Inquisition*; Bossu and 300 of his men were brought prisoner to Hoorn.

Bibliography

The maritime literature containing accounts of sea battles is so vast that it is possible here to list only a comparatively limited number of works for further reading.

ADMIRALTY, Naval Intelligence Department. *Modern Naval Operations* [1864–1900]. London: Admiralty, 1901
——. *The Russo-Japanese War.* Reports from naval attachés etc. 4 vols. London: Admiralty, 1904–7
ALBAS, Andrieu d'. *Death of a Navy. Japanese Naval Action in World War II.* New York: Devin-Adair, 1957
ALLEN, Gardner. *A Naval History of the American Revolution.* Boston and New York: Houghton Mifflin, 1913
ANDERSON, Dr Roger C. *Naval Wars in the Baltic in the Sailing Ship Epoch, 1522–1850.* London: G. Wood, 1910
——. *Naval Wars in the Lavant, 1559–1853.* Liverpool University Press, 1952
ANDERSON, Dr Roger C. (ed). *Journals and Narratives of the Third Dutch War.* London: Navy Records Society, 1946
AUPHAN, P., and MORDAL, Jacques. *The French Navy in World War II.* Annapolis: US Naval Institute, 1959
BALLARD, Admiral George A. *The Influence of the Sea on the Political History of Japan.* London: Murray [1921]
——. *Rulers of the Indian Ocean.* London: Duckworth, 1927
BALLHAUSEN, Phil Carl. *Der Erste Englische-Holländische Seekrieg, 1652–1654 sowie der Schwedisch-Holländische Seekrieg, 1658–1659.* The Hague: Nijhoff, 1923
BENNETT, Captain Geoffrey. *Coronel and the Falklands.* London: Batsford, 1962
——. *The Battle of Jutland.* London: Batsford, 1964
——. *Naval Battles of the First World War.* London: Batsford, 1968
——. *The Battle of the River Plate.* London: Ian Allan, 1972
BOYNTON, C. B. *History of the Navy during the Rebellion.* 2 vols. New York: Appleton, 1867
BRAGADIN, Commander M. A. *The Italian Navy in World War II.* Annapolis: US Naval Institute, 1957
BROOKS, Frederick W. *The English Naval Forces, 1199–1272.* London: A. Brown [1933]
CASSON, Lionel. *The Ancient Mariners: Seafarers and Sea-fighters of the Mediterranean in Ancient Times.* London: Gollancz, 1960
CHEVALIER, Captain Edmond. *Histoire de la Marine Française . . . 5 vols in 3.* Paris: Hachette, 1877–1902
CLOWES, Sir William Laird. *Four Modern Naval Campaigns, Historical, Strategical, and Tactical.* London and New York: Unit Library, 1902
CLOWES, Sir William Laird *et al. The Royal Navy: A History from the Earliest Times to the Present.* 7 vols. London: Sampson Low, 1897–1903
CORBETT, Sir Julian Stafford. *Drake and the Tudor Navy, with a History of the Rise of England as a Maritime Power.* 2 vols. London: Longmans, 1898
——. *The Successors of Drake (1589–1603).* London: Longmans, 1900
——. *England in the Seven Years' War: A study in Combined Strategy.* 2 vols. London: Longmans, 1907
——. *The Campaign of Trafalgar.* London: Longmans, 1910

——. *England in the Mediterranean: A Study of the Rise and Influence of British Power within the Straits, 1603–1713.* 2 vols. London: Longmans, 1914

CORBETT, Sir Julian Stafford, and NEWBOLT, Sir Henry. *History of the Great War. . . . Naval Operations.* 5 vols. London: Longmans, 1920–31

CRESWELL, Captain John. *Sea Warfare, 1939–1945.* Berkeley and Los Angeles: University of California Press, rev ed 1967

CUSTANCE, Admiral Sir Reginald. *War at Sea: Modern Theory and Ancient Practice.* London: Conway Maritime Press, 1971 [1st imp 1918]

DESBRIÈRE, Edouard. *Projets et tentatives de débarquement aux Iles Britanniques, 1793–1805.* 5 vols. Paris: R. Chapelot, 1900–2

——. *The Naval Campaign of 1805 – Trafalgar.* 2 vols. Oxford University Press, 1933

DUPUY, R. E. and T. N. *The Encyclopaedia of Military History from 3500 BC to the Present.* London: Macdonald, 1970

DURO, Cesaereo Fernandez. *Armada Española desde la unión de los reinos de Castilla y de León.* 9 vols. Madrid: Rivadeneyra, 1895–1903

EHRMAN, John. *The Navy in the War of William III, 1689–1697.* Cambridge University Press, 1953

EGGENBERGER, David. *A Dictionary of Battles.* London: Allen & Unwin, 1968

ELIAS, Johann E. *Schetsen uit de geschiedenis van ons Zeewezen.* 6 vols. The Hague: M. Nijhoff, 1916–30

FALK, Edwin A. *Togo and the Rise of Japanese Sea Power.* London: Longmans, 1936

FORESTER, C. S. *The Naval War of 1812.* London: Jonathan Cape, 1957

FROUDE, James Anthony. *The Spanish Story of the Armada, and Other Essays.* London: Longmans, 1892

GARDINER, Samuel R., and ATKINSON, C. T. (eds). *Letters and Papers Relating to the First Dutch War, 1652–1654.* 6 vols. London: Navy Records Society, 1899–1930

GREAT BRITAIN, Committee of Imperial Defence. *Official History of the Russo-Japanese War.* 3 vols. London: HMSO, 1910–20

GREEN, Peter. *The Year of Salamis 480–479 BC.* London: Weidenfeld & Nicolson, 1970

——. *Armada from Athens: The Failure of the Sicilian Expedition, 415–413 BC.* London: Hodder & Stoughton, 1971

GYLLENGRANAT, C. A. *Sveriges Sjökrigs-Historia.* 2 vols. Karlskrona: G. Ameen, 1840

HANNAY, David. *A Short History of the Royal Navy.* 2 vols. London: Methuen, 1898–1909

HOUGH, Richard. *The Fleet that Had to Die.* London: Hamish Hamilton, 1958

HOYT, EDWIN P. *The Battle of Leyte Gulf: The Death Knoll of the Japanese Fleet.* New York: Weybright & Talley, 1972

JACKSON, Vice-Admiral Sir T. Sturgess (ed). *Logs of the Great Sea Fights, 1794–1805.* 2 vols. London: Navy Records Society, 1899–1900

JAMES, William. *The Naval History of Great Britain from the Declaration of War with France in 1793 to the Accession of George IV.* 6 vols. London: Richard Bentley, 4th ed 1847

JAMES, Admiral Sir William M. *The British Navy in Adversity: A Study of the War of American Independence.* London: Longmans, 1926

JONES, VIRGIL CARRINGTON. *The Civil War at Sea.* 3 vols. New York: Holt, Rinehart & Winston, 1960–2

JONGE, J. C. de. *Geschiedenis van het Nederlansche Zeewezen.* 5 vols. Haarlam: Kruseman, 1858–62

JURIEN DE LA GRAVIÈRE, Vice-Admiral Jean P. E. *Les Marins du XVe et du XVIe siècles.* Paris: Plon, 1879

KLADO, Captain Nicholas. *The Russian Navy in the Russo-Japanese War.* London: Hurst & Blackett, 1905

——. *The Battle of the Sea of Japan.* London: Hodder & Stoughton, 1906

LACOUR-GAYET, Georges. *La Marine Militaire de la France sous la règne de Louis XV.* Paris: Champion, 1902

——. *La Marine Militaire de la France sous la règne de Louis XVI.* Paris: Champion, 1905

——. *La Marine Militaire de la France sous les règnes de Louis XIII et de Louis XIV.* 2 vols. Paris: Champion, 1911

LA JONQUIÈRE, C. de. *L'Expédition d'Egypte, 1798–1801.* 3 vols. Paris: Lavauzelle [1899–1907]

LA RONCIÈRE, Charles de. *Histoire de la Marine Française.* 6 vols. Paris: Plon, 1899–1932

LEWIS, Professor Michael. *The Navy of Britain, a Historical Portrait.* London: Allen & Unwin, 1948

——. *The Spanish Armada.* London: Batsford, 1969

LLOYD, Professor Christopher. *The Nation and the Navy.* London: Cressett Press, rev ed 1961

——. *Battles of St Vincent and Camperdown.* London: Batsford, 1964

——. *Sea Fights under Sail.* London: Collins, 1970

LORD, Walter. *Incredible Victory* [Midway]. London: Hamish Hamilton, 1968

MACINTYRE, Captain Donald. *The Battle for the Pacific*. London: Batsford, 1961

——. *The Battle for the Mediterranean*. London: Batsford, 1964

——. *Naval War against Hitler*. London: Batsford, 1971

MCKEE Alexander. *From Merciless Invaders: An Eyewitness Account of the Spanish Armada*. London: Souvenir Press, 1963

MACKESY, Piers. *The War in the Mediterranean, 1803–1810*. London: Longmans, 1957

——. *The War for America 1775–1783*. London: Longmans, 1964

MACLAY, Edgar Stanton. *A History of the United States Navy from 1775 to 1901*. 3 vols. New York: Appleton, 1901; new ed

MAHAN, Rear-Admiral Alfred Thayer. *The Influence of Sea Power upon History, 1660–1783*. London: Sampson Low, 1890

——. *The Influence of Sea Power upon the French Revolution and Empire, 1793–1812*. 2 vols. London: Sampson Low, 1892

——. *Sea Power and Its Relation to the War of 1812*. 2 vols. London: Sampson Low, 1905

——. *The Major Operations of the Navies in the War of American Independence*. London: Sampson Low, 1913

MARCUS, Geoffrey J. *Quiberon Bay: the Campaign in Home Waters, 1759*. London: Hollis & Carter, 1960

——. *A Naval History of England*. Volume I: *The Formative Centuries*. London: Longmans, 1961

——. *A Naval History of England*. Volume II: *The Age of Nelson*. London: Allen & Unwin, 1972

MARDER, Professor Arthur J. *From the Dreadnought to Scapa Flow: The Royal Navy in the Fisher Era, 1904–1919*. 5 vols. Oxford University Press, 1961–70

MARX, Robert F. *The Battle of Lepanto, 1571*. Cleveland and New York: World Publishing, 1966

MATTINGLEY, Professor Garrett. *The Defeat of the Spanish Armada*. London: Jonathan Cape, 1959

MELTON, Maurice. *The Confederate Ironclads*. South Brunswick and New York: Barnes/London: Yoseloff, 1972

MILLINGTON-DRAKE, Sir Eugene. *The Drama of the Graf Spee and the Battle of the River Plate*. London: Peter Davies, 1965

MORDAL, Jacques. *Twenty-five Centuries of Sea Warfare*. London: Souvenir Press, 1965

MORISON, Rear-Admiral Samuel E. *History of United States Naval Operations in the World War II*. Boston: Little, Brown, 1947–62

——. *The Two-Ocean War: A Short History of the U.S. Navy in the Second World War*. Boston: Little, Brown, 1963

NASH, Howard P. *A Naval History of the Civil War*. South Brunswick and New York: Barnes/London: Yoseloff, 1972

OGDEN, Lieutenant Commander Michael. *The Battle of North Cape*. London: Kimber, 1962

OWEN, J. H. *The War at Sea under Queen Anne, 1702–1708*. Cambridge University Press, 1938

PACK, Captain S. W. C. *The Battle of Matapan*. London: Batsford, 1961

PARKINSON, Professor Charles Northcote. *War in the Eastern Seas, 1793–1815*. London: Allen & Unwin, 1954

PARES, Richard. *War and Trade in the West Indies, 1739–63*. Oxford: Clarendon Press, 1936

POPE, Dudley. *The Great Gamble* [Copenhagen]. London: Weidenfeld and Nicolson, 1972

——. *At 12 Mr Byng Was Shot*. London: Weidenfeld & Nicolson, 1962

POTTER, E. B., and NIMITZ, CHESTER W. (eds). *Sea Power: A Naval History*. Engelwood Cliffs, NJ: Prentice-Hall, 1960

RICHMOND, Admiral Sir Herbert W. *The Navy in the War of 1739–1748*. 3 vols. Cambridge University Press, 1920

——. *The Navy in India, 1763–1783*. London: Benn, 1931

RODGERS, Vice-Admiral William Ledyard. *Greek and Roman Naval Warfare*. Annapolis: U.S. Naval Institute, 1939; repr 1970

——. *Naval Warfare Under Oars: 4th to 16th Centuries*. Annapolis: U.S. Naval Institute, 1939; repr 1970

ROSKILL, Captain Stephen W. *The War at Sea, 1939–1945*. 3 vols in 4. London: HMSO, 1954–61

——. *The Navy at War, 1939–1945*. London: Collins, 1960

RUGE, Vice-Admiral Friedrich. *Sea Warfare, 1939–1945: A German Viewpoint*. London: Cassell, 1957

SCHOFIELD, Vice-Admiral B. B. *The Loss of the Bismarck*. London: Ian Allen, 1972

——. *The Russian Convoys*. London: Batsford, 1964

SHEPARD, Arthur MacCartney. *Sea Power in Ancient History: The Story of the Navies of Classical Greece and Rome*. London: Heinemann, 1925

SOUTHWORTH, John V. D. *The Ancient Fleets: The Story of Naval Warfare under Oars, 2600 B.C.–1597 A.D.* New York: Twayne, 1968

——. *The Age of Sails: The Story of Naval Warfare under Sail, 1213–1853 A.D.* New York: Twayne, 1968

Starr, C. G. *The Roman Imperial Navy 31 B.C.–A.D. 324.* Cambridge: Heffer, 2nd ed 1960

Stenzel, Alfred. *Seekriegsgeschichte in ihre wichtigsten Abschnitten mit Berücksichtigung der Seetaktik.* 4 vols. Hanover and Leipzig: Hansche, 1907–11

Sue, Eugène. *Histoire de la Marine Française.* 4 vols. Paris: Perrotin, 1844–5.

Tedder, A. W. *The Navy of the Restoration, from the Death of Cromwell to the Treaty of Breda . . .* Cambridge University Press, 1916

Thomas, David A. *The Battle of the Java Sea.* London: A. Deutsch, 1968

Trammond, Joannès. *Manuel d'histoire maritime de la France.* Paris: Challamel, 1916

Troude, O. *Batailles navales de la France.* 4 vols. Paris: Challamel, 1867–8

US Naval History Division. *Civil War Chronology, 1861–1865.* 5 vols. Washington: Government Printing Office, 1962–5

Von der Porten, Edward P. *The German Navy in World War II.* London: A. Barker, 1970

Warner, Oliver. *Battle Honours of the Royal Navy.* London: G. Philip, 1956

——. *Trafalgar.* London: Batsford, 1959

——. *The Battle of the Nile.* London: Batsford, 1960

——. *The Glorious First of June.* London: Weidenfeld & Nicolson, 1964

——. *Nelson's Battles.* London: Batsford, 1965

Watts, A. J. *The Loss of the Scharnhorst.* London: Ian Allen, 1972

Weil, Alethea. *The Navy of Venice.* London: Murray, 1910

Westwood, J. N. *Witnesses of Tsushima.* Tokyo: Sophia University/Tallahassee: Diplomatic Press, 1970

Wilson, H. W. *Ironclads in Action.* 2 vols. London: Sampson Low, 1896

——. *The Downfall of Spain. Naval History of the Spanish-American War.* London: Sampson Low, 1900

——. *Battleships in Action.* 2 vols. London: Sampson Low, 1926

Winston, Graham. *The Spanish Armadas.* London: Colvin, 1972

Wolter, Gustav-Adolf. *See-schlachten als Wendepunkte der Geschichte.* Herford: Koehlers, 1972

Woodhouse, C. M. *The Battle of Navarino.* London: Hodder & Stoughton, 1965

Woodward, David. *The Russians at Sea.* London: Kimber, 1965

Acknowledgements

Many friends have contributed to the preparation of this book, which could never have been written without their help. I only regret that it is not possible to mention all of them by name. My particular thanks are due both to Commander David W. Waters, Deputy Director of the National Maritime Museum, Greenwich, and to Professor Christopher Lloyd for their valuable advice and for giving me the benefit of their profound knowledge of the whole field of naval history.

Although this has been an entirely personal undertaking, I am also deeply grateful to the Director of the National Maritime Museum, Basil Greenhill, CMG, for his constant interest and encouragement. Finally, all the illustrations in the book are from originals preserved in the National Maritime Museum and I am very grateful to the Trustees for their permission to reproduce them here.